Class Questions

THE GENDER LENS SERIES

The Gender Lens Series has been conceptualized as a way of encouraging the development of a sociological understanding of gender. A "gender lens" means working to make gender visible in social phenomena, asking if, how, and why social processes, standards, and opportunities differ systematically for women and men. It also means recognizing that gender inequality is inextricably braided with other systems of inequality. The Gender Lens Series is committed to social change directed toward eradicating these inequalities. Originally published by Sage Publications and Pine Forge Press, all Gender Lens books are now available from AltaMira Press and Rowman and Littlefield Publishers, Inc.

Books in the Series

Yen Le Espiritu, *Asian American Women and Men: Labor, Laws, and Love*

Judith A. Howard and Jocelyn A. Hollander, *Gendered Situations, Gendered Selves: A Gender Lens on Social Psychology*

Michael A. Messner, *Politics of Masculinities: Men in Movements*

Judith Lorber, *Gender and the Social Construction of Illness*

Scott Coltrane, *Gender and Families*

Myra Marx Ferree, Judith Lorber, and Beth B. Hess, editors, *Revisioning Gender*

Pepper Schwartz and Virginia Rutter, *The Gender of Sexuality: Exploring Sexual Possibilities*

Francesca M. Cancian and Stacey J. Oliker, *Caring and Gender*

M. Bahati Kuumba, *Gender and Social Movements*

Toni M. Calasanti and Kathleen F. Slevin, *Gender, Social Inequities, and Aging*

Judith Lorber and Lisa Jean Moore, *Gender and the Social Construction of Illness, Second Edition*

Shirley A. Hill, *Black Intimacies: A Gender Perspective on Families and Relationships*

Dorothy E. Smith, *Institutional Ethnography: A Sociology for People*

Joan Acker, *Class Questions: Feminist Answers*

Class Questions

Feminist Answers

Joan Acker

ROWMAN & LITTLEFIELD PUBLISHERS, INC.
Lanham • Boulder • New York • Toronto • Oxford

ROWMAN & LITTLEFIELD PUBLISHERS, INC.

Published in the United States of America
by Rowman & Littlefield Publishers, Inc.
A wholly owned subsidiary of The Rowman & Littlefield Publishing Group, Inc.
4501 Forbes Boulevard, Suite 200, Lanham, Maryland 20706
www.rowmanlittlefield.com

PO Box 317
Oxford
OX2 9RU, UK

British Library Cataloguing in Publication Information Available

Library of Congress Cataloging-in-Publication Data

Acker, Joan.
Class questions : feminist answers / Joan Acker.
p. cm.—(The gender lens series)
Includes bibliographical references and index.
ISBN 0–7425–4624–1 (cloth : alk. paper)—ISBN 0–7425–4630–6 (pbk. : alk. paper) 1. Social classes. 2. Feminist theory. 3. Women—Social conditions. 4. Minorities—Social conditions. 5. Capitalism. I. Title. II. Series.
HT609.A33 2006
305.5—dc22 2005018246

Printed in the United States of America

™ The paper used in this publication meets the minimum requirements of American National Standard for Information Sciences—Permanence of Paper for Printed Library Materials, ANSI/NISO Z39.48–1992.

Contents

Preface

In this book, I present my views on some long-standing feminist conceptual issues, building on the work of many others. Thus, my first thanks go to all whose thinking and writing about class, gender, race, and organizations made this contribution possible. Dorothy Smith is the one most immediately responsible for my writing this book. She insisted that I publish a collection of my essays, leading me to expand and develop the ideas in those essays into a book on gendered and racialized class. I also owe Dorothy much gratitude for her ideas that have so influenced me and for her friendship. Other friends who have been my co-researchers have contributed a great deal to my knowledge: Don Van Houten for his work with me on organizations, including much of the analysis in chapter 5 of this book; Margaret Hallock for all she taught me about unions and organizations as we tried to establish comparable worth in Oregon; Johanna Esseveld and Kate Barry for their critiques and discussions beginning in a project we did together long ago; Sandi Morgen for her partnership in studying welfare restructuring and many other projects. Thank you all for your excellent friendships and ideas. Many other friends have contributed to my thinking, including Cynthia Cockburn, Barbara Czarniawska, Nona Glazer, Harriet Holter, Wuokko Knocke, Elin Kvande, Arnlaug Leira, Judith Lorber, Patricia Martin, Carole Pateman, Frances Fox Piven, Bente Rasmussen, and Karin Widerberg. I also thank Joey Sprague for guiding me and this book through the process of writing and publishing, as well as Heidi Gottfried and Bill Martin for very helpful reviews of the manuscript. And thanks to the rest of the Gender Lens group, Judy Howard, Barbara Risman, and Mitch Allen, for all your help and support. Finally, thanks to Alan McClare, Alex Masulis, Jessica Gribble, and Marian Haggard at Rowman & Littlefield who turned my manuscript into a real book.

Series Editors' Foreword

It is now more than twenty years since feminist sociologists identified gender as an important analytic dimension in sociology. In the intervening decades, theory and research on gender have grown exponentially. With this series, we intend to further this scholarship, as well as ensure that theory and research on gender become fully integrated into the discipline as a whole.

In their classic edited collection *Analyzing Gender: A Handbook of Social Science Research* (1987), Beth Hess and Myra Marx Ferree identify three stages in the study of women and men since 1970. Initially, the emphasis was on sex differences and the extent to which such differences might be based on the biological properties of individuals. In the second stage, the focus shifted to the individual sex roles and socialization, exposing gender as the product of specific social arrangements, although still conceptualizing it as an individual trait. The hallmark of the third stage is the recognition of the centrality of gender as an organizing principle in all social systems, including work, politics, everyday interaction, families, economic development, law, education, and a host of other social domains. As our understanding of gender has become more social, so has our awareness that gender is experience and organized in race- and class-specific ways.

In the summer of 1992, the American Sociological Association (ASA) funded a small conference organized by Barbara Risman and Joey Sprague to discuss the evolution of gender in these distinctly sociological frameworks. The conference brought together a sampling of gender scholars working in a range of substantive areas with a diversity of methods to focus on gender as a principle of social organization. The discussions of the state of feminist scholarship made it clear that gender is pervasive in society and operates at multiple levels. Gender shapes identities and perception, interactional practices, and the very forms of social institutions, and it does so in race- and class-specific ways. If we did not see gender in social phenomena, we were not seeing them clearly.

The participants in the ASA-sponsored seminar recognized that although these developing ideas about gender were widely accepted by feminist sociologists and many others who study social inequalities, they were relatively unfamiliar to many who work within other sociological paradigms. This book series was conceived at that conference as a means of introducing these ideas to sociological colleagues and students and of helping to develop gender scholarship further.

As series editors, we believe it is time for gender scholars to speak to our other colleagues and to the general education of students. There are many sociologists and scholars in other social sciences who want to incorporate scholarship on gender and its intersections with race, class, and sexuality in their teaching and research but lack the tools to do so. For those who have not worked in this area, the prospect of the bibliographic research necessary to develop supplementary units or transform their own teaching and scholarship is daunting. Moreover, the publications necessary to penetrate a curriculum resistant to change and encumbered by inertia have simply not been available. We conceptualize this book series as a way of meeting the needs of these scholars and thereby also encouraging the development of the sociological understanding of gender by offering a "gender lens."

What do we mean by a *gender lens*? We mean working to make gender visible in social phenomena, asking if, how, and why social processes, standards, and opportunities differ systematically in women and men. We also mean recognizing that gender inequality is inextricably intertwined with other systems of inequality. Looking at the world through a gendered lens thus implies two seemingly contradictory tasks. First, it means unpacking the assumptions about gender that pervade sociological research and social life in general. At the same time, looking through a gender lens means revealing how central assumptions about gender continue to be the organization of the social world, regardless of their empirical reality. We show how our often unquestioned ideas about gender affect the words we use, the questions we ask, the answers we envision. The Gender Lens Series is committed to social change directed toward eradicating these inequalities. Our goals are consistent with initiatives at colleges and universities across the United States that are encouraging the development of more diverse scholarship and teaching.

The books in the Gender Lens Series are aimed at different audiences and have been written for a variety of uses, from assigned readings in introductory undergraduate courses to graduate seminars and as professional resources for our colleagues. The series includes several different styles of books that address these goals in distinct ways. We are excited about the series and anticipate that it will have an enduring impact on the direction of both the pedagogy and the scholarship in sociology and other related social sciences. We invite you, the reader, to join us in thinking through these difficult but exciting issues by offering feedback or by developing your own project and proposing it for use in the series.

ABOUT THIS VOLUME

Class questions is an urgent task at the beginning of the twenty-first century as global, national, and local inequalities escalate. Yet conventional conceptualizations of class are inadequate to the task because they illuminate the economic experiences of white men more clearly than those of white women or people of color. In this book, Joan Acker sounds the call for a return to questions of class while she deftly articulates a carefully reasoned resolution to the conceptualization problem. Acker proposes that we see class and capitalism as fundamentally gendered and racialized and powerfully shaped in work organizations.

Acker examines the efforts of feminist theorists, beginning in the late 1960s, to create theories of capitalism and class, or patriarchy and capitalism, as well as more recent efforts to integrate gender into class theory, to theorize the intersectionality of gender, race, and class, and to use other innovative approaches to account for the ongoing creation of gender and racial/ethnic differences within economic processes. She finds that attempts to integrate gender into class theories and to theorize the intersection of separate gender, race, and class structures both run into conceptual difficulties that can be resolved by analyzing class itself as thoroughly gendered and racialized.

Analyses of gendered and racialized class, Acker argues, must be based on concrete practices, not abstract structures, and on an expanded idea of the economy suggested by other feminist scholars that includes unpaid work and family forms of distribution. A feminist concept of gendered and racialized class relations spans production, reproduction, and distribution and includes the invisible work of linking households and paid workplaces.

Acker shows how capitalism was gendered and racialized historically, as it evolved in a process dominated by small groups of white men, and legitimated with images of masculinity. This process differed in various industrializing countries: the focus here is the United States. The subordination of white women, differing in various class situations, and the exploitation and enslavement of people of other race/ethnic groups were built into U.S. capitalism from the beginning. Capitalism developed with a gendered understructure anchored in divisions between the aims and organization of production and reproduction: production was organized to achieve profit, not to provide for and care for children and families. As women had the bulk of caring responsibilities, this was a gendered organization of necessary work.

With reproductive work relegated to women in the household, capitalist organizations could claim nonresponsibility for human reproduction, and nonresponsibility for the environment as well. Thus, capitalist claims to *nonresponsibility* are built into the basic aims of capitalist organizations and into society-wide gender and racial divisions of labor. The vast power of capitalist organizations in a highly monetized society, along with their nonresponsibility, continues to contribute to the devaluation of caring work and the women who do most of it. Such devaluation is central to women's class situations. Racial inequality and subordination are attributed to individual or group failings, thus are also outside the realm of corporate organizational responsibility.

Next Acker turns to the roles of powerful organizations and organizational actors in shaping gendered and racialized class. Organizations are the sites in which gendered and racialized class relations are created as integral to the ordinary business of getting the work done, accounting for the costs and revenues, hiring and firing, and setting wages. Acker examines these processes in greater detail, developing the concept of "inequality regimes." An inequality regime is the configuration of inequality-producing practices and processes within particular organizations at particular times. Class inequality is more legitimate than racial and gender inequality in the United States. This legitimacy of class and the strength of white, male gendered and racialized class interests often undermine efforts at organizational change, such as affirmative action, pay equity, and diversity projects.

Finally, Acker examines contemporary changes in work and employment in local, national, and global economic/political processes that are increasing inequalities and altering racialized and gendered class relations. Capitalist organizational processes have led to large-scale changes in the organization of production, the decline of manufacturing jobs, and the increase in service sector jobs. These changes have had gendered and racialized impacts. Changing work practices and employment contracts, facilitated by employer attacks on unions, have made work less secure for many. Gendered and racialized class patterns become more polarized as income and wealth inequality also increase and tax reductions favor corporations and the wealthy. These changes, plus the downsizing of the social safety net, mean that those already with poorer jobs and lower wages fall further behind. With so many women doing paid work, new questions emerge such as whether the male-breadwinner-family is a thing of the past and how people deal with the tasks of bridging family and work demands.

Changes are ongoing, Acker reminds us: white-collar and professional jobs are increasingly being moved offshore and Wal-Mart has emerged as the model of profitable organization. Both of these changes could mean further, serious alterations in gendered and racialized class configurations in the United States. Acker concludes by considering the implications of her conceptualization of class for progressive social change, outlining some proposals for decreasing gendered and racialized class inequalities.

Class questions are vital and immediate. In this book, Joan Acker develops an innovative and exciting feminist response that will change the way the reader understands how we got to this point and how we can most effectively respond to the challenges we face in the twenty-first century economy.

Judith A. Howard
Barbara Risman
Joey Sprague

1

Introduction—The Feminist Problem with Class

"Class matters" (hooks 2000; Phillips 1987; Wright 1997b) at the beginning of the twenty-first century. New class inequalities are arising from global, national, and local changes in capitalist production and politics, altering the daily lives of ordinary people in cross-cutting and contradicting patterns of gender, race, ethnicity, class, and nation. But, the concept of class is problematic. As some feminist scholars have argued, this concept illuminates the economic experiences of white men more clearly than those of white women or people of color because it was developed primarily within a privileged white male perspective. Exactly how class matters for white women and people of other racial groups is still an issue. In this book I examine feminist attempts to imagine a concept of class that resolves problems of combining gender, race, and class, and I argue for a concept of class as gendered and racialized as a solution. I also argue that class relations include not only relations of production and paid labor, but also relations of distribution and unpaid labor. I discuss gendered and racialized class processes and practices as fundamental in the emergence and ongoing structuring of various capitalisms, and as intrinsic to organizational processes. Finally, I examine some contemporary changes in work and employment and in local, national, and global economic/political processes that seem to be increasing inequalities and altering racialized and gendered class relations.

Class is a particularly important idea at the beginning of the twenty-first century as the bursting of the economic bubble of the late 1990s has severely undermined illusions in rich capitalist countries that everyone is becoming affluent. In other, less rich countries, extreme poverty is the fate for very large numbers of people. "Globalization," economic restructuring, and new technology continue to transform daily lives in many nations in multiple and widely different ways, sometimes for the better but often for the worse. Economic inequality is growing within nations and, globally, between nations. While those in the upper reaches of class structures enjoy incredible luxury, those at the bottom struggle to feed their families and may be hungry or even starving. In industrialized countries, class divisions between women are becoming greater as more and more women become paid workers, and some women enter well-paid professional and managerial jobs while a majority of women remain in low-paid "women's" jobs. Class divisions between men also become greater as some men direct large and increasingly powerful organizations in both public and private sectors, while many other men are unable to find work that pays a "family wage" as highly paid, secure production jobs disappear. At the same time, welfare state protections for single parent families, the unemployed, the destitute, the elderly, and the ill have been seriously undermined, particularly in the United States. These and many other transformations are visible evidences of political and economic processes in contemporary capitalism. "Class" is a central concept for comprehending these processes, although what is precisely meant by the term varies enormously.

Beginning with Marx and Weber, "class" has been at the center of efforts to understand systematic and systemic inequalities within capitalist societies. Class, as the concept that locates groups and individuals within ongoing capitalist processes, is essential for understanding gender and racial/ethnic differences in poverty and discrimination, and political/economic conflict around these issues, as well as issues of identity and consciousness. "Class" points to the economic realities which women and men of all racial and ethnic groups must contend with, whether they are living in rich capitalist countries, in countries still making a transition from socialism to capitalism, in not-so-rich countries, or in impoverished countries in the rest of the world. Thus, it is also an essential concept for understanding differences between peoples in varying global situations and the links across the boundaries of those situations.

Class, although essential for making sense of the contemporary world, is a highly contested concept and a curiously vulnerable idea, subject to reassessment as political climates and work structuring change. In the 1970s and 1980s, mainstream class theorists debated class theories, arguing about class consciousness, class formation, the possibilities of class action with the rapidly changing composition of the labor force, and whether relations of production or market relations were the best way to formulate the economic processes producing class structures. They also debated the merits of structural class analyses versus historical analyses.

Most male theorists ignored the question of women and gender. Thus, the feminist and nonfeminist discourses on class rarely intersected.

Mainstream sociologists and political theorists in the United States and in Britain, depending to a degree on their theoretical allegiances, have repeatedly proclaimed that class is dead or at least seriously ill (Crompton and Scott 2000). Such proclamations have usually been based on the decline of industrial working class employment in rich capitalist nations and diminishing union membership along with minimal success in working class mobilization. But, class survives. At the end of the twentieth century and the beginning of the twenty-first, new books and journal debates on class and class theory are again appearing (Baxter and Western 2001; Crompton, Devine, Savage, and Scott 2000; Hall 1997; Portes 2000),[1] reaffirming the relevance of class. Many of these discussions of class are little affected or disturbed by feminist critiques, as they continue to use notions of class and class processes that assume gender and race neutrality. Some, however, recognize that gender and race are important in understanding class, although they do not do much to bring that recognition into their analyses.

The history of feminist thinking about class shows a different pattern. Some feminists inside and outside academia criticized established, male-centered analyses of class at the beginning of Second Wave feminism. They argued that these analyses could not account for women's exploitation and inequality that was different from and more severe in its consequences than the exploitation and inequality suffered by working class men. Socialist and Marxist feminists, in particular, had intense debates on women, patriarchy, class, and gender from the late 1960s into the 1980s, criticizing concepts of class that made women invisible and proposing new approaches.[2] However, as solutions to conceptual and theoretical problems proved to be elusive, feminist debates about class almost disappeared. A few sociologists, anthropologists, and others (e.g., Acker 2000; Pollert 1996; Glucksmann 1995; Gottfried 1998) made new attempts to theorize gender and class, even as much attention moved away from class to issues of identity, diversity, race, discourse, and sexuality. Thus, class never completely evaporated from feminist scholarship and writing. In addition, a great deal of empirical work continues to be done on related issues such as sex segregation, wage inequalities, gender relations in work organizations, gendered effects of economy and production restructuring, and work-family connections, but theoretical issues having to do with economic relations were submerged as questions of culture and identity became more interesting. "Class" was no longer cutting edge.

As black and Third World feminists began in the 1970s to criticize feminist thinking for its location in a white, middle class consciousness that limited understanding of the lives of "others" (hooks 1984; Davis 1981;

Dill 1979; Collins 1990; Spelman 1989), many white feminist academics began to try to talk about race, gender, and class. I emphasize "try" because good intentions did not always result in substantial changes. The unmarked subject position of "whiteness" persists in a great deal of writing. Although white scholars began to recognize the necessity of understanding race as important in the structuring of class, in practice race was usually absent or a token presence along with sexuality in their analyses. These efforts to integrate gender, race, and class have revealed again how racial privileging along with the conventions of sociological theorizing about systems, structures, and levels still constrain efforts to rethink social life from perspectives of women located outside the "relations of ruling" (Smith 1999). The "race, gender, and class" discourses invented the notion of intersectionality, opening new ways of seeing how power, oppression, exploitation, and inequality work. However, these efforts to reconceptualize have, on the whole, paid little attention to what they mean by "class." They have not resolved the issue of how to think about class in ways that encompass the material/economic situations of women variously located in capitalist societies.

Now, feminist debates about class seem to be beginning again. bell hooks (2000) argues that "class matters" because, in her view, class has receded to the background in much feminist writing in the last ten years or so. She affirms the importance of class in her own life and in the lives of millions of other people who exist within growing insecurity and inequality. Nancy Fraser (1997), in a different feminist discourse, argues that a political and intellectual divide between redistribution (class) and recognition (culture/identity) must be bridged to develop a progressive politic of the future in a "postsocialist" world. To do this, she engages with "class" in arguments about types of remedies for injustices of distribution and recognition. Both hooks and Fraser bring our attention back to class, but without revisiting the earlier and unresolved feminist criticisms of class.

The same may be said for many feminist sociologists and other social scientists. Feminist scholars in the United States agree that gender, race, and class domination are intrinsically linked (Acker 2000; Collins 2000; hooks 2000; Weber 2001), but the "class" that enters that linkage is often unexamined, and is often some version of the same old, unreconstructed "class." An additional problem confronting these efforts to think about complex inequalities is how to specify what is meant by "intrinsically linked" or "intersectionality," how to see linkages in ways that do not ultimately give class or race or gender a privileged position as the most important element in understanding power and oppression. I think it is possible that solving those issues depends on solving the problems of "class." These problems are:

- Conceptualizing class and capitalism as gender- and race-neutral structures or processes, while implicitly modeling the class actor on a male worker or capitalist.
- Defining the capitalist economy, the basis of class, as encompassing only market-related activities, thus ignoring unpaid, reproductive, and subsistence work as economic and also basic to class.
- Ignoring the importance of state and family distributions for class relations.
- Failing to recognize the importance of masculine and white privilege in the historical development and contemporary functioning of class relations, as well as the importance of hegemonic masculinities in supporting exploitation and domination.

In this book, I present some solutions to these problems, using the scholarly work of others from the early (late 1960s and early 1970s) socialist feminist and Marxist feminist debates to the postcolonial feminist discourses of the beginning of the twenty-first century. I also use my own work on women, gender, and class, which began with an article in 1973. I build on the insights of the 1980s (e.g., Acker 1988; Phillips 1987) that class relations are always gendered and are constructed through gender. I also rely on my research on work and women for understanding and examples. This research includes a study of housewives attempting to return to work, a participatory study of a comparable worth project, a study of female bank workers in Sweden, a study of organizational restructuring in a college, and a study of welfare restructuring in the late 1990s. I learned a great deal from all these studies, including something of the complexity of the class relations within which the women (and men) were enmeshed, and how class, gender, and race are produced in work organizations. My sometimes abstract discussions are always informed by these realities, or so I hope. I next offer preliminary definitions of gender, race, and class. I end this introduction with a brief outline of my argument about how to resolve the issues listed above as it is developed in the following chapters.

Defining class, race, and gender. Class, race, and gender are conceptual categories, variously defined and debated from different theoretical perspectives. These words are often used as nouns, but such usage reifies processes and practices that are continually bringing into existence the situations, images, conditions, and relations that the words intend (Acker 1992a). I prefer verbal forms, such as gendering, or adjectival forms, such as racialized, that better capture the sense of process and diversity. Certain definitions are more amenable to an analysis of mutually constituting processes than are others.

Gender is best understood as pervasive patterns of difference, in advantage and disadvantage, work and reward, emotion and sexuality, image and identity, between female and male, created through practical activities and representations that justify these patterns that result in the social categories of women and men. Gender may include more than these two categories. Gender is a basic principle of social organization, almost always involving unequal economic and social power in which men dominate. Gender is socially constructed and diverse, and varies historically and cross-culturally.

Race is also socially and politically constructed around definitions of skin color and other physical characteristics; in particular, historical processes of war, colonization, slavery, immigration, and migration (for example, hooks 1981, 1984; Collins 2000; Bhavnani 2001; Glenn 2002). Race, too, almost always involves inequalities of power and material resources, resulting from and constituting relations of domination, exclusion, and exploitation. Racial representations in white society are primary ideological justifications for systematic exploitation and subordination. Historically, many different racial categories and identities have emerged, with members of the category "white" almost always in dominant positions in the northern industrial countries. Race, too, can be seen as a basic principle of social organization. Ethnicity differs from race, but is often associated with race. Ethnic differences are based on cultural and language traditions and do not always involve inequalities.

Class generally stands for economic/power inequalities structured by production, market, and/or occupational systems. Definitions of class, in my view, are more problematic than those of race and gender because the feminist critique of class theories did not lead to new feminist theories. Thus, certain conceptual problems remained unsolved: the invisibility of gender (and race) in class theories and the implicit male model of the class actor. Available class theories include structural Marxist approaches that specify some core set of class relations embedded in capitalist structures (e.g., Wright 2001a), historical materialist theories that emphasize economic structural change, class consciousness, and class conflict (e.g., Thompson 1963), Marxist theories of the labor process (e.g., Burawoy 1979), Weberian theories of class and status (e.g., Giddens 1973), occupational categorical schemes (e.g., Goldthorpe 1980), and relatively untheorized notions of positions in the economy related to income and wealth, such as lower class, working class, middle class, and upper class. I think that a feminist historical materialist approach, evident in much feminist historical and ethnographic work, holds the most promise for a class analysis that is compatible with the above concepts of gender and race. Below I outline the components of such an approach to a gendered and racialized class analysis, arguing that class is also socially constructed and processual, the outcome or effect of practices and relations that constitute the production and distribution of the means of survival. Class is, of course, a basic principle of social organization in capitalist societies.

Combining race, gender, and class. In pursuing an approach to class that displaces the white male model I have tried to develop the insights that class and capitalism are gendered, adding that class and capitalism are also racialized (see Omi and Winant 1994, 68). This way of combining gender, race, and class is different from arguing for intersections between systems or structures with their own, preexisting internal elements and dynamics. Rather than already existing, distinct systems, I see ongoing processes and practices in which gendering and racialization are integral to the creation and recreation of class inequalities and class divisions, emerging in complex, multifaceted, boundary-spanning capitalist activities. This is only one way to look at gender, race, and class. It is also partial, with a focus more on work relations than on other areas of daily life in which race, class, and gender also structure participation, inequality, and interpretation.[3] For example, I do not discuss how material and cultural consumption practices express and create gendered and racialized class distinctions and identities. I give little space to other important class processes, such as those in our schools, colleges, and universities. Lacking infinite space, I had to make choices about emphasis and inclusion of topics, and I chose to emphasize work and distribution in the following discussion.

In chapter 2, I discuss attempts to bring women into class analysis by both white feminist and nonfeminist class theorists. Most of these theoretical and empirical studies did not include race and racial inequalities. Other discussions and studies by women of color looked at race and its intersections with gender and class. General agreement emerged among all these scholars that gender and class, and then race, should be understood as mutually constituted and studied as lived experience or as practices in historically specific contexts. Some argued that reproduction and unpaid labor should be included in concepts of class relations. Problems remained in how to include reproduction and unpaid labor in understanding class practices and in how to give concrete meaning to metaphors such as "intersections" or "mutually constituting." This discussion of theorizing provides the basis for the ensuing chapters.

In chapter 3, I first discuss conceptual approaches to resolving some of the difficulties in thinking about class, gender, and race that were discussed in chapter 2. Thinking about the social as activities and practices is a basic step toward conceptualizing gendered and racialized class relations.[4] Embodied people engage in, coordinate, and interpret the practices of daily life within gendered and racialized distributions of power and inequality. Extended social relations, originating outside local places and specifying local practices, link those local practices into distant social spaces. What is often called "social structure," including class, gender, and race, is emergent in practices, produced and reproduced in ongoing human activities. Thus, people are not located in class structures, but enmeshed in class relations. To understand the complexity and variety of gendered and racialized class processes, investigations can begin in the standpoints of a variety of people who are enmeshed in class relations in different ways. To clarify the meaning of "gendered and racialized," investigations can look at how class experiences differ for white women, women and men of color, and white men, and how differences and persistent inequalities are explained and justified. To bring women of all races into class analysis, the notion of what counts as "economic" must be expanded to include unpaid work and other forms of unrecognized work. To expand the economic, I adopt economist Julie Nelson's (1993) concept of economic activity as processes of provisioning, providing what is socially defined as necessary to sustain life and ensure survival.

In the remainder of chapter 3, I outline the class practices and relations that accomplish provisioning. These include relations of paid and unpaid production and reproduction, relations of distribution, and relations that link paid work and unpaid family work. Class relations take place in the production of goods and services, both very broadly defined, and in the distribution of wages, taxes, and profits generated in production. Distribution is embedded in different forms of relations, including personal and intimate ties and impersonal, bureaucratic processes. Distribution through marriage and family relations is one way in which personal, emotional life is implicated in class relations. Linking activities create the infrastructure of scheduling, housework, and care of self and others that make it possible to be a paid worker. Thus, class relations are also produced and reproduced outside what are thought of as core capitalist processes, in unpaid work of various kinds. Class processes are gendered and racialized through many concrete practices that are based on assumptions about gender and race differences and inequalities, reproducing images and ideologies that support different outcomes and shaping interactions and identities. This chapter concludes with an outline of a conceptual approach to gendered and racialized class processes.

In chapter 4, I argue that capitalisms are gendered and racialized. I use the plural, capitalisms, because important national historical differences exist in the ways in which capitalism incorporated gendered and racialized practices and ideologies. As industrial capitalism emerged in Britain and the United States in the nineteenth century, differences in the aims and activities of production and household reproduction developed. Capitalist firms organized to achieve profits; families and households organized to provide for survival, raise children, and create a satisfactory daily life. Contradictions between these two modes of work organization were and are frequent. They were necessary to each other, but production often undermined the possibilities for survival, for example by paying wages too low to support a family. As many have argued, this was a gendered division. A relatively small group of white men drove the development of capitalist production, reworking forms of male domination as intrinsic to emerging class relations, and organizing the new factories and, later, the new offices based on assumptions about the masculine individual as the normal human being. Money and power were increasingly centralized in this male domain, while women were at least symbolically consigned to the domain with little power and money. Racial subordination, exploitation, and exclusion were also intrinsic to developing capitalism in the United States, providing a source of unpaid labor and, later, very low-wage labor based on racism and physical violence. White male workers accepted their dependence on wage labor partly through constructing their identities as different from and superior to women and African-American men.

Thus, white masculinity was central in the development of U.S. capitalism. As capitalist labor markets and wage practices became widespread and then bureaucratized, these were segregated and defined by gender and racial difference. These inequality processes, I argue, are also intrinsic to capitalist organizing. Although gender and race segregation and wage inequality have become less extreme, neither is disappearing, and instances of new forms of inequality and segregation are found in the "new economy."

Claims to corporate nonresponsibility for human and environmental survival and well-being, unless these goals happen to enhance profit, are an additional aspect of the gendering and racialization of capitalism. Claims to nonresponsibility are undergirded by the gendered separation between the aims of production and household reproduction. Such claims are particularly vociferous in the United States because of the dominance of neoliberal ideology in the last twenty-five years and the success of various capitalist organizations in fighting labor unions and achieving downsizing of both state and corporate welfare. Corporate nonresponsibility continually reinforces the responsibility of households, and mostly women within households, for survival and caring work. This is a process that pushes responsibility away from the centers of wealth and power and by implication devalues those who have little wealth and power but who must take on responsibility to preserve their lives and the lives of those around them. Women from poor and minority groups often have the greatest responsibilities and the fewest resources. These are both material and ideological processes that enshrine gender (male) and race (white) within capitalist organizing. Many white working class and middle class men have also been negatively affected by corporate nonresponsibility.

But, nonresponsibility is still based in the separations between the gendered organizing of production and the household and legitimated through laws and conventional practices that declare the private corporation to be a single-minded individual bent on getting the best deal in the market. Sometimes under pressure from reformers or social movements, governments attempt to control nonresponsibility with laws and regulations, with varying degrees of success. However, in the United States at least, the claims are continuously made and continuously countered, with a scarcely noticed gendered subtext to the arguments.

Chapter 5 deals with the role of work organizations in the structuring of gendered and racialized class processes. Powerful organizations and organizational actors, who are primarily white men, are central in the economic and political decision making that shapes class locally, nationally, and internationally. These actions maintain organizations' nonresponsibility, locate and relocate industries, and restructure jobs and workplaces. Large organizations control much of the media, and in other ways shape class processes. Organizations are also the sites in which gendered and racialized class relations are created as integral to the ordinary business of getting the work done, accounting for the costs and revenues, hiring and firing, and setting wages. I examine these processes in greater detail, developing the concept of "inequality regimes." An inequality regime is the configuration of inequality-producing practices and processes within particular organizations at particular times. Although common patterns exist, for example, in highly bureaucratic organizations, there are also many variations. Widespread attempts to restructure organizations, downsize management, and reorganize work in the last twenty years of the twentieth century and the first years of the twenty-first century contribute to variation. An inequality regime has a number of interconnected dimensions:

- The bases of inequality that may include, in addition to gender, race, and class, inequalities based on sexual orientation, age, differing abilities, and the like.
- Organizing practices that maintain inequalities, including hiring, job design, wage setting, and expectations about job performance based on a model of the worker as undistracted by outside obligations. Vertical and horizontal race- and gender-based segregation of jobs and positions, as well as functional segregation on the basis of race and gender, are produced and maintained through managerial and supervisory practices.
- The visibility and legitimacy of inequalities. Class inequality is much more legitimate than either race or gender inequality, but it may be more invisible because it is so widely accepted. Inequalities are legiti-

mated by gendered and racialized images and understandings, such as the widespread, still existing, image of the manager as a white male with certain characteristics.

- Methods of control, varying from consent based on worker identification with the organization, controls embedded in bureaucratic rules, to controls using implicit or explicit violence, such as sexual harassment. Unequal power based on racialized and gendered class disparities affects the efficacy of controls. Controls are created and recreated in interactions between workers, between workers and supervisors, and between managers and supervisors in which expectations of race-, gender-, and class-appropriate behaviors are covertly or overtly expressed, then complied with or opposed.
- Competing interests and organizing change. Intentional change may originate outside organizations by unions and/or social movements, or change efforts may come from inside, instituted by managers. In both cases, competing interests often limit the effectiveness of change efforts.

Efforts to increase equality in work organizations, such as affirmative action or pay equity projects, are efforts to change inequality regimes. These efforts often fail: Looking at how specific inequality regimes are constituted and function may help in understanding these failures, as well as those cases in which there was success.

Chapter 6 is a discussion of contemporary changes in gendered and racialized class relations in the United States. Large-scale changes in the organization of production, the decline of manufacturing jobs and the increase in service sector jobs, have had gendered and racialized impacts. Changing work practices and employment contracts have made work less secure for many. Income inequalities increased dramatically between top and bottom incomes, but decreased to a small degree between white women and men. Gendered and racialized class patterns became more polarized as wealth inequality also increased and tax reductions favored corporations and the wealthy. These changes, plus the downsizing of the social safety net, meant that those already with poorer jobs and lower wages, single mothers, African Americans, Hispanics, and other racial/ethnic groups, fell further behind than middle class and working class white families. With so many women doing paid work, new questions emerged, such as whether the male breadwinner family is a thing of the past and how people deal with the tasks of bridging family and work demands. Changes are ongoing, with recent employer initiatives increasing offshoring of white collar and professional jobs and with the emergence of Wal-Mart as the model of a profitable organization. Both of these changes could mean further, serious alterations in gendered and racialized class configurations in the United States. Gendering and racializing practices that I outlined in chapter 3 are still integral elements in the ongoing creation of class inequalities. Moreover, many of these changes are rooted in the underlying gendered and racialized processes that were part of the emergence of nineteenth-century industrial capitalism and that are still present in twenty-first-century capitalism.

Chapter 7 first summarizes my conceptualization of gendered and racialized class practices and relations. I then examine proposals for change in key areas of gendering and racializing processes. These are changes to support caring work, including funded parental leave and universally available day care. Reconstruction of work organization is necessary to move away from assumptions about ideal workers as males unencumbered by any obligations outside work. A shortened work day and flexible working arrangements would lessen gender inequality and would support efforts to get men to do their fair share of caring and other unpaid labor. Reinvigorating policies and programs to reduce inequalities in opportunities and pay are necessary to remove many practices that still discriminate against all women in racially specific ways and against racial/ethnic men. Measures to promote income equality and economic security are also important. These include rebuilding the fractured social safety net, instituting universal, single-payer health insurance, raising the minimum wage, and working toward a universal basic income or citizens' income as a right of citizenship. Finally, ways to increase and restore democratic participation and voice in decisions on the above issues is essential to achieving any of these policies.

I look at the possibilities for making any of these changes. In the present context of large capitalist organizations' global domination and control of economies and politics, with commitment to "free market" neoliberal ideology, the prospects for most of these changes look dim. Yet massive and diverse organizing against global capitalism's actions is also ongoing. It is possible that Karl Polanyi's (1944) observation, that at certain points capital has to act to save itself from the consequences of its own free markets, will again prove to be accurate. In any case, my revisionist reading of class may contribute to a concept of class that points us toward the fundamentally gendered and racialized constitution of global and national class society.

NOTES

1. A debate on how to conceptualize class appeared also in 2001 and 2002 in *Acta Sociologica*, volumes 44 and 45.
2. See Karen V. Hansen and Ilene J. Philipson (1990), *Women, Class, and the Femi-*

nist Imagination and Rosemary Hennessy and Chrys Ingraham (1997), *Materialist Feminism: A Reader in Class, Difference, and Women's Lives* for some of the most formative articles from this period and assessments of the contributions of these discussions to feminist thinking. See also Anne Phillips, 1987.

3. Evelyn Glenn's (2002) detailed history of gender and race in three regions of the United States gives a full picture of these processes in our past in which the focus is more on gender and race than on class.

4. Dorothy Smith's (1987; 1999) work on social relations and the relations of ruling is the basis for the conceptualization I propose here.

2

Feminists Theorizing Class—Issues and Arguments

Class and social stratification were central concepts in the study of economic and political inequality and domination when Second Wave feminism began in the late 1960s and early 1970s. But, these concepts did not deal with the subordinations and inequalities that faced women at work and in the home. Women were invisible or their subordination was seen as irrelevant to class and stratification in Marxist, Weberian, and occupational/status attainment theories. Thus, "class" was an object of scrutiny as feminists made intense efforts to understand the oppression and exploitation of women. In the social sciences, as in other academic areas, part of that process was an emerging awareness that accepted modes of thinking, theories of society that should help us understand our lives, were implicated in the processes of oppression. The very theories that had been accepted by academic women as well as men as explanations of inequality and exploitation were put into question. Feminist scholars queried and revised theory, as activists tried to unite theory and practice. Race was almost totally absent in the new (white) feminist theorizing,[1] as it was largely absent from the theoretical accounts of capitalist class structures that were feminists' objects of critique.

The outpouring of critical writing on class and gender subsided as new theories were also criticized and no solutions appeared to the problems of class and gender. Feminist theoretical concern turned to other issues, including the diversity of women's experiences and identities, sexualities and bodies, and racial oppression. In the context of political conservatism and the triumph of free market ideology, along with the emergence of postmodernism, mainstream interest in "class" also declined, beginning in the early 1980s. This decline was followed by the partial resurrection of concern with class in the 1990s.[2] As feminists also increasingly discuss class again in the twenty-first century, some of the earlier problems in the feminist class discourse persist. These include how to understand the differences and linkages between production and human reproduction, how to understand unpaid labor in relation to "the economy," how to analyze class, gender, race/ethnicity, and sexuality as mutually constituted in the overall processes of inequality, at what levels of social structure and theoretical abstraction analysis should proceed, and even how class should be defined, given the changing recognition of its relationship to gender, race, and sexuality. Recognizing that class still matters, these issues are relevant to understanding persistent and deepening exploitation and inequality in the twenty-first century.

In this chapter, I discuss early Second Wave feminist criticisms of class and stratification theory, proposals for new theory, and debates about that theory. I then move to more recent proposals for theorizing class and gender, postmodern/poststructural proposals and the conceptual problems encountered when race and other bases of inequality and domination are added to class and gender. Although many different theories of inequality exist, I focus on two dominant versions: stratification theory, in which inequality is rooted in hierarchies of categories or continuous variables such as income or prestige, and Marxist class theory, in which inequality is rooted in relations of capitalist production.

EARLY SECOND WAVE FEMINIST THINKING ABOUT CLASS

Early feminist class debates originated in allegations that women were absent or invisible and devalued in theories dealing with class and other large structures of society. These debates were initially in the context of the long traditions of Marxist and non-Marxist scholarship. Stratification structures based on hierarchies of income, education, or occupational prestige were, in the 1970s, dominant images of class in much U.S. sociology influenced by structural-functionalism. While "stratification" no longer stimulates much debate, continuous rankings along one or more dimensions of valued resources is implicit in many discussions of "inequalities." Marxist and Weberian discourses, although they differed theoretically in regard to class dynamics and conflict, saw classes as groups situated differently in relation to each other in terms of access to valued resources, including the means of production, markets, power, and wealth. During the same period, many nonfeminist theorists (for example, Giddens 1973) were discussing how to think about the new occupations in the rich industrial nations, the vastly expanded white collar work, service jobs, professional and expert occupations. These were and are the "middle," between the manual working class and the bourgeoisie. The middle is persistent, diverse, growing, and now, in the United States, constitutes the majority of those employed in paid occupations. The middle is also heavily occupied by women. In spite of that fact, many male theorists were and still are able to avoid discussions of gender. Race was also largely absent from these discussions.

Feminists did not immediately take up these changing contours of employment as issues in debates about class. Instead, they criticized stratification and class theories and proposed new theories of the political economy of domestic labor and of patriarchy and capitalism. This new thinking was then heavily criticized, with some critics arguing that theorizing as activity was a gendered and racialized process.

Gradational or Stratification Theories

Mainstream stratification research in the 1970s studied the social mobility of men using the "status attribution model," in which men's occupations were ranked according to judgments about their relative "status" or the respect they received in a ranking process. Status was correlated with incomes and education. Male occupations were taken to represent the stratification structure of the society as a whole. Women appeared in these and other stratification theories only as dependents of men and this dependent position was seen as natural or as functional for social stability (Acker 1973). The argument went as follows: the unit of stratification or class was the family; women lived in families; the family as a unit, including women within that unit, had the class position of the male head of household, usually the husband or the father. Inequality within the household was invisible or irrelevant. The fact that employed women earned less than men and were more economically vulnerable was not important for a theory of the society-wide structuring of inequality.[3]

Academic feminists using various occupational class schemes attempted to put women into stratification analysis by including the occupation "housewife" in occupational status hierarchies (Bose 1973; Acker 1980).[4] These empirical studies revealed anomalies when theoretical notions and methodological approaches developed for studying men were applied to women.[5] For example, survey respondents gave the occupation "housewife" unexpectedly high status rankings. As a result, "housewife" was placed near the middle of the stratification structure. Status or respect for men's occupations had high correlations with the income and education requirements for the occupations. But, "housewife" had no income and no education requirements. How could it have a status unrelated to other criteria? This occupation was an anomaly. In general, researchers found that "housewife" did not properly fit into stratification hierarchies. In addition, occupational status scores designed for men's jobs did not adequately describe occupational status hierarchies for women's jobs. Thus, claims that research using these measures was tapping into the inequalities of the society as a whole could not be supported. Status hierarchy theories could not explain why men's jobs were more highly valued than women's jobs.

After this initial success in challenging stratification theory, attempts to "gender" gradational sociological approaches to class and stratification in the United States almost disappeared, replaced with empirical studies that added significantly to knowledge about sex stratification and wage differences between women and men, both central components of the gender structuring of classes.[6] But, these studies did little to push toward greater clarity and inclusiveness in stratification theory.

In Great Britain, the feminist confrontation with gradational/categorical theories continued into the 1980s, when a sharp debate occurred between feminist sociologists and John Goldthorpe, a leading British sociologist, over the inadequacies of his research for understanding women and class. Goldthorpe developed a class scheme by aggregating occupations on the basis of employment relations, including employment status (Goldthorpe 1983; Crompton 1998, 64–69).[7] The classes he identified were the service class, divided into upper- and lower-level professionals, administrators, and managers; the intermediate class, divided into nonmanual clerical and administrative workers, small proprietors, and technicians; and the working class, divided into skilled, semi-skilled, and unskilled manual workers. His occupation-based class categories did not represent women's distributions across the occupational structure, and, as Crompton (2001) points out, the class meaning of a particular occupation varies by the gender of the person in the position. For example, a female nurse will probably spend her working life as a nurse; a male nurse will probably rise to a supervisory or administrative position rather rapidly. Scholars also debated whether or not married women have the class location of their husbands and whether the class of a family is affected by the wife's class if she is employed.[8] Goldthorpe defended his view that married women had the class positions of their husbands, while his critics argued that this could not be assumed because of the rising labor force participation of women and the increase in cross-class families. He attributed gender inequality in employment to "conventional norms" that require women to do the housework and child care (Goldthorpe 1983, 468), implicitly arguing that this inequality has nothing to do with class. In addition, Goldthorpe did not consider that gender might have been involved in the processes of creating the occupational positions and the employment relations that constituted his class scheme. Although this debate was not resolved, Goldthorpe later expanded his class scheme to better represent women and identified the class of the household as that of the "dominant" breadwinner who could be a woman or a man (Crompton 1998, 65). Such modifications were within a rather narrow definition of occupational class structure that could not adequately incorporate the restructuring of employment, new managerial strategies of control and flexibility, and changing interconnections of family and work (Crompton 2001).[9] A more basic problem may be that an idea of class that implicitly retains a dichotomy between a domestic and a public sphere in which the public is conceptualized as gender neutral can never account for the economic situation of women.

Marxist Class/Relational Theory

Feminists looked critically at two different aspects of Marxist theory: structural class theory based on Marx's (1906) *Capital* as developed by sociologists, and the historical materialist analysis of the subjection of women in Engels's (1972) *Origin of the Family, Private Property, and the State*. To simplify long and complex discussions, feminists attributed the absence of women in Marxist class theory to two basic omissions: The theories ignore 1) unpaid domestic labor and 2) the widespread sex segregation of jobs and the gender pay gap. A third criticism was that Marxist theory recognizes but does not sufficiently analyze the reproduction of human beings on a daily and intergenerational basis as an essential part of capitalism (Marx and Engels 1970). The importance of reproduction was grounded in a statement by Engels:

> According to the materialistic conception, the determining factor in history is, in the final instance, the production and reproduction of immediate life. This, again, is of a twofold character: on the one side, the production of the means of existence, of food, clothing and shelter and the tools necessary for that production: on the other side, the production of human beings themselves, the propagation of the species. The social organization under which the people of a particular historical epoch and a particular country live is determined by both kinds of production: by the stage of development of labor on the one hand and of the family on the other. (1972, 71–72)[10]

Engels's insights were not incorporated in later Marxist class theory that was based only in production.[11]

THEORIZING DOMESTIC LABOR

Marxist and socialist feminists pointed out that the unpaid work that women do in the home is essential to the economy and has value that is ignored in class analysis. Ignoring unpaid work followed from the way that the determinants of class are embedded in the core processes of capital accumulation.[12] Classes are rooted in the relations of commodity production. The capitalist owns the means of production and the product; the worker owns nothing but his labor power, which he is compelled to sell to the capitalist; the worker produces the value of his labor power, his wage, and surplus value that is appropriated by the capitalist. This appropriation is exploitation and lies at the center of the relations of production. The interests of the capitalist in maintaining exploitation and the worker in resisting it are, thus, in conflict at the core of the capitalist system, constituting two inherently oppositional classes. Unpaid domestic work does not directly enter the relations of commodity production and, therefore, does not produce surplus value (Benston 1969). Consequently, the work of full-time housewives does not provide a basis for locating them within the class system. Implicitly, their class positions are determined by the positions of their husbands. In this way, Marxist theory shared a fundamental problem with non-Marxist stratification theories.[13]

Feminists, primarily in Britain and Canada, proposed a new theory to solve the problem of unpaid labor. Unpaid domestic labor is essential to capitalism, they contended, because it reproduces the working class, contributing to the reproduction of labor power, class relations, and the accumulation of capital (e.g., Seccombe 1974; Gardiner 1975). Some theorists attempted to directly insert unpaid household labor into core capitalist processes of exploitation and the creation of surplus value. They argued that unpaid domestic work contributes to the production of surplus value but disagreed about whether this work contributes to profit by paying for part of the costs of labor, allowing capital to lower husbands' wages and thus add to its share of the surplus, or whether unpaid labor creates part of the value of husbands' labor power that capitalists actually pay for through a "family wage."

Critics pointed to the excessive abstraction and economism of the theorizing (for example, Molyneux 1979) and argued that the issue of how the value of labor power is affected by domestic production could not be decided. The argument failed for the additional reason that it is basically a functional argument—women are particularly placed in the system because their household work is necessary for the reproduction of the system itself. This has all the difficulties of functional explanations generally—it does not tell us why this, rather than some other way of reproducing the system exists, and it does not tell us how this situation is created—through what mechanisms or practices capitalism keeps women working in the home. With no resolution to the problems of fitting women's unpaid work into the abstract analysis of the production of value and the class concept to which it was linked, this direction in new theorizing disappeared.

Marxist theory also seemed problematic for explaining aspects of women's paid labor, such as persistent sex segregation and sex-based wage differences. Why should women's wages be systematically and persistently lower than the wages of men? If, as the theory said, wages roughly approximate over time, the value of the worker's labor power and that value is determined by the cost of the reproduction of that labor power, how is it that the wages necessary to pay for the reproduction of the female worker's labor power are lower than those necessary for the reproduction of the male worker's labor power? Perhaps women's labor power does cost less to reproduce because women are less skilled than men. Perhaps employers maintain sex segregation so that they can pay less to equally skilled women as a group and divide the working class. Veronica Beechey (1978), in a discussion of this problem, argued that, to explain the relative levels of women's wages, it is necessary to include the family and the sexual division of labor in the analysis. This means moving outside the core analysis of capitalist relations to understand "the specificity" of women's situations. Feminists might argue that explaining men's wages also requires looking at the family and the sexual division of labor, but that idea was not part of the theory.

Some versions of the domestic labor argument abandoned the economic analysis of value for a more general historical thesis that domestic labor is important for capitalism because it reproduces the working class and thus contributes to the accumulation of capital. This has become so widely accepted that versions of such reasoning, perhaps without the Marxist terminology, appear in many discussions of women's positions in society. Such arguments advanced our understanding of the linkages between unpaid labor and the rest of capitalist society, and they suggested questions we should ask whenever we are trying to analyze the situations of women in any particular society (Acker 1980). This debate also revealed some of the difficulties with the abstract structural Marxist approaches of the time, in particular the impossibility of inserting women into theories in which abstract, gender-neutral categories are implicitly based on images of the white male worker, assumed to have a housewife at home. I discuss this further below.

THEORIZING PATRIARCHY AND CAPITALISM

Another solution to the problem of the absence of women in theories of society and class was to see patriarchy and capitalism as separate but intersecting, even tightly interwoven, systems.[14] Patriarchy and capitalism or dual systems theories, were based on the insight that there are material relationships that are not directly grounded in production, whether paid or unpaid, but in human reproduction.[15] Sex, sexuality, conception, giving birth, nurturing children and adults are, without a doubt, concrete and material processes (see, for example, Mitchell 1971; Mackintosh 1979; McDonough and Harrison 1978). Patriarchy theories were at first constructed as analogies to Marxist theories of capitalism, positing a basic structural relation between women and men undergirding patriarchy in, for example, men's control over women's paid and unpaid productive labor or over women's bodies and their reproductive labor.[16] The structural bases of patriarchy, the roots of male dominance, were usually found in the relations of reproduction which are primarily located within the family or in the family conceived as the location of a domestic mode of production (Delphy 1984). Some, such as Heidi Hartmann (1976), located patriarchy in working men's interests in maintaining their advantages over women in both the labor market and the home, through protecting and extending sex segregation in paid employment and reinforcing the division of labor in the family.

Dual systems theories did not directly conceptualize class to include women's situations; instead, they placed their problems outside class, within a separate structure, patriarchy (Acker 1978; Kelly 1979; Petchesky 1979; Young 1981). Hartmann (1981) was explicit about this: "Marx's theory of the development of capitalism is a theory of the development of 'empty places.' . . . *Marxist categories, like capital itself, are sex-blind* [italics in original]. The categories of Marxism cannot tell us who will fill the empty places" (Hartmann 1981, 10–11). "Gender and racial hierarchies determine who fills the empty places" (18). Young (1981, 180) summed up the critique of this position: "The dual systems approach accepts the traditional Marxian theory of production relations, historical change, and analysis of the structure of capitalism in basically unchanged form. It rightly criticizes that theory for being essentially gender-blind, and hence seeks to supplement Marxist theory of capitalism with feminist theory of a system of male domination. Taking this route, however, tacitly endorses the traditional Marxian position that 'the woman question' is auxiliary to the central questions of a Marxian theory of society." Thus, the old theory of class was left intact, but it was still necessary to have an understanding of economy and class to understand women's situations (Acker 1989b). Class positions themselves, one could argue, were created through gendered processes. Notions of separate abstract structures could not capture the shifting, overlapping, processual nature of actual social life.

Although dual systems or patriarchy-capitalism arguments did not result in a new, gender-sensitive class theory, they made many contributions to feminist understanding of women and class, unearthing some of the history of working class women and men in nineteenth- and early twentieth-century capitalism, illuminating the importance of human reproduction and unpaid caring labor to the economy, and making visible the systematic devaluing of women's paid and unpaid labor. At the same time, much of this work raised questions about the claims of gender neutrality and adequate representation of social life of dominant modes of thought, including Marxism. These theories could not answer questions such as why women do most of the housework or why and how women are segregated from men and paid less in the world of employment.

GENDERED PROCESSES IN CLASS CONCEPTUALIZATION

While some feminists were trying to create new theories, others were asking questions about the conceptual practices that had made women invisible, creating barriers to inclusion that were very difficult to breach. Some feminists argued that concepts of class and class processes were not gender-neutral. The worker and the capitalist as prototypical subjects are modeled on the experiences and activities of men, as these experiences were changing in the nineteenth and twentieth centuries (Hartsock 1983). Images of these subjects are anchored in distinctions between production and reproduction, between the public and the private spheres, as they were becoming constructed ideologically and organizationally as separate and gendered in developing industrial capitalist society.[17] "Recent historical scholarship has documented that what social scientists came to identify as *the* public sphere was actually constructed by historical actors as a masculine domain during the eighteenth and nineteenth centuries. Historically, the oppositional construction of public/private was used to justify excluding women from both politics and the market" (Rose 1997, 142–43). While Rose examines the conceptual construction of the working class in historical scholarship, her observations are relevant to sociological constructions of class (see also Scott 1988). "Class" is about capitalist relations of production within an originally fairly narrow, but expanding, range of economic activities within the "public" sphere. Those who are defined as class actors were and are implicitly men, but discursively constituted as gender-neutral. The "individual" and the "human being," as well as the worker and the capitalist, are implicitly male, as Nicole-Claude Mathieu (1975–1976), a French sociologist, argued. In the language of sociology, Mathieu contended, the general is equated with the masculine, while the female is the particular. When sociologists talk about general social processes or the overall social structure, their referents are male, although perhaps not intentionally so. If "class structure" and "class relations" are to be seen as general, not partial, representations of social processes they must be seen as affecting all workers and thus as gender-neutral. But, women's lives and activities often do not conform to this "general;" women's complex responsibilities for production and reproduction were not like those of men. Women were seen as atypical, not general, and their lives and activities were not the model chosen for understanding the overall structuring of society.

The working class so conceived was not only made up of men, but of certain men, white and skilled. Rose (1997) argues that although unskilled men, along with many women, were also paid workers, it was white male skilled workers organized in trade unions who represented the working class in historical and sociological studies. This representation of a portion of workers as "the workers" was rooted in actual practices of exclusion and inclusion in working class history. Women and unskilled men were often intentionally excluded from trade unions and other working class organizations; white male working class identity was developed in processes that differentiated them from the "others," affirming the dignity and masculinity of white working class men (see, for example, Glenn 2002; Rose 1997). These processes were always racialized in the United States. As Brodkin (1998) argues, beginning with slavery, African Americans, as well as successive generations of immigrants, were defined as unskilled and either nonwhite or not-quite-white. This history is complex and long; the point here is that a certain concept of the working class and class organization as white and male informed and still informs research and theory in both Britain and the United States. Concepts of the ruling class, the entrepreneur, or the capitalist also have a gender-neutral status, although their masculine referents are clear.

Concepts such as class positions or class locations also contain unacknowledged gender assumptions, particularly when class positions are equated with "jobs" or positions in the division of labor. Many jobs are created as women's or men's jobs and gender-suitable workers are still preferred and recruited for these jobs. Criteria such as skill and responsibility are often used to classify jobs and occupations. Skill has been seen as a masculine attribute (e.g., Phillips and Taylor 1980; Cockburn 1983), as has responsibility and managerial expertise. For example, job evaluation studies done in the 1980s (e.g., Acker 1989a; Steinberg 1992) show how evaluation schemes systematically value responsibility for money, most often in the hands of male managers, much more highly than responsibility for the welfare of people, most often in the hands of women lower in work hierarchies. I discuss this issue further in later chapters.

An additional reason that class conceptualizations do not adequately incorporate the complex actualities of women's labor is that disciplines such as sociology are articulated to, even embedded in, the "conceptual practices of power" (Smith 1990). Smith (1999) argues that the discursive domain of political economy, including conceptualizations of class, is built upon the textual forms and the relevancies of "the main business" of organizing capitalist production and accumulation. "The main business" includes all the processes of organizing, regulating, controlling production, markets, distribution, labor, and consumption. Investigations of the theoretical entity "class" "build its textual correlates through a selective investigation of the already textual (census and department of labour statistics, economic reports of task forces, commissions, think-tanks, and so forth) and the extra-textual world mediated by interviews, observation, and person reports" (Smith 1999, 36).

In this process, the discourse of political economy defines its boundaries in terms set by the governing and organizing of "the main business." The topics that feminists have attempted to introduce are outside those boundaries. The problem, Smith argues, is one of a concealed standpoint, located in these processes of organizing and ruling, that is obscured by the objectifications of discourse. Efforts to introduce women into this discourse over the last thirty years have been relatively unsuccessful because the concealed standpoint has not been challenged. "The theoretical expansions of political economy introduced by white women have merely rewritten the boundaries" and a solution will be found in "the dissolution of objectified discourse, the decentring of standpoint and the discovery of another consciousness of society" (Smith 1999, 43).

CONTEMPORARY EFFORTS TO THEORIZE GENDER AND CLASS

The wide-ranging feminist criticisms of the concept "class" and of conceptualizing practices in academia continued to be addressed in a variety of ways, although the intense debates of the 1970s and early 1980s did not reemerge at a similar level of committed involvement.[18] "Class," as many have noted, was no longer at the top of the theory agenda (for example, Barrett and Phillips 1992; see also Crompton and Mann 1986). Political events, such as the breakup of the Soviet Union, and economic structural changes, such as the decrease of manufacturing jobs, in the 1980s and 1990s undermined for some scholars the relevance of the Marxisms of the 1960s and 1970s. Images of class became both more diverse and often more diffuse. Feminist scholars turned more and more to questions of identity, race, ethnicity, sexualities, and the body. Those who still identified themselves as "socialist feminists" continued to work with issues of gender and class, although ambitions to produce overarching theories of patriarchal capitalism declined as grand narratives were seen to be oversimplifications that often rested upon essentialist and universalizing concepts. As multiplicity and diversity were celebrated, the grounding of patriarchy in a universal imperative to mother, a universal male interest in controlling women's work and reproduction, the psychosocial structures of family life, or the functional "needs" of capitalism became untenable. One story did not fit all.

Efforts to put together gender and class and to understand the economic aspects of gender inequality went in a number of directions: theorizing structure and action, conceptualizing the relationship between production and reproduction, and bringing identities and meaning into thinking about class.

THEORIZING STRUCTURE AND ACTION

Erik Olin Wright and Gender

Marxist theorizing did not disappear, although debates on gender and class scarcely touched the class talk of male social scientists interested in capitalism and class. Erik Olin Wright, a leading U.S. sociologist, takes seriously the feminist criticisms of class theorizing. He recognizes the importance of gender, proposing a partial dual systems solution that maintains the integrity of his highly abstract analytical Marxist approach. I discuss his approach in some detail because it has been influential in U.S. sociology, is very clearly argued, and illustrates well the difficulties with abstract structuralism.

Wright has developed and modified his analysis of class over time, moving from a class scheme based on relations of domination to one based on a revised notion of exploitation. I will briefly summarize the outlines of his most recent approach (Wright 1997a, 2001a), recognizing that I inevitably eliminate much of the complexity of the argument. Wright argues that the social relations of production consist of rights and powers over resources used in production (Wright 2001a, 16). Class relations exist when there are "unequal rights and powers over the appropriation of the results" (17) of the use of the resources of production. Control over production resources, or assets, allows exploitation—some people appropriate the surplus from the labor of others. These assets are labor power assets, capital assets, organization assets, and skill or credential assets. Material interests are based on these productive assets, which are unequally owned. Those who control productive assets benefit in terms of income. They also control or dominate the activities of others who do not control such assets. Thus, class relations are maintained by exploitation and domination. Class locations are social positions occupied by individuals, and sometimes families, within class relations. Wright also distinguishes between macro-level and micro-level analysis. At the macro-level are the effects of class structures on the large unit of analysis, for example, the nation. At the micro-level are the effects of class structure on individuals. As Wright says, "The basic strategy for moving from *macro* to *micro* levels of analysis is to explore the ways these combinations of relations are embodied in *specific jobs*, since jobs are the essential 'empty places' filled by individuals within the system of production" (Wright 1997a, 45).

Using the criteria of different assets associated with different positions in interdependent processes of exploitation (e.g., capitalist and worker), Wright constructs occupational categories with different mixes of class assets. Empirical analysis using cross-national survey data examines the effects of membership in these class categories on dependent variables such as class identity or the gender division of household work.

Wright does not account for gender and the relative inequality of women within the abstract schema, although the empirical analyses of effects have had some interesting results. Wright is specific about the absence of gender: Within a Marxist class structure concept, at the level of abstraction of the pure capitalist mode of production, there are no "housewives" of "male breadwinners" (and equally, there are not male breadwinners as such). At this level of abstraction, it is impossible to specify the crucial differences in lived experiences of men and women in the working class that are generated by the concrete intersection of class relations and gender relations. Thus, while it is legitimate to insist on the importance of gender for understanding and explaining the concrete lived experiences of people, it does not follow that gender must or can be incorporated in the abstract concept of class itself (Wright 1997a, 49).

Earlier, Wright had proposed that economically dependent wives have an indirect relation to class structure through the mediation of marriage (Wright 1989). Mediated class locations are also occupied by others, such as children, who have no direct participation in "production." More recently, Wright has argued that class and gender are distinct systems that may be interconnected at the empirical level in several ways (Wright 2001b). He suggests a "conceptual menu" for studying these linkages. Gender may be a form of class relations; gender relations and class relations may have reciprocal causal effects; gender may be a sorting mechanism into class positions; gender may be a mediated linkage to class locations; and gender and class may have interactive effects.

Wright's efforts to modify his approach to include women and gender can be criticized by focusing on different stages of their development. The idea of mediated linkages is useful, but it does not capture the economic (class) consequences of dependence on a husband for women; it is simply a way of fitting women into a categorical structure based on male occupations, similar to the earlier status stratification theories. Wright continues to assume that the structure of positions or jobs is gender-neutral, that these are "empty places." He does allow that sometimes gender relations may help to explain why jobs with particular characteristics are available; for example, the supply of low-wage women workers in Third World countries stimulated the creation of certain jobs using this labor force (Wright 2001b). The insight that jobs may be gendered in the process of their invention and construction is not followed up as an entry into theorizing gender and class as more integrally related. Thus, Wright does not confront the possibility that, in general, jobs may be gendered, as many feminists have argued (e.g., Acker 1990). Nor does he confront the possibility that class structure, defined in his terms as employment structure, might be gendered, that is, historically constructed through a division of labor in which men and women were differently included and types of paid and unpaid work were defined as masculine and feminine. As Rosemary Crompton (1998, 2001) argues in an extensive discussion and critique of Wright's work, including his attempts to incorporate gender, "the separation of 'class' and 'gender' means that the genesis and development of the employment structure itself (which is being used as a proxy for class) is not addressed directly" (Crompton 2001, 42).

Wright's notion of productive assets exploited by individuals or position holders is rooted in rational choice theory. The central assumed actor, the rational individual making choices in his own self-interest, is undoubtedly a man, the "individual" of contract theory (Pateman 1988). He is certainly not a woman who often has affiliating and nurturing interests that contradict self-interest, however that is defined. In any case, the theory seems strangely disconnected from his "conceptual menu for studying the interconnections of class and gender." This may simply be an instance of what I see as a general disconnect between his abstract and macro-level theorizing and his empirical work at the individual level. However, the strategy of constructing abstract characteristics of positions that may have tenuous connections with what people actually do in these positions does not seem to be the most fruitful way of going about developing understandings of class that could inform organizing to improve societal democracy, one of Wright's stated goals. A different strategy might be to take the actual (gendered) construction of jobs and hierarchies as the object of investigation, as Crompton implies.

In summary, Wright responds to feminist criticisms by maintaining his view that gender and class are two separate systems that intersect at some times and places. He does not look at the actual, historical development of labor markets and occupations, so he does not deal with the possibility that gendered divisions and ideologies may have played a significant part in these processes. This neglect may be related to his analytic strategy that seems to jump from macro to micro levels, completely bypassing employing organizations and women's ongoing negotiations between work for pay and unpaid family work. His abstract analysis linking "production" to occupational categories assumes a narrow notion of production that cannot include, for example, unpaid household production. Such production and those who do it, therefore, have no relevance to class. His notion of class positions defined by different combinations of exploitation assets appears to be a notion that is gender-neutral. But, we could argue that this gender neutrality contains the same old hidden assumptions that conceal a male subject. His difficulties, indeed only minimal success, in reconciling gender and class illustrate the obstacles to a gendered analysis of class within the terms set by the conventional boundaries of "class," or, in Dorothy Smith's (1999) words, the boundaries set by the concealed standpoint within the conceptual practices of the relations of ruling.

Feminists on Structures and Practices

Wright's work shows again that structural Marxism is closed to the insertion of women into its gender-neutral but implicitly male terrain. But some sociologists did not abandon the idea of "structures" as an overall frame for understanding systematic inequalities.[19] A theory of gender structures developed by R. W. Connell (1987, 2000) is more amenable to bringing together gender and class (and race, sexuality, etc.) than is Wright's abstract structuralism or that of many patriarchy theories.

Connell brings together structure and practice: "To describe structure is to specify what it is in the situation that constrains the play of practice. Since the consequence of practice is a transformed situation which is the object of new practice, 'structure' specifies the way practice (over time) constrains practice" (Connell 1987, 95). This idea of structure as emergent in practice[20] allows for interventions to change structure, and for great variation in both structure and practice. Understanding structure and practice currently and historically requires looking at how practice occurs, how it is configured in particular times and places, and under what constraints. In industrial societies, three main gender structures can be identified: labor, power, and cathexis, or emotional relationships. Connell (2000) later added a fourth structure, symbolism. Understanding the configuration of gender relations in a particular society at a particular time can be achieved with a "structural inventory" of the three (or four) main gender structures. Such an inventory for a whole society is called the "gender order;" for an organization, he uses the term "gender regime." Connell emphasizes that none of the structures are independent of the other and that the structures are part of and specific to capitalist societies. He argues that within the structure of labor there is the gender structuring of production and accumulation. Thus, Connell (1987) suggests that there are fundamental connections between gender and class, and that gender divisions are as fundamental to capitalism as are class divisions. This insight, together with insights from Third World radical movements about capitalist imperialism, "suggest a new view of capitalism, as a system for the concentration and regulation of profits extracted by a number of qualitatively different mechanisms of exploitation, rather than a basically homogeneous structure implied by the concept of a 'mode of production'" (1987, 104).

Connell (2000) also discusses the importance of masculinities, especially hegemonic masculinity or the culturally authoritative masculinity, in constituting power relations such as those of globalizing capitalism. In summary, while Connell does not analyze in detail the intertwining of gender and class, he offers many resources for doing so in his approach to relating practice and structure, in his view of gender divisions as components of production, and in his analyses of the role of hegemonic masculinities in the history and present functioning of capitalism.

While the meaning of "structure" in feminist theorizing has had a number of interpretations, Connell represents the growing agreement that the complex intertwining of class and gender can be best captured through seeing them as mutually constituting processes rather than as more or less static structures, and that studying processes implies studying concrete practices that both reproduce and challenge oppressions and inequalities. Heidi Gottfried (1998), in a similar approach, argues that feminists do not have to choose between structure and agency. Instead, Gottfried suggests that a theory of practice can bridge the gap between structure and agency, and "can enable the study of *embedded* power relations without either reducing gender to class or detaching gender from class analysis" (455, italics in original). Gottfried's suggestions for a theory of practice point in the direction of solutions to the problems of combining gender and class that I use in later chapters.

REPRODUCTION RECONSIDERED

How to bring "reproduction," unpaid work, caring work, or "domestic production" into the analysis of class processes continues to be a problem. This is partly because these concepts are built on gendered dualities: production/reproduction, paid/unpaid, caring/noncaring, domestic/market. The boundaries implicit in these dualities are unstable and often dissolve. For example, reproductive labor may be commodified at one time and place and decommodified at another. Child care is a major, if low-paid, industry. Even conception, pregnancy, and giving birth are commodified in some ways. Women buy the services of doctors and hospitals. Some medical specialists make a lot of money providing fertility treatments. One approach is to analyze how transitions across these boundaries are accomplished, as Nona Glazer (1993) does in the cases of retail sales and medical care. Another approach that attempts to dissolve the duality between production and reproduction is developed by Miriam Glucksmann (1990, 1995, 2000), a British sociologist, in her analysis of the total social organization of labor. The total social organization of labor "refers to the manner by which all the labour in a particular society is divided up between and allocated to different structures, institutions, activities and people" (Glucksmann 2000, 19).

The total social organization of labor is highly differentiated by gender and includes productive and reproductive work, paid and unpaid, wherever it is carried out, in different relations and settings, in changing networks and connections. For example, caring work may occur in both unpaid domestic and paid market sectors and may move across sector boundaries, as much caring work has been pushed into the unpaid sector with the devolution of the welfare state (Glazer 1993). Inevitably, some activities may be work under some circumstances and something else, perhaps recreation, under other circumstances.

The total social organization of labor is a conceptual framework for understanding how labor is organized on a societal scale at any one historical moment and for facilitating understanding of transformations in this organization. This framework makes possible the tracing of complex and changing interconnections between work in the money economy and work in the domestic or nonmoney economy by recognizing both as elements in the broader organization of activities. Glucksmann emphasizes that this is not a theory of determinant relations but a way of looking at empirical material about what women and men do as they weave together their work in different sectors.

Glucksmann developed this framework to analyze working class women's experiences with intersecting domestic, paid, and casual (part-time, informal) labor. In her empirical study (2000), she also examines the effects of time, both on a daily basis and over a lifetime, on the interweaving of different forms of labor, as well as the effects of place, the local configurations of community and work. Glucksmann points out the implications of her framework for understanding class, arguing that class relations of workers cannot be explained independently of the work they do in the nonmarket economy.

As a conceptual tool, the total social organization of labor attempts to erase the privileging of paid work in accounts of the everyday processes of class, bringing unpaid work into the same analytic plane as paid work.

It also attempts to erase the conceptual boundaries between family, community, and "work," boundaries that still persist in academic constructions in spite of the recognition that in the lives of many people, especially women, those boundaries are extremely porous and shifting.

Feminists continue to use the concept of "reproduction" in spite of earlier discussions about its imprecision, its multiple meanings, and some difficulties in drawing boundaries between production and reproduction, defined as bearing children, caring for them and for adults, and doing the tasks of daily life. A great deal of unpaid production goes on in the household; much reproduction is organized in the market, for money. In spite of these and other difficulties, reproduction remains a useful component of a theory of gender and class, race, and sexuality, although the difficulties with the concept should be explored through concrete, empirical studies of the kind that Glucksmann (2000) has done. Many other relevant empirical and theoretical studies now exist, dealing with caring work (e.g., Uttal and Tuominen 1999), family-work intersections, and the household division of labor (e.g., Gerstel, Clawson, and Zussman 2002; Jacobs and Gerson 2004; Moen 2003; Presser 2003), revealing a daily reality that is complex and varying and not simple to integrate into conceptions of gendered and racialized class processes.

IDENTITIES, MEANING, AND CLASS

Postmodern, poststructural criticisms of modernist thinking and theorizing also criticized structural theories, emphasizing that "reality" is constructed through discourse and that to understand society, it is necessary to understand how meaning and identity are produced (e.g., Butler 1990). Some feminist scholars have responded with new efforts to rethink class. These efforts are scattered and emphasize different strands in postmodernism and poststructuralism. All attempt to go beyond the limits of structural class concepts to include the ongoing social construction of meaning and identity and the fluidity of gender and class processes. I discuss only two of a number of different approaches, Nancy Fraser's concepts of recognition and redistribution and Beverley Skeggs's research on British working class women's constructions of identity.[21]

Nancy Fraser produces a discourse on class that is different from most other feminist views. She attempts to bridge the divide between postmodern emphasis on justice through cultural and identity politics and the old emphasis on justice through economic and class politics (1995). Fraser contrasts these two approaches as demands for redistribution from class-based movements and demands for recognition from social movements based on race, ethnicity, gender, and sexuality. She argues that both redistribution (class) and recognition (status) are essential to achieving justice, including feminist aims of gender justice. But, redistribution and recognition have often been positioned in opposition, which undermines political effectiveness. For analytic purposes, she constructs a hypothetical thought experiment, "a conceptual spectrum," with class or economic injustice at the redistribution end and sexuality, specifically homosexuality, at the recognition end. In between are gender and race which, sharing both political-economic dimensions and cultural-valuational dimensions, are "bivalent modes of collectivity." Although Fraser repeatedly confirms that maldistribution and misrecognition are always intertwining, she argues that their structural roots are separate. She positions class, gender, race, and sexuality as separately located in theory, even as she recognizes that empirically these separations are complicated and unclear. Class is more purely economic than gender or race, while homosexualities are basically cultural and evaluative, although often with severe material consequences. Misrecognition and maldistribution are also contradictory in that achieving redistribution means eliminating or reducing class difference, while achieving recognition means accepting and honoring differences based on gender, race, and sexuality. Fraser goes on to analyze and propose political remedies for the two types of injustice which will overcome the contradictions between them.

Fraser rethinks her analysis, particularly the analysis of the politics of recognition in several later discussions (for example, 1997, 1998, 2003). She argues that the identity politics or cultural politics model of misrecognition is problematic. This model has two difficulties. First, it tends to place the problem entirely in cultural devaluation and ignore the intersecting economic injustices or assume that distributional injustice will be remedied when respect and positive evaluation are achieved for the group. Second, by stressing the need for an authentic group identity defined only by the group itself, the model tends to support pressures for conformity within the group and the ignoring of intergroup differences such as gender subordination. Such a model could lead to serious contradictions for supporters of gender equality, as demands for respect by patriarchal groups could be seen as legitimate. This model of identity politics can also lead to separate groups in hostile competition with each other. Fraser (2003) proposes that recognition should be seen as a matter of social status, the status of individuals as full participants in social interaction. Misrecognition is, then, the denial of participation, or "an institutionalized relation of social subordination" (Fraser 2003, 27). Changing negative evaluations requires institutional changes, for example, in laws, policies, or associational rules.

For Fraser, in capitalist society there is "a partial uncoupling of economic distribution from structures of prestige" (Fraser 2003, 31). This sort of society is highly differentiated, with "gaps" between the status order and the class hierarchy. At the same time, status and economic arrangements are complexly interconnected and both must be considered in specific efforts to redress injustice.

In sum, Fraser uses an eclectic mix of Weberian concepts of class (as market-based) and status with a Marxist view of the capitalist economy, rejecting the view that Marx and Weber are incompatible theorists. Fraser argues that both gender and race are "basic structuring principle(s) of the political economy" (1997, 19); they also involve cultural devaluations (misrecognitions) that are analytically distinct from economic processes. At the same time, she recognizes that in the real world almost all oppressed groups suffer from both maldistribution and misrecognition that are highly interconnected. I think that Beverley Skeggs's book could be read as a comment on Fraser, as she gives a concrete but nuanced picture of how class and gender are intrinsically connected, as they are produced and experienced in daily life.

The feminist retreat from class motivated Beverley Skeggs to study the search for respectability of young, white, working-class women in the northwest of England. For her, "class is a discursive, historically specific construction, a product of middle-class political consolidation" (1997, 5). At the same time, class inequality with all its deprivations and exclusions exists beyond its theoretical representations. "To understand the intersections of class and gender in subjective productions" (7), she uses Bourdieu's (1977, 1987) metaphors of capital, constituting a model of class as forms of capital moving through social space. The forms of capital are economic, cultural, social, and symbolic. Social space is historically produced; we are born into various social spaces that give access to varying amounts of capital assets. Skeggs uses these ideas, which I have only superficially represented here, in drawing out the complexity and the difficulties the young women in her study face as they strive for subjectivities as respectable persons. Part of that is trying to distance themselves from identifications as working class, to deny, to disidentify with the shame of such an identity. Some tried to pass as middle class, but did not have the cultural capital to do so. Gender is ever present in the efforts to move beyond the identification as working class. The body is important here, for "Bodies are the physical sites where the relations of class, gender, race, sexuality and age come together" (82). One of the strengths of this perspective on class and gender is the ease with which central issues in feminist thinking, such as the body and its cultural/social production, can be brought into the realm of class and economic inequality. Skeggs effectively brings back class as lived experience, reproduced constantly at the same time that gender in the form of caring, femininity, and heterosexuality is also reproduced.

In summary, the postmodern, poststructural feminist approach presents several different visions of class. These theories draw on the work of a number of male scholars other than Marx, including Max Weber and Pierre Bourdieu. Each approach indicates a way out of the limitations of previous theorizing. However, none of them pay substantial attention to the role of race/ethnicity in the structuring of inequalities, nor do they pay much attention to the economic processes that underlie status injuries.

THE INTERSECTIONALITY OF RACE, GENDER, AND CLASS

While some feminist scholars concluded that class and gender should be theorized as mutually constituting practices and processes, a parallel discourse developed on the interrelations of gender, class, and racial/ethnic processes, emphasizing the experiences of women from a variety of subordinated racial/ethnic groups in both the rich Northern countries and in Third World countries affected by globalization (for example, Collins 1995; Glenn 1999, 2002; Bhavnani 2001; Rowbotham and Mitter 1986). How best to conceptualize the intersections of race, gender, and class, became a major issue (Collins 1995, 2000; Glenn 1999, 2002; West and Fenstermaker 1995a; Fenstermaker and West 2002). This discussion occurred in an intellectual arena somewhat separate from the gender and class debates, but shares some of the same dilemmas about intersecting structures versus mutually constituting processes and uses a concept of class that still carries the marks of its origins in a theory implicitly modeled on certain white men's work relations.

Feminist scholars of color and Third World feminist scholars in both Britain and the United States had made clear for years that much feminist theorizing ignored race and ethnicity and thus helped to perpetuate racism (e.g., Davis 1981; hooks 1984; Joseph 1981; Higginbotham 1992). Feminists of color argued that, in practice, most (white) feminist theorizing assumed a white, middle class woman similar to the women doing the theorizing (e.g., Joseph 1981), and that theories about this middle class woman do not represent the experiences of women in other racial and class situations. Although white feminists recognized that race should be part of their analyses, they did not appreciate how deeply a white racial perspective was built into their analyses of gender and class.[22] Feminist critiques of essentialist and/or universalizing theory that posits a universal (white and middle class) man or woman contributed to the growing understanding among many feminist scholars that no one image of gender relations or women's situations could represent the diversity of racial/ethnic, economic, social, and cultural processes (e.g., Harding 1991). Diversity or multiplicity of oppressions had to be recognized in theory and in research.

One way to recognize multiplicity was to bring together concepts representing different forms or social bases of oppression. Thus, connections between gender, class, and race, as well as other bases of discrimination and inequality such as sexuality, became the focus of empirical studies and theorizing. By the mid-1980s, sociological (e.g., Dill 1979), anthropological (e.g., Sacks and Remy 1984), and historical (e.g., Janiewski 1985) studies were making these connections. By the 1990s, many contemporary empirical studies documented the intertwining of gender, race, and class (e.g., Baca Zinn and Dill 1994; Smith 1995). But, exactly how to theorize the interconnections continued to be a problem.

Most scholars rejected an additive model of gender, race, and class because such a model assumes an internal coherence or commonality of experience within each category. An additive model fails to recognize that gender relations differ within different race and class situations; that "race" encompasses many racial/ethnic groups and racial processes vary in many ways, including on the basis of gender and class; and that class processes are integral to the production of both gender and racial oppressions, while class relations (and capitalism) are shaped in turn by both race and gender processes. As Spelman (1989) pointed out, sexism is not just another burden added to racism for African-American women, it is a different burden shaped by the history and present practice of racial and class subordination. The life situations of women (and men) are not the sum of disconnected segments of gender, race, ethnicity, and class; rather, all these elements are produced and reproduced within the same everyday, historically and locally varying, processes. Society-wide patterns of segregation, inequality, exploitation, and oppression are, in concrete historical processes, constructed and reconstructed within and along class, race, and gender divides. Feminist theory would have to take account of these claims.

Solutions began to emerge in the work of Third World feminists and other feminists doing research on women and development (for example, Benería and Sen 1982; Mohanty 1991) and in the work of feminists of color (for example, Collins 1990; Brewer 1993) who began to see race, class, and gender as intrinsic to each other, as social constructions, realities of power and reward, identities emerging in particular historical moments and local places, but shaped by changing social relations and material realities that we designate as, for example, colonialism, capitalist expansion, and demographic and technological change. Rose Brewer (1993), for example, argued that race, class, and gender processes should be seen as simultaneous forces, and that theorizing must be historicized and contextualized.

"Gender takes on meaning and is embedded institutionally in the context of the racial and class order" (239). However, how to develop the comprehension that race, class, and gender are somehow intrinsic to each other, how to move theoretically beyond the demonstration that this is so in concrete historical instances, has not been easy to elaborate.

The lack of agreement on how to construct such a formulation of complex interrelations was clear in the 1995 symposium on the issue in *Gender & Society* (9 [4]) and the book from that symposium (Fenstermaker and West 2002). For some, the interconnections occur within individuals in processes of identity construction or in face-to-face interactions in which shared or reciprocal identities are produced. For example, West and Fenstermaker (1995a) argued that race, class, and gender are experienced simultaneously and that to capture that "compels us to focus on the actual mechanisms that produce social inequality" (Fenstermaker and West 2002, 60). They outlined an ethnomethodological approach in which these interconnections occur most basically as "situated accomplishments" in interactions in which race, gender, or class categories are enacted and reproduced. West and Fenstermaker emphasize that the process is institutional as well as interactional, and "its idiom derives from the institutional arena in which those relationships come to life" (West and Fenstermaker 1995a, 21). One of their crucial arguments about the interrelations of gender, race, and class is that these categories are reproduced in the same way, "just as the mechanism for accomplishment is shared, so, too, is their simultaneous accomplishment ensured" (30).

Patricia Hill Collins (1995), in a critique of West and Fenstermaker, argues that such an approach, couched in the language of "doing difference," erases the knowledge of institutional power and oppression (see also Weber 1995; Winant 1995). This is particularly clear in their discussion of class: They note but do not discuss "the different material realities imposed by differing relations under capital" (70), suggesting, however, that these realities have little to do with processes of class categorization in daily life. In later work, Fenstermaker and West (2002) reply to their critics and emphasize again that interaction always occurs within institutions or social structures in which power differences exist. However, what constitutes institutions or structures is not clear, and how power differences are produced is also unclear. They imply that structures are normative systems, but the processes generating normative systems are not spelled out.

Collins proposes that, instead of seeing interconnections as situated accomplishments, interlocking oppressions should be conceptualized as macro-level structures that link "systems of oppression such as race, class, and gender" (Collins 1995, 492). Individuals and groups occupy positions "within interlocking structures of oppression described by the metaphor of intersectionality" (Collins 1995, 492). Together, interlocking macro-level systems and intersectionality shape oppression, Collins argues. This approach has some of the problems encountered in efforts to link gender and class as separate systems of patriarchy and capitalism. How macro-level systems are actually linked is unclear. How intersectionality at the micro-level is put together is also unclear, as are the processes that connect macro and micro levels. The meaning of class remains unspecified.[23]

The notion of interrelated systems of oppression that operate on both macro–social structural and micro–social psychological levels is elaborated by Lynn Weber (2001, 71–72). These interactions are historically and geographically specific, socially constructed, and consist of power relations of dominance and subordination. Gender, race, class, and sexuality operate simultaneously at both the societal and individual levels. Weber (19) defines class as hierarchical ranking based on "position in the economy—in the distribution of wealth, income, and poverty: in the distribution of power and authority in the workforce." She uses empirical examples, such as the situation of women receiving welfare benefits, to illustrate the intersections of gender, class, and race. Weber develops the notion of intersectionality but still leaves unresolved issues about how "systems" are put together and how macro and micro processes are connected. Nevertheless, she lays out in clear terms the arguments for and the elements in an intersectional analysis of concrete experience.[24]

Implicitly addressing the problem of levels, a first step in conceptualizing "interacting, interlocking structures," in Evelyn Nakano Glenn's terms (2002, 6), "is to bring race and gender within the same analytic plane." Glenn does this by using a social constructionist approach that "provides a common vocabulary and set of concepts with which to look at how gender and race are mutually constituted—that is, at the ways in which gender is racialized and race is gendered" (7). Further, in Glenn's analysis, race and gender are relational, for example, woman and man as categories gain meaning in relation to each other. Race and gender involve representations and material relations and are importantly constituted through power relations. Gender and race are both fundamental principles of social organization and sources of meaning and identity. The processes of their constitution take place in many, or most, areas of social life, at all levels of structure. Both race and gender are variable and shifting historically.

Glenn does not ignore class, discussing it as the development of the labor system of the United States, within which the meaning and materiality of both gender and race were constructed and changed. She discusses the interweaving of gender and race in the development of segregated labor markets, fights for unions and the family wage, debt bondage, and racial oppression. However, Glenn does not theorize class in a way that is comparable to her theorizing of gender and race. She does not suggest that class is gendered and racialized, nor does she argue that class is mutually constituted along with gender and race. This absence of class from the usual tripartite construction raises a question: Is class exploitation, oppression, and inequality so different from race and gender that it cannot be seen as comparable enough to be analyzed within the same analytic plane? Or, differently stated, can class be conceptualized as also socially constructed, gendered, and racialized? The answer can be a qualified "yes." But to accomplish such a notion of class requires thinking about class in the particular ways that have been developed by many of the feminist scholars whose work I discussed above (e.g., Rose 1997; Connell 1987; Gottfried 1998; Acker 1988, 2003). The task is to liberate the concept from its implicit grounding in white male experience during a particular historical period and redefine it in ways that permit analysis of a broad range of actually existing class relations.

In summary, scholars working on the interweaving of race, class, gender, and other axes, dimensions, or forms of inequality or exploitation agree that these are simultaneous processes, socially constructed, historically and geographically specific, and involving material, ideological, and psychological elements which create and recreate unequal economic and power distributions. These differences must be analyzed together if we are to understand the complex lived realities of women (and men) and the social/economic processes that set the conditions for their/our lives. But, precisely what is meant by class and by embedded, mutually reinforcing, and simultaneously reproducing systems are still issues. Class is defined in a variety of ways: as position in a system of economic inequality that involves power differences in workplaces, as a dichotomous measure of education, as material differences related to capitalism. Or class is simply left unspecified, thereby remaining implicitly grounded in assumptions that class actors are men. The linkage to the capitalist economy, necessary, I believe, to an understanding of class, is often not apparent or only implicit. Because class is my primary interest here, I have focused on the problems with that concept in this discussion of the idea of intersectionality, neglecting other contributions of this work that push forward the recognition of the complexity of the task of combining in one analysis what scholars and activists have defined as multiple and different forms of oppression.

CONCLUSION

"Class" is still a necessary category of analysis. As economic inequality and severe poverty deepen, as middle class families face increasing stress over time and money, while redistribution to the corporate rich increases its pace in the United States and most other countries, any idea that class and capitalism are no longer relevant concepts must be seen as a delusion. But, the old notions of class, implicitly based on images of male lives, are what should be abandoned. This inventory of feminist thinking about class shows that there is no generally accepted theoretical solution to the criticisms feminists made in the late 1960s and 1970s. At the same time, agreement among many of the authors discussed here seems to exist on some issues. Most would abandon abstract structuralism in favor of more concrete notions of class, based in "lived experience," practice, or historically specific accounts.[25] Dual systems theories, most agree, are not useful. The linkages are more fundamental. The ongoing and simultaneous production of gender and class, along with race/ethnicity and sexuality, are named in various ways—embedded, mutually constituting, intertwining, intersecting. In addition, many would expand their notions of what constitutes class relations, ending the privileging of production and bringing in reproduction, distribution, and consumption to expand the relevant economic processes.

Unresolved problems persist. Reproduction in the sense of human reproduction and unpaid labor in general has not been successfully integrated into class understandings. A substantial amount of variation exists about the precise meanings of class and gender relations. Adding race and sexuality to class and gender and conceptualizing intersectionality raises again some of the old issues about class and gender: If dual systems theories placing gender (women's) subordination in one system and class (economic) subordination in another system were unsatisfactory, are multiple systems theories any more successful? How can class, race, and gender be understood in one conceptual frame? What do the metaphors of mutually constituting, intertwining, intersecting mean in terms of concrete analysis of social practices? While most feminists theorizing class have abandoned abstract structuralism, the issue of how to think about "structures" or "structuring" persists. Although the critiques of particular Marxisms are compelling, class is still the concept that links economic inequalities to capitalist processes. Thus, there are reasons for feminists to continue to locate their understandings of class within a broadly conceived Marxist perspective. I think that a historical-materialist analysis is still useful for feminism; the starting place must be the material conditions of life and the relations involved in the production of those conditions in particular historical moments. Feminist issues can be addressed with this general methodological perspective, including questions of how race is integral to historical and daily class/gender processes, and how questions of identity, sexuality, bodies, and violence (for example) are involved. Building on the theoretical work I have briefly summarized here, I develop one version of this approach in the following chapters.

NOTES

1. Both Heidi Hartmann (1981) and Zillah Eisenstein (1979) recognized that race is an important system of oppression, but did not develop this insight in their analyses of patriarchy and capitalism.

2. Portes 2000; Baxter and Western 2001; Hall 1997; Crompton, Devine, Savage, and Scott 2000; Esping-Andersen 1993.

3. See Nancy Folbre (1994), *Who Pays for the Kids?* for an economist's interpretations of these debates.

4. These issues are not only old history: The same measures, the same approach to mobility, and the same erasure of women still appear in articles in top journals. See for example, Thomas A. Diprete's (1993) discussion of mobility of men workers in the *American Sociological Review*.

5. These anomalies helped to undermine these approaches in quite a Kuhnian way. Thomas Kuhn (1962) in *The Structure of Scientific Revolutions* argued that scientific revolutions occur partly as a result of anomalies that accumulate as research more and more explores the implications of the dominant paradigm.

6. See Irene Padavic and Barbara Reskin (2002) for an inventory of research on women's labor force participation, sex segregation, the gender pay gap, and the mutual impacts of work in the labor market and work in the home.

7. I include Goldthorpe's class scheme here as a gradational scheme, although he sees it as a relational scheme. Crompton (1998, 66) notes that other critics have seen it as hierarchical and gradational.

8. Goldthorpe 1983, 1984; Britten and Heath 1983; Heath and Britten 1984; Stanworth 1984; Erikson and Goldthorpe 1988; Leiulfsrud and Woodward 1987.

9. A very long discussion on the technical points of this debate can be found in the references already listed and in Rosemary Crompton's and Michael Mann's (1986) *Gender and Stratification*.

10. Engels theorized women's subordination through a historical materialist analysis of the development of the family. He argued that in the historical development of production and the single monogamous family, "the wife became the head servant, excluded from all participation in social production" (Engels 1972, 137). Engels clearly understood the contradictions for women who, at the time he was writing in the second half of the nineteenth century, were going to work in "social production;" "if she carries out her duties in the private service of her family, she remains excluded from public production and unable to earn; and if she wants to take part in public production and earn independently, she cannot carry out family duties. . . . The modern individual family is founded on the open or concealed domestic slavery of the wife, and modern society is a mass composed of these individual families as its molecules" (Engels 1972, 137). Thus, he located the problem in women's exclusion from production and the fact that the monogamous family was the economic unit of society.

Engels's belief that women's entry into "social production," into the paid labor force, would end male dominance in the working class family was not confirmed by the history of either capitalist or socialist countries. Women continued to carry the double burden of paid and domestic labor; men continued to be privileged heads of households. Moreover, the transformation to socialism and the eradication of private ownership of the means of production, legal equality between the sexes, and the widespread full-time labor force participation of women did not create equality. The oppression of women was more complex and more persistent than Engels had imagined. Nevertheless, Engels conceptualized women's oppression and exploitation as systematically rooted in basic political/economic/historical processes, a view that is central to most feminist sociology.

11. *Of Marriage and the Market* (1981), edited by Kate Young, Carol Wolkowitz, and Roslyn McCullagh, contains a series of complex papers on women's economic and sexual subordination, production, and reproduction, which critique and extend Marxist arguments.

12. This is a short version of the theory that was current in the early 1970s. A huge literature on interpretations of Marx and Engels existed then and has become more vast in the intervening years. Early feminist criticisms were directed primarily at the versions of Marxism then fashionable in the new left movements and in academia that did not include the more historical and humanistic interpretations, such as the work of E. P. Thompson (1963).

13. The critical feminist literature on Marxist class theory is voluminous, providing the starting point for widely differing efforts to include women in analyses of class structure. See Sandra Morgen (1990) for a summary of this literature. See also Jaggar (1983) and Hansen and Philipson (1990).

14. Rowbotham 1973; Delphy 1984; Hartmann 1976, 1981; Eisenstein 1979; McDonough and Harrison 1978; Kuhn 1978. The extensive debates around this theorizing have been summarized and assessed by, among others, Michèle Barrett (1980), Veronica Beechey (1978), and Sylvia Walby (1990) in Britain and in the volumes edited by Heidi Hartmann (1981) and Karen Hansen and Ilene Philipson (1990) in the United States. I will not replay these extended discussions here.

15. Reproduction is an ambiguous concept, and its use is frequently confusing. In Marxist theory, reproduction refers to the reproduction of the means of production and of class relations, as well as the reproduction of labor power. Most feminists have used reproduction to mean human reproduction, raising children, caring for their needs as well as caring for other adults and doing the concrete work of reproducing daily life, such as cooking, cleaning, and doing the laundry. Most of these activities reproduce labor power, but they seem rather distant from the reproduction of the relations of production. Production or products are necessary for reproduction of human beings and their labor power. When the concept refers to the reproduction of human beings, including childbearing and nurturing, and is used to explain the continuing secondary place of women in employment (and class), the danger exists of falling back into a biological reductionism with the implication of the inevitability of subordination. "Reproduction" used in this way is also an element in a functional explanation: Women are subordinate to men because their unpaid reproductive work is necessary for the functioning

of the economic system. See Michèle Barrett (1980) for a more complete discussion of the usages and difficulties of the notion of "reproduction."

16. See Mary O'Brien, *The Politics of Reproduction* (1981), for a complex discussion of the centrality of relations of reproduction in human history.

17. Public and private spheres have existed in other societies such as ancient Greece and Rome. This discussion refers to the modern development in which the public and private were differentiated as production moved out of the household and family establishment.

18. Some Marxist feminist scholars reject the proliferation of critiques of Marxism and the socialist feminist efforts to reconstruct class theories to account for women and gender in capitalist societies. Martha Gimenez (2001), for example, argues that although race and gender domination are significant forms of oppression, class is the more fundamental form of power and that "class relations . . . are of paramount importance, for most people's economic survival is determined by them" (Gimenez 2001, 31). Class as a system of oppression is not equivalent to gender and race. In addition, Marxist analysis is necessary to understand the historical development of class relations and the ways in which these relations are related to both gender and race.

19. For example, Sylvia Walby (1986, 1989) developed a model of six gender structures, or patriarchy, to analyze the forms of women's oppression in Britain. These were "a patriarchal mode of production in which women's labour is expropriated by their husbands; patriarchal relations within waged labour; the patriarchal state; male violence; patriarchal relations in sexuality; and patriarchal culture" (Walby 1989, 220). These six structures are analytically independent of capitalism and class, but often interact with capitalist processes. See Pollert (1996) and Acker (1989b) for criticisms of this approach.

20. Connell credits the ideas of the presence of structure in practice and the constitution of structure through practice to Anthony Giddens (1979) and Pierre Bourdieu (1977). He is also critical of their different versions of the structure-practice ties for their inabilities to successfully integrate history into the theory.

21. Gibson-Graham's (1996) reformulation of Marxist capitalism and class theory aims to open spaces for innovation and change in capitalism that, they argue, is discursively constructed as an oppressing and inescapable totality. Harriet Bradley (1999), responding to poststructuralist critiques of realist notions of class, develops an analysis of both material relations and representations of those relations in working life in specific organizations.

22. This was not true of all white feminist scholars. Anthropologist Karen Brodkin Sacks, for example, analyzed gender, race, and class in the 1980s (Sacks and Remy 1984; Brodkin 1988). However, I include myself among those white feminist scholars who gave a nod to race without seeing that I spoke from a privileged white location (e.g., Acker 1973; 1988).

23. Kimberlé Crenshaw (1995), writing from the perspective of critical race theory, uses "intersectionality" somewhat differently, referring to structural and political intersectionality in concrete terms. Structural intersectionality can include poverty, unemployment, lack of good housing, insufficient child care, and legislation discriminating against immigrants, all of which have varying impacts

based on race, gender, and class. Political intersectionality refers, for example, to the situation of women of color who may be situated within two or more subordinated groups with political organizations that conflict in some ways.

24. Intersectionality is an important but difficult focus for feminist economists as well as sociologists and anthropologists, as Rose M. Brewer, Cecilia A. Conrad, and Mary C. King point out in a special issue of *Feminist Economics* (2002) dealing with the "mutually constitutive nature of color, caste, race, gender, and class" (5). A primary problem is "contending with the deep intersectionality of these social forces" (4). How to think about categories and how to use them in analyses are other problems. Having added caste and color to the list, how to define and differentiate between categories becomes an issue. And again, what is meant by "simultaneity" and "inextricably intertwined" is at issue.

25. Feminist historians such as Jane Lewis (1985), Judy Lown (1983), and Joan Scott (1988) had made this argument for some time, as had other scholars, such as Lourdes Benería and Gita Sen (1982), Cynthia Cockburn (1983, 1985), and Anne Phillips (1987).

3

Thinking about Gendered and Racialized Class

The old notions of gender-neutral class structures, with their sometimes hidden white male class actors, were implicitly gendered and racialized class concepts. Explicitly thinking about class as gendered and racialized is one way of making visible all the "others" not represented in those now outmoded views of class.[1] Thinking about gendered and racialized class may also be a way to replace the metaphors of intertwining, intersecting gender, race, and class. This approach expands the insight that class is gendered and gender is produced through class by adding processes of racialization. In this chapter I first discuss some conceptualizing practices that contribute to developing such a view of class. Then I outline a view of class relations, suggesting the ways in which they are gendered and racialized, and conclude with a sketch of a theory of racialized and gendered class processes.

THINKING ABOUT CLASS—CONCEPTUALIZING PRACTICES

The review in chapter 2 of feminist writing on class, gender, and race suggested that certain conceptual approaches would contribute to developing an analysis of gendered and racialized class. These approaches are: first, thinking about social relations and structures as active practices, occurring in specific historical and geographical places; second, beginning the exploration of class from the standpoints of women and men located differently from white male class actors; third, clarifying the meaning of gendering and racializing; and fourth, broadening the understanding of the economic relations that constitute class and extending the analysis of gendering and racializing processes beyond production.

PRACTICES, RELATIONS, AND STRUCTURES

Thinking about "the social" or society as human practice, rather than as abstract structures, is necessary for developing the idea that class is gendered and racialized, partly because race and gender seem to disappear in structural class analyses. Heidi Gottfried (1998), using the work of Bourdieu (1977) and Gramsci (1971), proposes a theory of practice to direct "attention to embodied activity rather than sterile structures, shifting our gaze to gender and class relations as embedded in everyday practices" (464). Gottfried uses the metaphor of excavation to describe the methodology of unearthing gendering practices that perpetuate male power. Racializing practices can be excavated, together with gendering, in the same way.[2]

The idea of the "social" as practice has roots in Marxist historical materialism.[3] The social arises in the concrete activities of human beings as they produce and reproduce their lives, within conditions they did not create, but which they often attempt to change. Thus the social is human practice, existing in the sentient activities of living, embodied beings. The social exists in concrete, time- and place-defined locations, and thus it is always historically located and historically specific. Practice, as I use the term, includes production of material "things," virtual nonmaterial "things," the material and emotional production of human beings, and all the ordinary activities of daily living. Practice is always infused with meaning, and usually informed by thought, although many ordinary activities are guided by tacit knowledge, not consciously invoked. Thought, language, and meaning are also practices and can be understood "as what people do, as existing in time, and as integral constituents of social relations and organization" (Smith 1990, 202).

The concept of "social relation" extends this way of seeing social life. "Social relations" can be thought of as bundles of interrelated practices that organize social life and connect people with one another (Smith 1990). "Extended social relations," often mediated through documents and other texts, link practices in the local and concrete place with other distant practices that may be invisible from a standpoint in the local everyday world (Smith 1999). For example, supervisors in a call center may try to increase the number of calls per hour each worker should answer. The workers feel pressured and hurried, but may be unaware that these pressures originate with the managers of large mutual funds who invest in the company and who are demanding better returns of company executives, who consult with lower-level managers and come up with the demand for increased productivity. Extended class relations thus help to organize and constrain local practices. At the same time, what I/we do here today influences the practices that shape our own and others' local lives. For example, welfare workers sometimes find ways around the rules imposed from remote and unknown members of Congress and filtered through layers of bureaucracy, paper, and e-mail to the local desk in the local welfare office where the worker and the aid recipient are sitting. These social relations extend across the legal and conceptual boundaries of organizations and institutions. Extended social relations are generalized and generalizing, operating to create similar situations across many local places, across regions and national boundaries.

Large "social structures" can be understood in terms of social relations, particularly extended social relations that link the local to the extra-local. These relations are multiple, often contradictory, constantly being constructed and reconstructed, knitting together the activities in widely separated places. At any particular moment, and often for long periods, they have identifiable and repetitious forms. Most of us participate in these processes, creating local forms, adaptations, and innovations, and sometimes fundamental changes. But fewer create and have the power to enforce the practices which guide the creation and coordination of the concrete activities. Still, conflicts over power to define and implement organizing practices are endemic. Corporations struggle to keep governmental controls at a minimum, labor unions fight to gain or maintain power over wage setting, environmental organizations campaign for more governmental controls.

I think it is important to recognize that local, embodied, concrete activities of people constitute many of the links in extended relations; there is always the local and the particular within the extra-local. Extra-local places are local for the people, such as top managers, legal teams, and legislators, who are actively creating the practices that constrain and structure the local. Of course, their actions do not always translate to other local places, but they often do. The local places within the extra-local are connected in dense webs of practice. In other words, social structures are not just out there, bearing down on us, but consist of the real consequences of things that people do in real historical time. Important aspects of gender, race, and class are produced in these complex webs of social relations linking local and extra-local sites. This conceptual move suggests a shift in terminology—we are enmeshed in class relations, not located in class structures.

This way of looking at large structures, at the local and the extra-local, provides an alternative to the concepts of macro, meso, and micro often used to talk about social processes, such as class processes, extending across time and space. While thinking in terms of macro, meso, or micro can be a useful simplification when discussing very complex processes, this usage obscures the practical activities that interconnect the "levels." Another problem is that what is taken to be micro, whether the individual actor, a small group, or relations between individuals and groups, is always present within macro or meso processes. Meso processes or structures often refer to organizations in which managers, technical staff, supervisors, and workers all are busily carrying out the activities that constitute the organization. While talking about the meso level as though the organization is a decision-making actor can summarize actions and their effects, to understand what happened it is necessary to go behind the summary to look at what people were doing. Organizations could better be seen as fields of coordinated and controlled activities and practices than as a level of social structure. Macro structures or processes are either statistical aggregates expressing the compilation or outcomes of many actions, such as unemployment rates, or representations of outcomes of actions taken by powerful groups that affect large numbers of people, such as "economic restructuring." Some of these outcomes are unintentional for some or all group members and are the results of uncoordinated actions, for example, the U.S. stock market decline in 2001. Thinking in levels tends to reify these social practices and processes as "forces" that seem to operate independent of human actions.[4]

This understanding of social relations as practical, concrete activities, that of necessity involve thinking and feeling, allows discovery of class relations rather than deriving them from abstract, a priori formulations. This makes possible a dynamic and multifaceted picture of class, gender, and racial/ethnic processes, dramatically different from a categorical approach that assigns individuals and families to theoretical class positions and then investigates the correlations of class position with other variables.[5]

BEGINNING IN THE STANDPOINTS OF WOMEN (AND MEN)

Feminists have argued that to develop knowledge about different women's situations, the social world must be viewed from their racially, ethnically, and sexually diverse standpoints.[6] A similar argument can be made in regard to some men from nondominant groups who have been invisible in previous class analyses. Using this strategy, the implicit modeling of "class" on the situations of certain white men can be altered. Standpoints can be seen as points of entry into gendered and racialized class relations. Thus, this use of the notion of "standpoint" is methodological.

It potentially directs our view to relations that have been relatively unobserved by beginning in the everyday experiences of real women and men belonging to different racial and ethnic groups and asking what practices or social relations their experiences are created through, thus taking their standpoints.

From the standpoints of a variety of women and men, many issues may be critical class issues, although they are probably of little interest from the perspectives of the white male managers of capital or of white male workers. From these many different standpoints, it is possible to look back at the relations of ruling to see how local class situations are being constructed. Two examples from my own research show, I believe, the insights that can be gained from this approach. The first example is from a study done in the late 1970s and early 1980s of the impact of feminism on middle-aged women (Acker, Barry, and Esseveld 1981). A substantial number of the women we interviewed were full-time housewives married to men with adequate incomes. They had few economic worries, but they felt insecure. Some looked back with regret at their younger selves who, during World War II, had been independent, self-confident, working at interesting jobs, traveling alone across the country. They couldn't believe that they had ever been such independent, fearless people. Now some were afraid to go out by themselves in the evening, afraid to try to get a job. They could be seen as examples of women suffering from Betty Friedan's (1963) "problem that has no name," caught in economic powerlessness and isolation. I wanted to understand these existential dilemmas in terms of class processes, rather than in terms of psychological reactions to lonely affluence. What were the relations within which this disempowering experience was produced? One answer was that these women were enmeshed in particular relations of distribution, the society-wide relations in which money was transferred from wages to the support of children and their mothers/caretakers through husbands' earnings. The women's own efficacy in assuring their economic security was weak. Their interactions with much of the surrounding world were mediated through their husbands. They felt insecure in distribution relations that produced both insecurity and security.

Another example comes from research on women who receive welfare (Acker and Morgen 2001; Edin and Lein 1997). From the perspective of capital, poor mothers on welfare in the United States are of little interest, at best members of an economically draining "underclass," caught in webs of dependency. From the perspectives of those women, their class as well as gender and racial situations look quite different. In complex interactions with public bureaucrats, private charity personnel, employers, lovers, husbands, other family and friends, they put together a livelihood from a number of sources—public assistance, wages, charity, support payments, and gifts (Edin and Lein 1997). Public assistance payments are never enough to cover the cost of living, but neither are wages from the jobs usually available to them. The costs of health care and day care are high and cannot be covered by minimum wages. The only feasible avenue is to combine income from various sources in varying mixes over time (Acker et al. 2001; Hartmann and Spalter-Roth 2003). A lot of effort goes into maintaining this pattern of survival as these women negotiate within complex relations of ruling. All of this work constitutes their gendered and racialized class situations. They are not marginal to capitalism, as "underclass" implies, because they are enmeshed within its relations. But, they are marginal from the standpoint of capital, serving an ideological function as images of sin and failure.

DEFINING GENDERED AND RACIALIZED CLASS PRACTICES

The idea of racialized and gendered class practices is an alternative to conceptualizing race, class, and gender as intersecting or interlocking systems or structures. To say that class is racialized and gendered means that gender and racial/ethnic divisions, subordinations, and meanings are created as part of the material and ideological creation and recreation of class practices and relations. Class processes are shaped by gendered and/or racialized practices and privileges, justified and explained within discourses that define gender and sexuality in racial terms (Higginbotham 1992).

I distinguish between 1) class practices, 2) gendering and racializing processes, and 3) effects of gendered and racialized class practices. Class practices are all those activies that organize and control production and distribution. I discuss these in some detail below. Gendering and racializing processes shape class practices. I also discuss these below. The effects of gendered and racialized class practices are diverse forms of inequality: gender and racial/ethnic segregation in employment, both hierarchical and horizontal, unequal distributions of power, types of work, and monetary rewards. For example, employers in certain restaurants and resorts hire only young, white, attractive women as waitresses or hostesses (Adkins 1995). These hiring practices are gendered and racialized and result in a gender-, race-, and age-segregated work force. Effects and their severity change over time, and vary within and between localities and nations. People often see gender and race effects as natural, just the way things are. The naturalization of inequalities then influences subsequent gendering and racializing processes, as assumptions about what is natural shape perceptions and actions. That is, there are reciprocal, or feedback, influences between effects and practices. For example, secretaries in the nineteenth century were usually white men. As businesses became more complex and larger, record keeping tasks expanded and changed, particularly with the development of the typewriter. Employers turned to relatively well-educated young white women for a labor force that was less expensive and more available than a male labor force. As the occupation expanded and became a segregated white female job, the image of the secretary changed (Kessler-Harris 1982). That image and the division of labor it represented then became part of selection and choice practices, essentially regendering and racializing those practices, and helping to maintain "secretary" as a highly segregated and relatively low-wage occupation.

A focus on economic class inequalities constituted as gendered and racialized does not explore all facets of race and gender. The historically and discursively established categories of class, race, and gender stand for different avenues of entry into complex ongoing practices. Each entryway directs us to particular facets of social relations, to particular practices. Class provides the entry point into complex webs of relations in which capital is accumulated, inequalities are generated, work is accomplished, and gendered and racialized people put together ways of surviving. Class involves the production and distribution of material and nonmaterial things, in which gender and race processes shape class practices and their outcomes.

Analysis could also begin from the entry point of gender relations. From such a beginning, attention would focus on practices involved in, for example, human reproduction, sexuality, and family, as these are implicated in and affected by divisions of labor, exclusions, and inequalities of race and class. "Race relations" as an entry point directs the view to exclusions, inequalities, and separateness in many areas of social life based on racial/ethnic divides and difference within both class and gender. Such an elaboration would make explicit, but with different points of departure, the processes of mutual creation of race, class, gender, and perhaps also sexuality, suggested in the work of many feminist sociologists (e.g., Brewer 1993; Collins 2000; Weber 2001; Williams 1997; Brodkin 1998). Description and analysis of an actually existing issue, for example, abortion rights, welfare "reform," or corporate scandals, might begin from a particular starting point and then expand to look at how the issue is constituted and dealt with, using mutually constituting gender, class, and racial processes to comprehend the practices of oppression and power.

Although the concept of gendered and racialized class relations depicts class, gender, and race as inherently interconnected, these concepts also represent differences that may be lost to view in the effort to approach them as mutually constituted. One problem is that both gender and race stand for extremely diverse realities. "Gender" represents historically varying differences across class and racial/ethnic divides, as many have pointed out. Simplifying this complexity by talking about "gender" as a general term may mean that a white, middle-class woman is still the hidden referent. Race is similarly complicated. Different racial/ethnic groups have different histories and present conditions. Differences within groups also cut across class and gender lines. For many in the United States, "race" had been historically defined as black. African Americans are in different situations than other racial/ethnic groups in this white-dominated society. As Andrew Hacker (2003, 22) has said, "none of the presumptions of inferiority associated with Africa and slavery are imposed on these other ethnicities." Studies of whiteness (e.g., Frankenberg 1993) have begun to raise the consciousness of whites about their own race privileges. Yet, as with "gender," simplifying the complexity by talking about "race" may obscure the complexity behind the category.

An important difference between gender, race, and class as processes of inequality and exploitation is the degree to which they are defined as legitimate and enforced both formally and informally. In the contemporary United States, class relations are legitimate and regulated by laws, governing practices, regulations and rules, supervisory procedures, and union-management agreements that specify, support, and sometimes limit the power of employers to control workers and the organization of production. Class-based inequalities in monetary reward and in control over resources, power, and authority, and the actions and routine practices that continually recreate them, are accepted as natural and necessary for the ongoing functioning of the socioeconomic system.

In contrast, inequality and exploitation based on gender or race are not legitimated and regulated by law, although gender and race discrimination and inequality are, of course, institutionalized in other ways and widely practiced. At one time in the not too distant past, race- and gender-based exclusion and subordination were legitimate and were written into laws in the United States. A civil war, many years of struggle by African Americans culminating in the civil rights movement, and two mass women's movements extending over a century were necessary to remove these bases for discrimination and subordination from the laws of the land and to lay the basis for a decline in their legitimacy. Thus, at the beginning of the twenty-first century in the United States, class exploitation and inequity have far more legitimacy than gender- and race-based exploitation and inequity, which are illegal and defined as discrimination, although white privilege and male privilege are ubiquitous. The legitimacy of class is, at the present time, so self-evident that no one with any political or economic power, at least in the United States, discusses eliminating wage labor and mandating a communal and cooperative organization of production, although many at least claim to be in favor of eliminating gender and race inequality, discrimination, and segregation.

BROADENING "THE ECONOMY"

The economy is conventionally defined as the production of goods and services, of material and nonmaterial things, their exchange for money in markets, and the distribution of the surplus from that exchange. Paid employment in production of goods and services for markets has defined "work" and "class." As I discussed in chapter 2, feminists have contended, since the 1970s, that other sorts of paid and unpaid production are part of the economy: unpaid domestic production (or reproduction) that includes bearing and caring for children and others,[7] subsistence production for the household and sometimes the community, and volunteer work (Benería 2003). These activities can be seen as economic, whether or not they contribute to the profits or the value produced by capital. Another type of unpaid work contributes to the profits of capital: all the tasks that once were done by paid employees but are now done by customers, clients, and family caretakers (Glazer 1993). We load and unload our groceries, find our size in the bathing suit department, wait in a queue for computerized information because no one answers the telephone, take care of very ill people at home, buy our own airline tickets on a computer screen, check in at the airport by ourselves. All of these activities reduce the wage bill that employers must pay, increasing the surplus that goes to capital.

Informal economic activities that provide goods and services for money are also parts of economies.[8] Alejandro Portes and Saskia Sassen (1987) define the informal sector as "the sum total of income-earning activities with the exclusion of those that involve contractual and legally regulated employment" (31). Informal activities, in their definition, are all the work that is off-the-books, for which no taxes or Social Security payments are made. Informal work may be, for example, manufacturing or construction labor, restaurant or catering labor, household or domestic labor, yard work, or selling at flea markets. Some of these activities are more visible than others to those who theorize about class. Informal economies exist in the rich nations of the North and West as well as in the less wealthy countries.

Many state activities are economic in nature. "The economy," as many have argued (e.g., Polanyi 1944), is embedded in social, political, and cultural processes. Boundaries between economic and certain political processes are, I think, particularly difficult to determine. Clearly, industrial capitalism emerges through political as well as economic activities. The state is a major facilitator of capitalist accumulation, providing the legal and material infrastructure, as well as subsidies and other economic guarantees to businesses. The state also determines major aspects of the employment relation. Boundaries between state and economy seem to collapse in the case of some distributions of money. In particular, states in their taxation, welfare, and insurance functions distribute money to selected groups. Thus, state distributions to low- and middle-income individuals, such as unemployment compensation, Social Security payments, or welfare are economic transfers that provide support when income is lost. State distributions also go to the wealthy and to corporations. These, too, should be seen as part of the economy and components of class relations.

Feminist economists have attempted to redefine the economic. For example, Julie Nelson defines economic activity as "the provisioning of human life . . . the commodities and processes necessary to human survival" (1993, 32). "Voluntary exchange is part of the process of provisioning, but so are gift-giving and coercion. Organized, impersonal markets are one locus of economic activity, but so are households, governments, and other more personal or informal human organizations" (Nelson 1993, 33). The idea of provisioning is a promising approach to expanding the understanding of economic practices which are part of the production of class.[9] Provisioning can also include those activities that link work to the rest of life. They are, for example, organizing child care, coordinating work and family schedules, arranging transportation, taking care of conflicts between work requirements and family emergencies. These unpaid activities are necessary to facilitate and accomplish provisioning. They were not counted as economic as long as they were part of the invisible work of housewives. These activities become visible as economic as they became commodified in the service sector.

One implication of this discussion is that economic activities and class relations are not always embedded in practices that directly contribute to the accumulation of capital, but may be, nevertheless, practices constrained and influenced by capitalist processes. In the above discussion of the methodological approach of taking the standpoints of "others," I described how low-wage mothers of young children often put together their economic survival. Their multiple methods reveal the class relations in which they are enmeshed—wage relations, informal economic activities such as babysitting or selling at garage sales, distributional relations such as those embedded in families or welfare programs, and complicated arrangements to take care of children and work at the same time. These are components of the provisioning of human life and ensuring survival.

In summary, an expanded definition of the "economy" as processes of provisioning includes production for markets and for immediate use, of products and processes, including caregiving, as well as various forms of exchange and distribution. Those practices that link paid work and the rest of life should also be seen as economic. Capitalist production and accumulation are central economic processes, but do not exhaust the meaning of economy. Capitalist control is not total: People keep inventing economic activities outside capitalist control and these play a part in constructing class practices.[10] I view this as a tentative definition of the economic, open to revision. This understanding of what is meant by economic practices leads to a diverse overall picture of class practices and relations. But, it is potentially an inclusive and dynamic view, within which there is space for women as well as men, for those whose economic/political situations are deeply shaped by racism, as well.

Based on this view of the economy, I define class as differing and unequal situations in access to and control over the means of provisioning and survival. Capitalist control of production and finance to achieve the goals of profit and accumulation also controls and shapes provisioning practices, providing many with adequate resources, but undermining the abilities of many others to provide adequately for themselves and their families. The definition of "adequacy" is socially constructed and historically varying, a subject of disagreement and contention. Minimally it includes food, shelter, clothing, and the resources, such as education, to participate in the society. The definition of adequacy that I use later in this book is empirical, estimates of living wage budgets made by economists and sociologists. In the following section, I discuss class practices in more detail.

CLASS PRACTICES AND RELATIONS

The concept of "racialized and gendered class relations" stands for the multiple practices that create[11] differing and unequal situations in access to and control over the means of provisioning and survival. There are three main configurations of class practices: those associated with paid and unpaid production, broadly defined to include reproduction, those associated with distribution, and those associated with articulating paid and unpaid work. Class divisions also arise in other institutions, shaping access to provisioning. Education is a powerful influence in shaping access, as are family and community resources. Racial and ethnic variations are great. I don't analyze education and other resources here, but note that the very basic likelihood of finding paid work at a "living wage" may depend on these resources. In general, those who have the most power in the realm of production receive the largest returns in the realm of distribution.

RELATIONS OF PRODUCTION AND REPRODUCTION

Production and human reproduction are accomplished through both paid and unpaid work. Although much reproduction is unpaid, a great deal of it is paid labor, including employment in education, health care, child and elder care, food preparation, and house cleaning. I temporarily bracket unpaid domestic and caregiving labor in order to focus on the practices that constitute class relations in paid work.[12] This is only for the purpose of this discussion, for in the "total social organization of labour" (Glucksmann 1995) market work and unpaid domestic work are closely interconnected and cannot be understood in isolation from each other. "The class relations of wage workers . . . could not be explained independently of the factors underlying their mode of insertion in the market economy" (Glucksmann 1995, 69). That mode of insertion has to do with their participation in unpaid domestic work and with the ways in which they reproduce their own capacities to work.

The Practices of Paid Labor

The relations within which paid work is performed have a number of different forms. Class practices tie workers into capitalist processes, but some ties are direct, others indirect. For example, the daycare provider who takes children into her home works as an independent contractor, selling her services. Her ties to capitalist processes are indirect, as she is paid from the wages of others who are in formal employment. Such ties do not define boundaries of class as some sort of totality, nor do they define boundaries of distinct classes, as groups and individuals may be involved, at the same time or over time, in more than one "class relation."[13] For example, a part-time worker may get wages from capital in the morning, but work as an independent babysitter in the afternoon. Similarly, jobs in the public and the nonprofit sectors are not directly tied to capital, but work processes often facilitate capitalist processes and the relationships between workers and employers, the organization of work, and the expectations for performance tend to be very similar.

The practices of paid labor include the gendered and racialized hiring processes, constructions of work hierarchies and jobs, the wage relation, the employment contract, the work process itself, how it is organized and controlled, how autonomy and control are allocated to the worker and to management, and how conditions are set for coordinating paid work and life outside of work. I briefly discuss employment contracts, including wage provisions, and their implementation, because these play a central role in constructing differences in access to and control over the means of provisioning.

Employers and employees make employment contracts in local places. Such contracts are formal and informal, explicit and implicit. Formal and explicit contracts are made within extended social relations that link the participants into state and federal offices where rules and regulations about such matters as working hours and pay, or safety and health on the job, are made, or that link professional and technical jobs into credentialing bodies such as universities and professional associations. Bureaucratic texts and messages often link these agreements into other areas of the large organizations of which they are often a part and from there into global relations. Employment contracts specify, or are assumed to specify, what work the worker is to perform, what the work hours and schedule will be, what fringe benefits are included, and the pay. Contracts also specify that whatever is produced is the property of the employer, although this may be an unspecified assumption of the contract. In other words, employment contracts implicitly set the terms of exploitation. Agreements also deal with the security and stability of employment. Informal, often implicit, contracts specify and extend formal agreements. Informal contracts include expectations that are taken for granted, such as obligations to follow the orders of supervisors, respect those in higher positions, come to work on time and work hard, and behave appropriately in terms of gender, race/ethnicity, sexuality, and age. Employment contracts, both explicit and implicit, can be seen as gendered and racialized agreements that define, distribute, and use gendered and racialized bodies.[14] Implementation of these agreements is often through highly bureaucratic processes, using practices that replicate gender and race inequalities as they organize work processes (Acker 1990).

Middle-class professional, technical, and managerial workers have employment agreements that differ from those of clerical, service, and manufacturing workers. Although "middle class" is a large and heterogeneous category, jobs so designated are generally less routinized, less closely supervised, and offer more employee control over the work process than do jobs that are not defined as professional, technical, or managerial.

Wage setting, as part of the implementation of employment contracts, is also often bureaucratized in processes that result in gender- and race-based wage inequalities (Acker1989a, 1991). Many studies show that the proportions of men or women in a job affects the level of pay: The higher the proportion of women, the lower the relative pay (e.g., Kilbourne,

England, and Beron 1994; Tomaskovic-Devey 1993; England, Christopher, and Reid 1999).[15] Further evidence that the wage relation is gendered and racialized is provided by studies showing the erosion of white men's pay over the 1970s and 1980s in occupations with a large share of white women and African-American workers (Catanzarite 2003). Similarly, wages in minority-dominated jobs are lower than wages in similar white-dominated jobs, and this wage disadvantage applies to white workers as well as minority workers in these jobs (Kmec 2003). In other words, wages are attached to jobs and occupations, not to individuals, and jobs that are stereotyped as female, black, or Hispanic have lower wages even for white men. The persisting wage gaps between white men and all other gender/race categories of workers (Mishel, Bernstein, and Boushey 2003, 170–171) also suggest that gender and race are built into wage-setting procedures. The wage relation is also gendered and racialized, as it involves the sale of control, not over abstract gender-neutral bodies, but concrete gendered and racialized bodies.

Employment agreements are now widely categorized as "standard" and "nonstandard." Standard employment involves the exchange of labor for monetary compensation from an employer, work on a fixed schedule, usually full-time, at the employer's place of business, under the employer's control, and with mutual expectations of continued employment (Kalleberg et al. 2000). Standard employment usually also includes health and retirement benefits. Nonstandard work does not have the security of tenure and benefits of standard employment. These agreements and the wage relations they include may be affected by the gender and/or race of typical job holders and their relative power in organizations and the labor market. Gendered and racialized images lurk behind the gender- and race-neutral language of "standard" and "nonstandard" employment. The idea of standard employment with its steady living wage is linked to the image of the ideal male breadwinner household; nonstandard employment is linked to the image of the married woman who does some part-time work, or to the image of the immigrant farm laborer picking strawberries.[16]

The power to set the terms of the employment contract is overwhelmingly in the hands of employers, particularly for blue collar, clerical, and lower-level service jobs. Relatively little room for individual variation exists when wages are set in bureaucratic systems, although manipulations of bureaucratic systems exist (Acker 1989a). In addition, workers' lack of alternatives to waged work increases employers' power (Perrow 2002). Professional and managerial employees have more possibility than lower-level employees to set the terms of employment. Union membership increases the control of workers over the pay, the benefits, the security of the employment, and the ability of the worker to have some say in, or at least to be able to predict, hours, schedules, and tasks. That is, union jobs tend to be "standard" employment with higher pay than nonunion jobs (Mishel, Bernstein, and Boushey 2003, 189–196).

Nonstandard work includes part-time, temporary, on-call, self-employed, and contract jobs. Nonstandard work also includes contingent work, defined as temporary or short-term work. Contract workers may be employed and dispatched by an agency or they may be self-employed. Many nonstandard workers find their own work with the help of networks of family, friends, and former colleagues. This is the way that many domestic workers, whether immigrants or native-born, find their jobs (Romero 1992).[17] Elite professional independent contractors earn high incomes: They are disproportionately white men (Kalleberg et al. 2000). However, most nonstandard jobs have lower pay than comparable standard jobs, fewer benefits, less security of employment, and often extreme demands for flexibility or variable and unpredictable hours of work (Mishel, Bernstein, and Boushey 2003, 250–261). Some nonstandard work is in the informal economy of "black" or off-the-books production, street vendors, and microenterprises (Benería 2003). Such work is totally unregulated, usually paid in cash, with no withholding of taxes and no reporting to any state authorities.[18] "Nonstandard" is a catch-all category including the illegal immigrant from Guatemala doing domestic work in Los Angeles and the high-priced business consultant flying from one global city to the next. What they have in common is the absence of an agreement that they will have work with a particular employer for the foreseeable future.

Other types of employment relations and agreements exist in the informal economy. Most of these are not accounted for in official statistics. Sweatshops, small manufacturing establishments that avoid government oversight, have reappeared in the apparel industry (Rosen 2002; Bonacich and Appelbaum 2000), employing primarily immigrant women in work conditions reminiscent of the worst nineteenth-century worker exploitation. Employment, often unpaid, in small, family-run businesses, is another form of relation in which culturally diverse ideologies of mothering, heterosexuality, family, and marriage converge to create a racial/gender dividend for capital (Mohanty 2002). Such employment may take place within the home, contributing to its invisibility. Other almost invisible payments are made for informal, casual services and production, such as babysitting, cleaning a friend's house ostensibly as a favor, or mowing the neighbors' lawn. Some of these payments may be difficult to categorize as market exchanges because they are made within personal helping relations with kin, friends, and neighbors (Williams and Windebank 2003), but they may be important as individuals put together enough cash to buy the groceries. In other sorts of informal work the agreement may be implicit and the activities are either illegal or on the edge of illegality. Prostitution (and other forms of sex work) is one such area,[19] and the drug trade is another. Criminal activities are not usually included in class analyses, except as deviant behavior associated with an "underclass." A case has been made, however, that the international illegal drug system, from small farm producer to final customer, distributes drugs and money in ways that have multiple connections to class and to capitalism across national boundaries (Stares 1996).

The above discussion uses bureaucratic language to describe the skeleton of employment agreements, but, of course, these are agreements between real people acting within concrete workplaces. These people have bodies, are aware of their own and others' bodies. Images and evaluations of gendered and racialized bodies often frame the ways in which employment contracts are transformed from texts into actions.

The Practices of Unpaid Labor

A very large, but difficult to measure, proportion of the work of the world is unpaid. One estimate is that "between 40 and 60 percent of the total value of all U.S. output" is from nonmarket (unpaid) work (Folbre and Nelson 2003, 113). As I outlined above, much unpaid labor in Northern wealthy nations is domestic labor, including care work. The work necessary to organize daily activities so that adults can do both unpaid and paid work is an additional form of unpaid work. Subsistence production and volunteer work are other forms of unpaid labor. In every country, women do a large proportion of this work, especially of child care (Benería 2003). Subsistence production, often seen as characteristic of societies with large peasant sectors and relatively little industrialization, still exists in rural areas of the so-called advanced societies.[20] For example, in our study of the consequences of welfare reform in the state of Oregon (Acker and Morgen 2001), we interviewed several women who supplemented their low wages with produce from large gardens they maintained, usually with their mothers or other female relatives. Subsistence production is also reappearing in some parts of former socialist countries now in transition to market economies (Kandiyoti 2002). Volunteer work, such as running food banks or community kitchens, provides important income replacement for people with low money incomes and little access to state income supports. At the other end of inequalities, volunteer work can function primarily to maintain status and class distinctions, as in the activities of some upper class women (Kendall 2002).

Unpaid labor presents problems in conceptualizing class in the wealthy countries in which wage labor is at the center of class processes and money is necessary for provisioning.[21] A primary question about unpaid domestic labor for understanding class is how this work affects the gender and race structuring of inequalities, and thus affects the abilities of different groups to obtain the resources to support daily life and survival. Women still do the bulk of unpaid labor in the home, as many studies show (e.g., Presser 2003). When the demands of family and work conflict too much, many women adapt to these double demands by leaving the labor force for periods of time or working part time, if they can afford to do so. Because doing unpaid caring work is the major reason that women do not work for pay, caring work has a negative impact on earning ability in the paid labor market. Michelle Budig and Paula England (2001, 219) found "a wage penalty of approximately 7 percent per child" inflicted on mothers. In addition, part-time and sporadic paid work reduces the likelihood of promotion to more demanding and more secure jobs.

In general, then, dedication to family and unpaid domestic and caring work leads to a deterioration of earnings and authority prospects in the paid labor market. Unpaid family work, no matter how satisfying to the individual, how central to child and family well-being, or how important to the society, increases gendered economic inequalities as well as racial and class inequalities between women. Thus, doing unpaid caring work enmeshes the care provider in insecure class relations in which the carer's ability, in a totally monetized economy, to provide the necessities of survival is undermined. To reiterate, this outcome is a result of gendered and racialized class practices, and constitutes a class, not an individual family, problem (Crompton 2001).

RELATIONS OF DISTRIBUTION

The ongoing class processes in capitalist societies involve those who are not employed, such as children and many women and men who are out of the labor force, including older people who have retired.[22] Taking the standpoints of single mothers on welfare, of other mothers and housewives, the elderly poor, the chronically ill, or the unemployed reveals that relations of distribution other than wages, salaries, and profits are essential to survival in contemporary societies, and thus can be seen as economic and as components of class structuring (Acker 1988). While distribution through wages, profit, interest, and rent are all important, distribution through marriage and other family relationships and through the state are essential economic transfers, and most of these are patterned along lines of gender and race as well as class.

Relations of distribution are sequences of linked practices through which people share the necessities of survival and divide, usually unequally, the fruits of production. Distribution, along with production, is shaped by politics, by contests for power over who should control the processes and to whom should go what share. All societies have some distributional arrangements, which vary with other aspects of social organization and culture. In some, production and distribution are embedded within kinship groups that at the same time define gender and determine rights or entitlements to subsistence. In others, production takes place outside the family or kin group and much of distribution to individuals is in the form of wages. In the latter type of industrial, now almost always capitalist, society, distribution to nonwage earners is through family and marriage or partner relationships, through welfare state programs, or through the channels of stocks, bonds, rent, and other forms of wealth transfer such as subsidies and tax structures. These different forms of distribution result in huge, and in the United States in the beginning of the twenty-first century, rapidly growing inequalities of income, wealth, and well-being (Keister 2000). Distribution relations vary in the ways in which they are legally regulated, in their legitimacy, and in the concrete practices through which they are constituted. The structure of distribution relations varies in wealthy capitalist countries, depending upon political history, the relative power of capital and labor, welfare state differences, and differences in the earnings patterns of women and men. In all complex societies whose inhabitants have diverse racial/ethnic histories, distribution relations are also racialized. On a global basis, large differences in distribution exist with extreme distribution deficits in some countries, particularly in the Third World. Below I briefly comment on some forms of distribution.

The wage is both an aspect of production and a mechanism of distribution. It is the major way that production becomes the means of subsistence for the majority of men and women in twenty-first-century industrial societies. The wage is represented as a market exchange and, in the wealthy capitalist nations, becomes the personal property of the wage earner. As I discussed above, wages are socially produced within gender and racial differences and serve to reproduce and reinforce those differences as economic conditions change. Health insurance, retirement plans, and other benefits provided by employers can be considered part of wages and salaries in the United States.

Personal relations of distribution through marriage, other intimate relations, and kin relations are primary ways that wages and wealth are distributed to those who do not have their own resources for survival. This distribution is often legally regulated and sometimes required by law, although legal obligations have changed historically and vary widely between states. Child support laws are an obvious example. These are personal relations in the sense that they occur in interpersonal contexts culturally defined as based on caring, love, commitment, and often sex.

At the same time, personal relations are linked into distant economic and political processes, including social movements and state interventions to support social reproduction that was in jeopardy as capitalist industrialization developed. Distribution to children in the United States is primarily accomplished through family relations and responsibilities, resulting in severe inequalities between children (see chapter 6). Family and kin networks continue past childhood to distribute cash and emotional support to those whose economic survival is threatened by unemployment or illness. Family and kin networks also distribute wealth at the upper levels of the income structure; indeed, family-based distribution is one way that extreme differences in wealth are maintained. Gender is often an organizing principle in these distributional relations: Housewives depend on husbands for money income in the male breadwinner household where it still exists, but in a growing minority of households, the woman is the primary breadwinner (Rose and Hartmann 2004). In other families, the woman and the man are coproviders. Women are most frequently the ones who organize distribution to children and to other family and kin, even when it is the male wage that is distributed.

Despite the variety of forms, for most people in wealthy capitalist countries, personal relations of distribution depend upon the existence of the wage-based system of distribution. If the wage declines or is destroyed, the personal relations are changed, even severely threatened. Low wages or unemployment often undermine marriage stability, particularly in the absence of other sources of support such as a welfare state safety net or personal savings.[23] While all personal relations of distribution are ensconced within emotional-moral ties, marriage may be the most problematic. In marriage, the exchange of money and unpaid labor is an integral part of society's system of distribution. Yet this exchange is accomplished within an intimate, ideally sexual, relationship. A societal and structural relationship appears as a relationship specific to two people. Negotiation over money and unpaid labor can undermine the sharing, commitment, and sexual mutuality prescribed in ideologies about marriage. In addition, issues about how industrial societies should arrange distribution and ensure survival are often obscured as such issues are redefined as interpersonal conflict or instances of individual parental irresponsibility.[24] Intergenerational distribution goes in both directions, to children and to parents.

The full-time housewife is enmeshed in the practices of unpaid labor, personal distribution, and the articulation between work and life outside work, part of her unpaid labor. Her situation in class processes is risky and potentially financially disastrous because she depends for income upon personal relations of distribution within marriage, giving her little power and control over, or access to, the means of provisioning (Bergmann 2003). The situation of a housewife married to a wealthy businessman is, of course, very different from that of a housewife married to a clerk at Wal-Mart. But, whatever the income and the status of her husband, her unpaid labor does not enhance her ability to earn a wage, but detracts from it, as discussed above. If she and her husband divorce, she is likely to see her income fall rapidly. Depending on her age and education, she may have great difficulty in finding a job. Her years of unpaid work are only a negative factor in the job market. Her identity, sense of efficacy and independence, and confidence in the future can suffer as she is enmeshed in these personal relations of distribution, as my study of housewives, discussed above, showed (Acker et al. 1981). The life of a full-time economically dependent housewife may become more and more a prerogative of women married to wealthy men. African-American women have pointed out that housewifery as a full-time job has been a white privilege; it may also become an elite class privilege.

State relations of distribution are usually conceptualized as the welfare state, transfers to middle and working class people, distinct from state transfers to corporations and wealthy individuals. If we include the latter kind of transfers, we may have a more accurate accounting of how state policies shape class processes. Some welfare state transfers to individuals and families substitute for wages when these are not available to support families and individuals. Such transfers "decommodify" labor (Esping-Andersen 1990). That is, such payments protect workers against being forced to sell their labor at any price employers offer. Some transfer programs support those who are poor, often single mothers and their children, but also those who are unable to work because of injury, illness, or age. Services such as universal medical care and child care are also distributed by governments in almost all wealthy countries except the United States. Some benefits are allocated on the basis of needs, others are allocated universally as rights of citizenship, while others are allocated as a reward for service or on the basis of inability to participate in paid labor because of unemployment, disability, or age. The latter are often based on previous earnings and funded by contributions from employers and individuals. White women and persons from racial and ethnic minorities are almost always disadvantaged in earnings-based transfers because their prior earnings were lower than those of white men.

Welfare distributions vary dramatically in form and adequacy in the different welfare states, as voluminous literature on the topic shows (for example, O'Connor, Orloff, and Shaver 1999). Welfare state benefits are often gendered and influenced by race in their structures and effects, even when laws and rules are written in race- and gender-neutral vocabularies.[25] For example, the Social Security retirement system in the United States originally excluded agricultural and domestic workers who were disproportionately African Americans, contributing to the perpetuation of extreme poverty among elderly African Americans. These exclusions were the result of political compromises to ensure the support of Southern legislators (Quadagno 1994). Income support programs for the poor in the United States, such as Temporary Assistance to Needy Families, are primarily directed at women, while others, such as military retirement and military medical programs, are primarily directed at men (Nelson 1990; see also Gordon 1994). These gender-focused programs may reinforce particular gender relations, such as the male breadwinner model, by, for example, either making women's survival possible outside marriage or by restricting support, forcing them into marriage to a breadwinner. Historically, one of the largest U.S. welfare programs ever implemented, the GI Bill of Rights for veterans of World War II, was a program primarily for white men, as the U.S. military in World War II had not integrated either men from racial minorities or women into its ranks. The GI Bill included transfers for education and training, loans for home purchase, employment services, and unemployment insurance, which contributed to the expansion of the racialized and gendered postwar middle class (Axinn and Levin 1992).

Income support transfers have an impact on inequality, on the relative proportion of populations living in poverty, and on the gender and racial structuring of class differences. As many studies have shown, women, especially single mothers, have higher poverty rates than men in all nations except Sweden (Christopher, England, Smeeding, and Phillips 2002), where generous welfare benefits support single mothers' labor market participation in a number of ways. Post-tax, post-transfer poverty rates are lower in countries with more extensive welfare state distribution programs, with higher union density rates, and with social democratic governments (Moller et al. 2003; Gustafsson and Johansson 1999; Korpi and Palme 1998). Welfare state distributions affect class structures, but the existence and level of those distributions is profoundly affected by politics, including the power of labor unions and left political parties in comparison with the power of capitalist organizations.

Tax expenditures are another form of state distribution, with most benefits going to relatively affluent individuals, small businesses, and large corporations, influencing the contours of gendered and racialized class. "Tax expenditures are tax credits, exemptions and deductions that simultaneously lower tax liability, subsidize 'preferred activities' and reduce the revenues available to the U.S. Treasury" (Morgen 2004). For example, an income tax deduction for the interest on mortgages is available to homeowners in the United States. Owners of a second home also receive the deduction on this home. People too poor to own a home, disproportionately women and minorities, do not receive this tax deduction, which amounts to a subsidy for home ownership. Low-income families with children may receive the Earned Income Tax Credit, a refundable credit, meaning that those without a tax bill still receive a refund. Child care tax credits, deductions for dependents, and education tax credits are other benefits to families. These credits are transfers to people who owe taxes, not to those whose incomes are too low to pay taxes. Higher incomes and expenses result in higher credits. These are only a few of the tax expenditures that constitute a hidden welfare state (Morgen 2004; Howard 1999). In the United States, massive state subsidies go to corporations in the form of contracts, direct subsidies, and grants, for example, to large agricultural firms, or in the form of tax loopholes and reductions (Johnston 2003).

Taxes are also distributed through the provision of community resources, such as education, housing, services such as street maintenance, and transportation. Distribution to working class and racial/ethnic minority communities is often less adequate than distribution to more affluent communities. Differential community resources contribute to racialized class differences. For example, unemployment of African-American working class men increased in the post–World War II period as manufacturing moved out of the cities to the suburbs, racist barriers preventing their moving to find new jobs, and lack of public transportation made it difficult to get to suburban jobs (Brown et al. 2003, 90–96).

Financial wealth may be distributed directly, rather than being channeled through the state, to those who do no work for this largesse. They are investors, whether of their own earned money or of inherited wealth. Wealth also comes from savings and home ownership. Wealth is defined as net worth, a family's assets, including a house, savings account, retirement accounts, stock ownership, minus debts, including mortgages, credit card debt, and other debts. In the United States, wealth inequality is more extreme than income inequality and has increased over the last forty years (Keister 2000). In addition, wealth is very unequally distributed by race, with African American households having very little wealth compared with whites (Mishel, Bernstein, and Boushey 2003, 283). The intergenerational inheritance of wealth is an important mechanism in reproducing racialized class inequalities.

Articulating Paid and Unpaid Labor

Managing the interface and the daily transitions between the paid workplace and life in a family and a home involves scheduling, arranging for care of children in some cases, monitoring children's after-school activities from the workplace, arranging transportation, getting and maintaining clothes for work, actually traveling from home to work, and in some cases, arranging social events related to paid work. This work is shaped by the organization of the job and the paid workplace, its proximity to the living place, and by the composition of the household and the work that needs to be done there. Much of this work is done by women and is usually invisible. Those with high incomes can pay others to do much of this work. Stay-at-home wives often do this work for their husbands and it becomes part of unpaid domestic duties. Single mothers with low incomes have the fewest resources for this work. Their difficulties in putting together paid and unpaid work are often the reason that low-income women lose their jobs. These are economic activities that are unpaid, but that have a hidden relation to capitalist production because they deliver workers to their workplaces on a daily basis. These activities also contribute to survival within a capitalist society.

Class Structures and Class Locations

Three additional issues are: 1) how to conceptualize the class situations of individuals, 2) whether the unit of class analysis should be the individual or the family, and 3) how to talk about the larger class picture or "class structure."

Individuals can be seen as enmeshed in complex webs of racialized and gendered practices that change over the course of the lifetime. These webs are not endlessly varied, as many people are enmeshed in the same practices. But, they are too multidimensional, complex, and shifting to be described as "locations" in "class maps."

Analyses of inequality, including class inequality, often focus on inequalities between families. This focus obscures differences between family members in access to and control over the means of provisioning in both paid work and in intrafamily exchanges. Thus, to understand class inequalities it is often important to focus on individuals. However, sometimes comparisons between family types, such as two adult worker versus single adult worker families, or comparisons between working-class and middle-class families, or comparisons between families with different racial/ethnic identities reveal severe gendered and racialized inequalities. For such analyses, families can be considered "the unit" of class analysis. In addition, people as members of families play a significant part in perpetuating class inequalities. They may share resources or put great effort into preserving the status and economic power of the family when there are status and power to preserve. Parents try to assure that their children get good educations and good jobs, to achieve easy access to the means of provisioning. Thus, family ties are important in understanding these processes.

I think we can talk about overall class configurations in terms of aggregates of people or groups similarly embedded or enmeshed in webs of practice. Because practices are gendered and racialized, there are probably considerable differences within any one grouping. Or, a more accurate picture might be attained by using gender and race/ethnicity as criteria for placement in an aggregate. This is a fluid notion of fragmented aggregates, with shifting boundaries and shifting practices, particularly during times of economic and employment restructuring, such as at the beginning of the twenty-first century. Although I am committed to this notion of class as relations always in process, there are times when a shorthand way of indicating location can be very useful. Therefore, I will sometimes use the designations manual working class, service and clerical working class, middle class—a large and heterogeneous grouping (Bradley 1999)—and capitalist class to designate very large aggregates with similar situations of access to and control over the means of provisioning

SUMMARY: THEORIZING GENDERED AND RACIALIZED CLASS: A PRELIMINARY SKETCH

1) "Class" stands for practices and relations that provide differential access to and control over the means of provisioning and survival. This is a relational, rather than a categorical, view of class. For example, class practices take place in the ongoing relations between employers and employees, or in the ongoing relations between citizens/workers and the state. These relations include: 1) paid and unpaid production/reproduction practices; 2) distribution practices through wages, personal relations, the state, and financial institutions; and 3) practices in the workplace and the home that link and coordinate these sites.
2) These relations are gendered and racialized through a number of processes:
    - *Pursuing material interests*. Corporate leaders and their political allies, acting on their interests, make decisions that shape the availability and character of gendered and racialized jobs and distribution systems. Employers acting on their perceived economic interests often hire people from particular racial/gender groups: Seeking low wage costs they may hire white women, blacks, or Hispanics, or relocate jobs to other countries with low-wage women workers. Seeking stability in a white male workforce, they may hire only, or primarily, white males. Employers may change the gender of their workforce. The gender of the new workers then becomes identified with the job (Reskin and Roos 1990). Once

particular jobs are gendered, racialized, and segregated, employers may have economic interests in maintaining segregation. Pursuing material interests and making political compromises to protect those interests, as in the design of Social Security and unemployment insurance discussed above, may gender and racialize state distribution relations. Managerial economic decisions that are apparently gender and race neutral can have gendering and racializing effects. Workers, too, pursuing their perceived economic interests may contribute to creating, maintaining, or changing gendered and racialized class practices. For example, in local places, some male workers resisted pay equity policies because they feared their own wages would be lowered to achieve equality with women's wages (Acker 1989a).

- *Organizing work, constructing rules and unwritten expectations, on the implicitly male model of the worker* who is unencumbered with caring responsibilities and ready to devote his life to the job. This worker is also usually implicitly white. This model of the workplace and the worker, institutionalized as the way (gender-neutral) things just are, places women on the periphery, a bit out of place, even when they have no caring responsibilities. Of course, some men, particularly minority men, can also be out of place. This model also implicitly casts caring work as less important than paid work. Women must comply with the expectations of this model. If they are managers, they must "manage like a man" (Wacjman 1998). I discuss this model of work and the worker further in chapter 4.
- *Constructing and using images, stereotypes, and ideologies about race and gender*. These constructions guide, justify, and legitimate gendered and racialized decisions, ways of organizing, and divisions of labor. Images of masculinity and femininity may be crucial in developing new occupations and even whole industries. For example, Karen Ashcraft and Dennis Mumby (2004) show that in the emerging airline industry, class, gender, and race were consciously used to create images of the professional (white male) pilot and the reliable company that customers could trust with their lives. The stewardess, as caring and attentive white female, was created in the same process. Class inequalities are often justified through gendered and racial images. The poor single mother is portrayed as black, lazy, and sexually irresponsible (Roberts 1999; Dill, Baca Zinn, and Patton 1999) and the cause of her own difficulties. Top corporate managers and entrepreneurs, along with their political friends, are portrayed as rational, competent, aggressive, white, and masculine (Kanter 1977; Collinson and

Hearn 1996). Deeply held and unquestioned assumptions about gender and race differences often shape class practices (Reskin 2003; Charles and Grusky 2004). For example, assumptions about bodily differences between women and men, or assumptions about differences in reliability and intelligence between whites and people not defined as white may underlie decisions. The assumption that men "naturally" have a talent with tools, or that women are "naturally" good with human relationships, caring relations in particular, often underlies the gender stereotyping of jobs and the assignment of women and men to different jobs.

- *Interacting in and outside paid workplaces on the basis of conscious or nonconscious gendered and racialized assumptions.* Gendered and racialized assumptions and interests influence and shape the ways in which people relate to each other and carry out the ordinary work of daily life. Men often prefer to interact with other men: Homosocial patterns of informal interaction may exclude women and consolidate images of the masculine as the normal worker or manager (Kanter 1977). Bodies are always present in face-to-face interactions; the gender and race of bodies influences the class-related outcomes of interaction. For example, having a black male body reduces the possibility of getting hired for certain jobs (Royster 2003; Hossfeld 1994). Feminist scholars have done a great deal of both theoretical and empirical work on these interactional processes, including Sarah Fenstermaker and Candace West (2002), Patricia Martin (2003), and Barbara Reskin (2003).
- *Constructing and adjusting identities as gendered and racialized.* Identity, as the sense of who one is and is not, where one fits, how one should function in social life, what is appropriate behavior, can be seen as a socially produced aspect of individual consciousness. Identities may be contradictory, fluid, changing with situation and experience. Particular employers, or the culture of particular work places, may require particular identities (Gottfried 2003). Identities are important in maintaining and/or changing patterns of domination and inequality. For example, seeing the self as the head of the household and the breadwinner provided a positive identity for many white working-class men, while helping them to adjust to their powerlessness as workers (Sennett and Cobb 1972). Such male identities also assumed the relative subordination of wives and their unpaid labor in the home. Changing identities may be embedded in social movements aimed at changing gendered and racialized class inequalities. For example, participation in the feminist movement changed the identities of many

women from diverse racial/ethnic groups and these altered identities contributed to the strength of the movement that, in turn, had a significant impact on the situation of middle-class women in the gendered and racialized class processes in the United States. The diversity of identity processes in a multiracial society such as the United States contributes to the debate around redistribution and recognition (Fraser 2003, 1997) that I discussed in chapter 2.

3) The effects of gendered and racialized class practices are inequalities of power and money, segregation of jobs and occupations, and inequalities in access to education, housing, health care, and safe community environments. The effects of class practices support or sometimes undermine the gendered and racialized images and ideologies, feeding back into these processes. For example, high proportions of women in particular jobs tend to confirm the image that these jobs are gendered as female, particularly appropriate for women.
4) Gendered and racialized class practices and inequalities are historically produced in the development of capitalism, a process dominated and defined by white masculinity. These patterns have a gendered understructure in the ways in which production is organized and in the goals of production, aimed at profit and not at provisioning ordinary people. One manifestation of this way of organizing is that organizations claim nonresponsibility for human and environmental reproduction. The vast power of capitalist organizations in a highly monetized society, along with their nonresponsibility, contributes to the devaluation of caring work and women who do most of this work. I discuss this in chapter 4.
5) Organizations are a primary location of the ongoing creation of gendered and racialized class relations, locally, nationally, and globally. Large organizations, in particular, can be conceptualized as inequality regimes, or ongoing practices and processes in which racialized and gendered class relations are reproduced. I discuss this in chapter 5.
6) Class relations are not only at the point of production, in the wage relation or the relations of unpaid work, in personal and welfare state distributions, but are embedded in the extended global relations that link the low-paid worker in a nursing home in the United States to another low-paid worker manufacturing her uniform in southeast Asia, as both are linked to U.S. and Asian corporations. I discuss this further in chapter 6.

CONCLUSION

In summary, class practices and relations are gendered and racialized historically and in contemporary social life in processes of inclusion, exclusion, sorting, and segregation based on economic and cultural interests, justified through beliefs and images of racial/ethnic masculinity and femininity, reproduced in interaction patterns and through identity constructions.

All of these class practices occur in local places, influenced, shaped, and often determined by actions, intended and unintended, occurring in such places as corporate management suites, congressional committees, and the offices of business consultants. Some work relations, some distribution practices, and many articulation practices fall outside the boundaries of the institutionalized political economy. These may be increasingly important as people in many places innovate ways of surviving economically in a global system that does not place their survival high on its list of priorities.

In the next chapter, I look at the history of capitalism as fundamentally gendered and racialized ways of organizing economic activities. I argue that capitalism developed under the leadership of white men in a process that violently displaced, exploited, and in some cases enslaved people defined as racially and ethnically different and inferior to whites. The process was supported by ideologies of masculinity and femininity, casting women, within racial/ethnic and class differences, into subordinate and economically powerless situations. Further, capitalism was built on a particular gendered organization of production and reproduction in which production was aimed at profit and expansion, and providing for human reproduction was often irrelevant. The organization of wage work was based on the assumption that reproduction is done by women outside the money economy. Large corporations have historically operated on the assumption that they are not responsible for reproduction of human beings or the natural environment. Maintaining nonresponsibility continues as a basic orientation of capitalist organizations, helping to perpetuate gendered and racialized class processes.

NOTES

1. Floya Anthias (1998) has suggested another solution to this problem.

2. My understanding of the "social," social relations, and social practices owes a great deal to the work of Dorothy Smith, especially her *The Conceptual Practices of Power* (1990) and *Writing the Social: Critique, Theory, and Investigations* (1999). R. W. Connell's (1987, 1995, 2000) writing on gender emphasizes practice,

crediting Pierre Bourdieu (1977) and Anthony Giddens (1979) for the ideas of the presence of structure in practice and the constitution of structure through practice. The relationship between structure and practice has generated much discussion in which the meaning of structure is often unclear. I will not try to resolve this question in this discussion.

3. This is not a new approach. Marxist historians such as E. P. Thompson (1963) and labor process theorists such as Michael Burawoy (1979) have investigated class as practices.

4. An even more fundamental criticism of the macro/micro distinction is that it has "underlying premises: that, in fact, there exist two social worlds which interact. The micro world consists of individuals, be that persons or organizations. The macro-world consists of macro-actors such as state, society, market or United Nations. The two worlds coexist in a causal loop: macro-actors establish the constraints for micro-actors, whereas micro-actors change the macro-scene only by their aggregate action" (Czarniawska and Sevón 1996, 7). Admitting that this sounds like a caricature, Czarniawska and Sevón observe, accurately I think, that this view is taken for granted in much social analysis. But, they argue there are no macro-actors, only micro-actors creating very large networks that are perceived to be macro-actors. Czarniawska and Sevón draw upon the work of Callon and Latour (1981) in this discussion.

5. Rosemary Crompton (1998) argues that these are two different ways of looking at class that have different purposes and are not comparable.

6. "Standpoint theory" has been constructed as a perspective from very different feminist uses of the essential women's movement insight that women's experiences were—and are—invisible in much of academic scholarship. Sandra Harding's work was central in constituting very diverse approaches into a "perspective," as Dorothy Smith (1997) points out. For some aspects of debates around "standpoint theory" see the symposium in *Signs* volume 22, number 2 (1997). I use the concept of standpoint as developed by Smith as a "method of developing investigations of the social" (1997, 396).

7. In chapter 2, I reviewed some of the ways in which feminist scholars have attempted to reconceptualize women's unpaid reproductive labor (for example, Glucksmann 1995). One of the ambiguities of this discourse revolves around whether this labor should be called productive or reproductive.

8. Lourdes Benería (2003, 134) discusses these forms of unpaid economic activity and efforts to measure them in national and international statistics. See also Marilyn Waring (1988), *If Women Counted: A New Feminist Economics.*

9. Feminist economists have contributed a great deal in recent years to a broader understanding of the economy. See, for example, Nancy Folbre (2001), Marianne A. Ferber and Julie A. Nelson (1993), Ellen Mutari and Deborah M. Figart (2003). The journal *Feminist Economics* volume 9, numbers 2 and 3 (2003) recently devoted an issue to the work of economist Amartya Sen, especially his concept of human capabilities as the basis for assessing the adequacy with which human needs are met.

10. J. K. Gibson-Graham (1996) in *The End of Capitalism (As We Knew It)* makes an extended argument about many forms of noncapitalist production existing within capitalist societies.

11. Sonya O. Rose (1997) provides an insightful discussion of class as the effects of practice.

12. I also bracket the question of the importance of domestic labor for the reproduction of labor power as argued by feminists since the 1970s. As Sarah Fenstermaker Berk (1985) defined it, domestic work is the unpaid production of goods and services using materials purchased in the market. This may be the most important aspect of household labor from the perspective of the capitalist economy, for the buying (and using) of manufactured products is an essential step in the realization of surplus value. Buying and using are gender differentiated; markets for certain goods are also differentiated by race. This is another way that capitalism is gendered and racialized.

13. Gibson-Graham (1996) also makes this point, although she extends the idea of class relations to a much wider area of activities than I do here. That is, she talks about class relations in the household, in cooperative community ventures, and in other collective and individual activities.

14. See, for example, Adkins (1995), Pierce (1995), Gottfried (2003).

15. England, Christopher, and Reid (1999) show that gender and race/ethnicity function differently in different gender and racial/ethnic combinations in influencing wage differences.

16. For example, Guy Standing (1989) argued that the drive toward labor flexibility was "feminizing" world labor, meaning that men as well as women were increasingly in part-time, temporary, insecure employment.

17. For a perceptive discussion of the competing and contradictory emotional demands facing paid child carers, see Uttal and Tuominen (1999).

18. This is often associated with Third World countries, but occurs everywhere, of course. A recent IMF survey reports that in the United States in 2003, 8.6 percent of GDP came from the underground economy (Akst 2003).

19. Some sexual services, such as pornography videos available in top-ranked hotels, are products marketed by major corporations (Connell 2000, 52).

20. Many researchers, beginning with Ester Boserup (1970), have shown how "development" of various kinds has undermined women's subsistence production by shifting production to commercial agriculture under the control of men, or undermining the environmental conditions for women's subsistence production.

21. This was one of the primary difficulties that Marxist feminists had in producing a gendered theory of class and capitalism in the 1970s, as I discussed in chapter 2.

22. The following discussion is based on my article "Gender, Class, and the Relations of Distribution" (Acker 1988).

23. Michelle Fine and Lois Weis (1998), in an ethnographic study of poor and working-class young adults, show the complex impacts on family and marriage relationships of poverty and unstable, low-wage jobs. They document differences between the ways in which African-American and white women cope with these pressures. Kathryn Edin (2000) in a study of attitudes toward marriage among low-income mothers shows that they see a man's lack of a well-paying and stable job as a major impediment to marriage. Of course, marital instability exists in all class situations, but the economic resources to deal with it vary widely.

24. The 1996 welfare restructuring law clearly shows the substitution of concern about marriage conflict and parental responsibility rather than concern about a broader social responsibility for children. This law emphasizes the importance of pursuing absent fathers for child support and getting mothers into the labor market, rather than a concern for the adequacy of economic support for children.

25. A voluminous literature exists on the gendering and racializing of welfare state programs. See, for example, for the United States, Piven and Cloward (1993), Mimi Abramovitz (1996), Gwendolyn Mink (1999), Piven, Acker, Hallock, and Morgen (2002). Gendering European welfare states is discussed by Arnlaug Leira (2002), Jane Lewis (1992), and Diane Sainsbury (1999), among many others. O'Connor, Orloff, and Shaver (1999) provide a comprehensive and in-depth analysis of gender and welfare states, as well as a broad overview of debates in the area.

4

Is Capitalism Gendered and Racialized?

The class practices, or practices of provisioning, I outlined in chapter 3 are, of course, aspects of the ongoing functioning of capitalism. In this chapter I make the claim that capitalism as an organization of production and distribution is gendered and racialized. I argue, along with R. W. Connell (1987) that "gender divisions . . . are a deep-seated feature of production itself. . . . They are not a hangover from pre-capitalist modes of production" (103–104). The same is true for race divisions. I explore the ways in which capitalism can be seen as gendered and racialized and what this analysis means for understanding the ongoing production of gendered and racialized class practices and outcomes such as continuing gender and race segregation and divisions of labor. This exploration builds upon the valuable insights in socialist feminist work of the 1970s and early 1980s.

Although talk about globalizing capitalism is common today, class relations are usually seen as situated within particular nation-states and are usually analyzed within national boundaries. Good reasons exist for doing this: Nation-states and their gendered and racialized class structures have differing national characteristics produced by different political, social, and economic histories. However, to see the historical relations through which capitalism emerged in different countries as gendered and racially structured, a broader view is helpful. Therefore, in the following discussion, which deals primarily with the United States, I give some attention to processes that span state boundaries, or are transnational from the beginning. Organizations are critical locations for many of the activities and practices that comprise capitalism and class. The development of large organizations shaped and still shapes changing class processes (Perrow 2002) that are at the same time gender and race processes. Therefore, looking at these processes requires paying attention to organizations and what people do within them to create, implement, or oppose the practices that constitute relations of power and exploitation. I discuss some actions taken in the name of organizations in this chapter, but develop a detailed analysis of organizations in chapter 5.

Capitalism is racialized and gendered in two intersecting historical processes. First, industrial capitalism emerged in the United States dominated by white males, with a gender- and race-segregated labor force, laced with wage inequalities, and a society-wide gender division of caring labor. The processes of reproducing segregation and wage inequality changed over time, but segregation and inequality were not eliminated. A small group of white males still dominate the capitalist economy and its politics. The society-wide gendered division of caring labor still exists. Ideologies of white masculinity and related forms of consciousness help to justify capitalist practices. In short, conceptual and material practices that construct capitalist production and markets, as well as beliefs supporting those practices, are deeply shaped through gender and race divisions of labor and power and through constructions of white masculinity.

Second, these gendered and racialized practices are embedded in and replicated through the gendered substructures of capitalism. These gendered substructures exist in ongoing incompatible organizing of paid production activities and unpaid domestic and caring activities. Domestic and caring activities are devalued and seen as outside the "main business" (Smith 1999) of capitalism. The commodification of labor, the capitalist wage form, is an integral part of this process, as family provisioning and caring become dependent upon wage labor. The abstract language of bureaucratic organizing obscures the ongoing impact on families and daily life. At the same time, paid work is organized on the assumption that reproduction is of no concern. The separations between paid production and unpaid life-sustaining activities are maintained by corporate claims that they have no responsibility for anything but returns to shareholders. Such claims are more successful in the United States, in particular, than in countries with stronger labor movements and welfare states. These often successful claims contribute to the corporate processes of establishing their interests as more important than those of ordinary people.

THE GENDERED AND RACIALIZED DEVELOPMENT OF U.S. CAPITALISM

Segregations and Wage Inequalities

Industrial capitalism is historically, and in the main continues to be, a white male project, in the sense that white men were and are the innovators, owners, and holders of power.[1] Capitalism developed in Britain and then in Europe and the United States in societies that were already dominated by white men and already contained a gender-based division of labor. The emerging waged labor force was sharply divided by gender, as well as by race and ethnicity with many variations by nation and regions within nations. At the same time, the gendered division of labor in domestic tasks was reconfigured and incorporated in a gendered division between paid market labor and unpaid domestic labor. In the United States, certain white men, unburdened by caring for children and households and already the major wielders of gendered power, buttressed at least indirectly by the profits from slavery and the exploitation of other minorities, were, in the nineteenth century, those who built the U.S. factories and railroads, and owned and managed the developing capitalist enterprises.[2] As far as we know, they were also heterosexual and mostly of Northern European heritage. Their wives and daughters benefited from the wealth they amassed and contributed in symbolic and social ways to the perpetuation of their class, but they were not the architects of the new economy.[3]

Recruitment of the labor force for the colonies and then the United States had always been transnational and often coercive.[4] Slavery existed prior to the development of industrialism in the United States: Capitalism was built partly on profits from that source.[5] Michael Omi and Howard Winant (1994, 265) contend that the United States was a racial dictatorship for 258 years, from 1607 to 1865. After the abolition of slavery in 1865, severe exploitation, exclusion, and domination of blacks by whites perpetuated racial divisions cutting across gender and some class divisions, consigning blacks to the most menial, low-paying work in agriculture, mining, and domestic service. Early industrial workers were immigrants. For example, except for the brief tenure (twenty-five years) of young, native-born white women workers in the Lowell, Massachusetts mills, immigrant women and children were the workers in the first mass production industry in the United States, the textile mills of Massachusetts and Philadelphia, Pennsylvania (Perrow 2002). This was a gender and racial/ethnic division of labor that still exists, but now on a global basis. Waves of European immigrants continued to come to the United States to work in factories and on farms. Many of these European immigrants, such as impoverished Irish, Poles, and eastern European Jews were seen as nonwhite or not-quite-white by white Americans and were used in capitalist production as low-wage workers, although some of them were actually skilled workers (Brodkin 1998). The experiences of racial oppression built into industrial capitalism varied by gender within these racial/ethnic groups.

Capitalist expansion across the American continent created additional groups of Americans who were segregated by race and gender into racial and ethnic enclaves and into low-paid and highly exploited work. This expansion included the extermination and expropriation of native peoples, the subordination of Mexicans in areas taken in the war with Mexico in 1845, and the recruitment of Chinese and other Asians as low-wage workers, mostly on the west coast (Amott and Matthaei 1996; Glenn 2002).[6]

Women from different racial and ethnic groups were incorporated differently than men and differently than each other into developing capitalism in the late nineteenth and early twentieth centuries. White Euro-American men moved from farms into factories or commercial, business, and administrative jobs. Women aspired to be housewives as the male breadwinner family became the ideal. Married white women, working class and middle class, were housewives unless unemployment, low wages, or death of their husbands made their paid work necessary (Goldin 1990, 133). Young white women with some secondary education moved into the expanding clerical jobs and into elementary school teaching when white men with sufficient education were unavailable (Cohn 1985). African Americans, both women and men, continued to be confined to menial work, although some were becoming factory workers, and even teachers and professionals as black schools and colleges were formed (Collins 2000). Young women from first- and second-generation European immigrant families worked in factories and offices. This is a very sketchy outline of a complex process (Kessler-Harris 1982), but the overall point is that the capitalist labor force in the United States emerged as deeply segregated horizontally by occupation and stratified vertically by positions of power and control on the basis of both gender and race.

Unequal pay patterns went along with sex and race segregation, stratification, and exclusion. Differences in the earnings and wealth (Keister 2000) of women and men existed before the development of the capitalist wage (Padavic and Reskin 2002). Slaves, of course, had no wages and earned little after abolition. These patterns continued as capitalist wage labor became the dominant form and wages became the primary avenue of distribution to ordinary people. Unequal wages were justified by beliefs about virtue and entitlement. A living wage or a just wage for white men was higher than a living wage or a just wage for white women or for women and men from minority racial and ethnic groups (Figart, Mutari, and Power 2002). African-American women were at the bottom of the wage hierarchy.

The earnings advantage that white men have had throughout the history of modern capitalism was created partly by their organization to increase their wages and improve their working conditions. They also sought to protect their wages against the competition of others, women and men from subordinate groups (for example, Cockburn 1983, 1991).

This advantage also suggests a white male coalition across class lines (Connell 2000; Hartmann 1976), based at least partly in beliefs about gender and race differences and beliefs about the superior skills of white men. White masculine identity and self-respect were complexly involved in these divisions of labor and wages.[7] This is another way in which capitalism is a gendered and racialized accumulation process (Connell 2000). Wage differences between white men and all other groups, as well as divisions of labor between these groups, contributed to profit and flexibility, by helping to maintain growing occupational areas, such as clerical work, as segregated and low paid. Where women worked in manufacturing or food processing, gender divisions of labor kept the often larger female work force in low-wage routine jobs, while males worked in other more highly paid, less routine, positions (Acker and Van Houten 1974). While white men might be paid more, capitalist organizations could benefit from this "gender/racial dividend." Thus, by maintaining divisions, employers could pay less for certain levels of skill, responsibility, and experience when the worker was not a white male.

This is not to say that getting a living wage was easy for white men, or that most white men achieved it. Labor-management battles, employers' violent tactics to prevent unionization, massive unemployment during frequent economic depressions characterized the situation of white industrial workers as wage labor spread in the nineteenth and early twentieth centuries.[8] During the same period, new white-collar jobs were created to manage, plan, and control the expanding industrial economy. This rapidly increasing middle class was also stratified by gender and race. The better-paid, more respected jobs went to white men; white women were secretaries and clerical workers; people of color were absent. Conditions and issues varied across industries and regions of the country. But, wherever you look, those variations contained underlying gendered and racialized divisions. Patterns of stratification and segregation were written into employment contracts in work content, positions in work hierarchies, and wage differences, as well as other forms of distribution.

These patterns persisted, although with many alterations, through extraordinary changes in production and social life. After World War II, white women, except for a brief period immediately after the war, went to work for pay in the expanding service sector, professional, and managerial fields. African Americans moved to the North in large numbers, entering industrial and service sector jobs. These processes accelerated after the 1960s, with the civil rights and women's movements, new civil rights laws, and affirmative action. Hispanics and Asian Americans, as well as other racial/ethnic groups, became larger proportions of the population, on the whole finding work in low-paid, segregated jobs. Employers continued, and still continue, to select and promote workers based on gender and racial identifications, although the processes are more subtle, and possibly less visible, than in the past (for example, Brown et al. 2003; Royster 2003).[9] These processes continually recreate gender and racial inequities, not as cultural or ideological survivals from earlier times, but as essential elements in present capitalisms (Connell 1987, 103–106).

Segregating practices are a part of the history of white, masculine-dominated capitalism that establishes class as gendered and racialized. Images of masculinity support these practices, as they produce a taken-for-granted world in which certain men legitimately make employment and other economic decisions that affect the lives of most other people. Even though some white women and people from other-than-white groups now hold leadership positions, their actions are shaped within networks of practices sustained by images of masculinity (Wacjman 1998).

Masculinities and Capitalism

Masculinities are essential components of the ongoing male project, capitalism. While white men were and are the main publicly recognized actors in the history of capitalism, these are not just any white men. They have been, for example, aggressive entrepreneurs or strong leaders of industry and finance (Collinson and Hearn 1996). Some have been oppositional actors, such as self-respecting and tough workers earning a family wage, and militant labor leaders. They have been particular men whose locations within gendered and racialized social relations and practices can be partially captured by the concept of masculinity. "Masculinity" is a contested term. As Connell (1995, 2000), Hearn (1996), and others have pointed out, it should be pluralized as "masculinities," because in any society at any one time there are several ways of being a man. "Being a man" involves cultural images and practices. It always implies a contrast to an unidentified femininity.[10]

Hegemonic masculinity can be defined as the taken-for-granted, generally accepted form, attributed to leaders and other influential figures at particular historical times. Hegemonic masculinity legitimates the power of those who embody it. More than one type of hegemonic masculinity may exist simultaneously, although they may share characteristics, as do the business leader and the sports star at the present time. Adjectives describing hegemonic masculinities closely follow those describing characteristics of successful business organizations, as Rosabeth Moss Kanter (1977) pointed out in the 1970s. The successful CEO and the successful organization are aggressive, decisive, competitive, focused on winning and defeating the enemy, taking territory from others.[11] The ideology of capitalist markets is imbued with a masculine ethos. As R. W. Connell (2000, 35) observes, "The market is often seen as the antithesis of gender (marked by achieved versus ascribed status, etc.). But the market operates through forms of rationality that are historically masculine and involve a sharp split between instrumental reason on the one hand, emotion and human responsibility on the other" (Seidler 1989). Masculinities embedded in collective practices, are part of the context within which certain men made and still make the decisions that drive and shape the ongoing development of capitalism. We can speculate that how these men see themselves, what actions and choices they feel compelled to make and they think are legitimate, how they and the world around them define desirable masculinity, enter into that decision making (Reed 1996). Decisions made at the very top reaches of (masculine) corporate power have consequences that are experienced as inevitable economic forces or disembodied social trends. At the same time, these decisions symbolize and enact varying hegemonic masculinities (Connell 1995). However, the embeddedness of masculinity within the ideologies of business and the market may become invisible, seen as just part of the way business is done. The relatively few women who reach the highest positions probably think and act within these strictures.

Hegemonic masculinities and violence[12] are deeply connected within capitalist history: The violent acts of those who carried out the slave trade or organized colonial conquests are obvious examples. Of course, violence has been an essential component of power in many other socioeconomic systems, but it continues into the rational organization of capitalist economic activities. Violence is frequently a legitimate, if implicit, component of power exercised by bureaucrats as well as "robber barons." Metaphors of violence, frequently military violence, are often linked to notions of the masculinity of corporate leaders, as "defeating the enemy" suggests. In contemporary capitalism, violence and its links to masculinity are often masked by the seeming impersonality of objective conditions. For example, the masculinity of top managers, the ability to be tough, is involved in the implicit violence of many corporate decisions, such as those cutting jobs in order to raise profits and, as a result, producing unemployment. Armies and other organizations, such as the police, are specifically organized around violence. Some observers of recent history suggest that organized violence, such as the use of the military, is still mobilized at least partly to reach capitalist goals, such as controlling access to oil supplies. The masculinities of those making decisions to deploy violence in such a way are hegemonic, in the sense of powerful and exemplary. Nevertheless, the connections between masculinity, capitalism, and violence are complex and contradictory, as Jeff Hearn and Wendy Parkin (2001) make clear. Violence is always a possibility in mechanisms of control and domination, but it is not always evident, nor is it always used.

As corporate capitalism developed, Connell (1995) and others (for example, Burris 1996) argue that a hegemonic masculinity based on claims to expertise developed alongside masculinities organized around domination and control. Hegemonic masculinity relying on claims to expertise does not necessarily lead to economic organizations free of domination and violence, however (Hearn and Parkin 2001). Hearn and Parkin (2001) argue that controls relying on both explicit and implicit violence exist in a wide variety of organizations, including those devoted to developing new technology.

Different hegemonic masculinities in different countries may reflect different national histories, cultures, and change processes.[13] For example, in Sweden in the mid-1980s, corporations were changing the ways in which they did business toward a greater participation in the international economy, fewer controls on currency and trade, and greater emphasis on competition. Existing images of dominant masculinity were changing, reflecting new business practices. This seemed to be happening in the banking sector, where I was doing research on women and their jobs (Acker 1994a). The old paternalistic leadership, in which primarily men entered as young clerks expecting to rise to managerial levels, was being replaced by young, aggressive men hired as experts and mangers from outside the banks. These young, often technically trained, ambitious men pushed the idea that the staff was there to sell bank products to customers, not, in the first instance, to take care of the needs of clients. Productivity goals were put in place; nonprofitable customers, such as elderly pensioners, were to be encouraged not to come into the bank and occupy the staff's attention. The female clerks we interviewed were disturbed by these changes, seeing them as evidence that the men at the top were changing from paternal guardians of the people's interests to manipulators who only wanted riches for themselves. The confirmation of this came in a scandal in which the CEO of the largest bank had to step down because he had illegally taken money from the bank to pay for his housing. The amount of money was small; the disillusion among employees was huge. He had been seen as a benign father; now he was no better than the callous young men on the way up who were dominating the daily work in the banks. The hegemonic masculinity in Swedish banks was changing as the economy and society were changing.

Hegemonic masculinities are defined in contrast to subordinate masculinities. White working class masculinity, although clearly subordinate, mirrors in some of its more heroic forms the images of strength and responsibility of certain successful business leaders. The construction of working class masculinity around the obligations to work hard, earn a family wage, and be a good provider can be seen as providing an identity that both served as a social control and secured male advantage in the home. That is, the good provider had to have a wife and probably children for whom to provide. Glenn (2002) describes in some detail how this image of the white male worker also defined him as superior to and different from black workers.

Masculinities are not stable images and ideals, but shifting with other societal changes. With the turn to neoliberal business thinking and globalization, there seem to be new forms. Connell (2000) identifies "global business masculinity," while Lourdes Benería (1999) discusses the "Davos man," the global leader from business, politics, or academia who meets his peers once a year in the Swiss town of Davos to assess and plan the direction of globalization. Seeing masculinities as implicated in the ongoing production of global capitalism opens the possibility of seeing sexualities, bodies, pleasures, and identities as also implicated in economic relations.

In sum, gender and race are built into capitalism and its class processes through the long history of racial and gender segregation of paid labor and through the images and actions of white men who dominate and lead central capitalist endeavors. Underlying these processes is the subordination to production and the market of nurturing and caring for human beings, and the assignment of these responsibilities to women as unpaid work. Gender segregation that differentially affects women in all racial groups rests at least partially on the ideology and actuality of women as carers. Images of dominant masculinity enshrine particular male bodies and ways of being as different from the female and distanced from caring. In the following section, I argue that industrial capitalism, including its present neoliberal form, is organized in ways that are, at the same time, antithetical and necessary to the organization of caring or reproduction and that the resulting tensions contribute to the perpetuation of gendered and racialized class inequalities. Large corporations are particularly important in this process as they increasingly control the resources for provisioning but deny responsibility for such social goals.

THE GENDERED SUBSTRUCTURES OF CAPITALISM

The ongoing processes of gender and racial segregation, wage inequalities related to the segregation patterns, and the ideological and practical dominance of white masculinities are components of capitalist organizing supported and perpetuated by a gendered and racialized break between processes of production and reproduction. The idea that there are two domains of human activity, material production and human reproduction, has been important in feminist thinking and much criticized. This idea formed the basis for theories of patriarchy and capitalism, or gender and class, dual systems theories that were discarded as unsatisfactory, as I discussed in chapter 2.[14] Although the objections are valid, I still think the idea of reproduction can be helpful if it is anchored in history, time, and place, and defined as biological reproduction, the raising of children, caring labor of other kinds, and domestic tasks. Used in this sense, the distinction between production and reproduction is important in understanding historical processes in the United States, as well as other countries, in which unpaid family work and paid market work were divided and capitalist organizations came to effectively determine the fates of families and reproduction. In the process, gendered and often racialized segregation and inequities were, and are, produced. These processes constitute a gendered and racialized substructure of capitalism and its class relations.

The concept "substructure" stands for practices, arrangements, and ideologies that organize the broad parameters of daily life. I discuss several components of this substructure: the nature of the division between production and reproduction; the conceptual consequences of the location of capitalist organizing in the worlds of male entrepreneurs and managers; the organization of work processes and practices based on gender assumptions arising from the separations of production and reproduction; and the activities of corporations that maintain the subordination of reproduction to production.

The Separation of Production and Reproduction

The emergence of industrial capitalist economic organization created a break between material production and human reproduction, as has been frequently argued. Here I briefly retell this story to make the point that reorganized gender relations, with racial and ethnic variations, are built into capitalist processes. My retelling is primarily based on the United States.[15] The break consists of a divergence between the aims and modes of organizing of capitalist production and the aims and modes of organizing of families and reproduction. This is a gendered process, as it reorganizes the divisions of labor between women and men. This break creates an immanent contradiction between the work of production and the work of reproduction in capitalist class societies. Although creating material goods and bearing and raising children are both essential to human life and thus ultimately necessary to each other, the goals and organization of activities in these life processes begin to conflict as well as to diverge.[16] The aims of capitalist production are to create profit and to extend the control of capitalist organizations, either in competition or collusion, over larger and larger geographic areas and domains of activity.[17] Production is organized, work processes are invented, to achieve these aims. The aims of the complex and multiple activities summarized as reproduction are the social/physical reproduction of human beings, including the provision of the necessities of daily life and of the possibility of pleasure, love, and creativity. In other words, as many have pointed out (e.g., Polanyi 1944), with the coming of industrial capitalism, production no longer directly provided the means for subsistence or provisioning, but the means for the accumulation of capital. Production might or might not provide for subsistence and reproduction of ordinary laboring people through wages and consumption. Money became the link between material production and reproduction.

Intrinsic to this separation was the transformation of human labor into a commodity sold in a market at the lowest price the buyer could manage. Karl Polanyi (1944), analyzing the emergence of industrial capitalism in England, argues that the large-scale, factory organization of production required, in order to turn a profit, a reliable supply of the factors of production, most importantly labor, land, and money. In the commercial society of the time, this meant that these things must be for sale, commodified. To commodify labor and establish a labor market, the old impediments to a freely varying price, such as poor relief, had to be removed. In Polanyi's account, the Poor Law Reform of 1834, mirrored in similar reforms in states such as New York and Massachusetts,[18] was the defining legislation that allowed the labor market to develop. As Polanyi (1944, 82) points out, the abolition of poor relief was the abolition of the "right to live." This and the effects of the new labor market discipline were catastrophic for ordinary people, especially in England in the nineteenth century. Those now dependent on the wage did not cease to eat when there was no demand for their labor. The results were so appalling that almost immediately measures to protect society set in. The consequences of living in societies built on this separation and the concomitant commodification of labor were and are often dire, especially for single women with children, for both women and men from subordinated minorities, but also for workers in general. In periods of capitalist crisis and high unemployment, some literally starve in the midst of plenty. State interventions, including new forms of distribution, necessarily develop almost everywhere to ameliorate the destructions of the market, Polanyi contends. Diane Elson (1994) deals with some of the same issues, emphasizing the interdependence between the productive or monetary economy and the reproductive or nonmonetary economy. She also recognizes a contradiction in "that monetized production is subject to inherent dislocations and crises" (40), necessitating the intervention of the state and community to meet essential needs and avoid social breakdown.[19]

Women's unpaid work in the garden, the henhouse, and the kitchen often mediated this contradiction, providing some of what the market failed to provide. Women also continued to do the work of nurturing and caring. Much of reproductive work remained the responsibility of women even when they worked for pay, while white men in increasing proportions were only employed in capitalist enterprises. But, as money income became more necessary to family survival, women's unpaid work was seen less and less as "economic." The emergence of an economy seen as separate from the household is part of the same historical and discursive processes that produced the gender-coded distinction between production and reproduction, between the public and the private.[20] "The economy" can be seen as a discursive construction with a gendered undergirding: As industrial capitalism developed, male activities organized around money became defined as the "economy," seen as a separate realm responding to its own laws. This definition was reified in capitalist practice and in social theory. The separation between production and reproduction of aims, locations, rewards, and organization of tasks incorporated women's responsibilities for reproduction and unpaid production as outside of and less important than the "the economy," or profit.[21] In the process, the intrinsic connections between reproduction and the "economy" were obscured, made invisible.

Once the "market" and the "economy" were seen as separate spheres and of primary importance, those whose main involvements were elsewhere, in the family for example, were less visible, less valued, to paraphrase Ann Jennings (1993). But the separation that hides the value of women's unpaid labor did not, perhaps, occur as an unintended consequence of changes in production. As Viviana A. Zelizer (2002) argues, drawing on the work of Reva Siegel (1994), "splitting the family and market spheres took painstaking legal effort. Focusing on nineteenth-century debates over the valuation of household labor, Siegel shows how courts carefully kept that labor as non-market exchange" (291). The decisions, in cases of interspousal contracts for labor, reinforced the belief that domestic labor is done for love and nurture and that this structure would be undermined by market exchange. Male privilege, men's economic interests, and their gender identities could also have been involved. Using changing census definitions in Great Britain and the United States, Nancy Folbre (1994, 95–96) documents the redefinition of domestic labor in the nineteenth century from economically important labor to unproductive labor and finally to nonexistent labor.

The pattern was established that reproductive activities and those with most responsibilities for reproduction—women—were devalued in comparison with men and their market work. This devaluation exists today in the low pay for domestic and caring work.[22] Evelyn Glenn (2002) points out that the domestic duties, especially mothering, of white women were valued, whereas the same duties of African-American women were not so honored. She is correct that white, especially middle class, motherhood was idealized in various ways that emphasized racial devaluation of African-American women. But this idealization was also part of placing white women in a different realm of economic and social value than that of men. It did not confer economic power or economic returns to white women that were equal to those of white men. I think that lack of access to and control over money by people who do caring work has a great deal to do with the social evaluation of domestic and caring work. However, race and class subordination create extreme differences among women. In some parts of the United States, many middle class white women as late as the early 1940s ruled their domestic domains, but did not actually do all of their own housework. They had servants, often African-American women, for that work.[23] Such middle class white women's unpaid work was not as devalued as that of the low-paid servants they employed. Thus, race structures class domination among women. In some parts of the United States, particularly the South, paid domestic labor was almost the only occupation other than farming open to African-American women. White working class women were too poor to hire "help," they did their own housework. The identification of this work with women who lacked power and money may also have been a factor in its low status and low monetary value.

Such differential evaluations based on class and race are rampant in the twenty-first-century United States. Poor mothers on welfare, disproportionately African Americans, Hispanics, or other women of color, are expected to work for money without much regard to the welfare of their children. Although the expectation that children come last is not explicit in most welfare policies, work is a requirement for receipt of Temporary Aid to Needy Families and assistance to pay for child care is frequently inadequate (Acker and Morgen 2001). In practice, mothering is almost totally devalued (Roberts 1999). At the same time, middle class, disproportionately white, mothers who quit well-paying jobs to take care of their children receive no reprimands, and are actually seen as good mothers. The difference is class, which determines access to money, as well as race. In summary, I am arguing that separating the aims and organization of paid production from those of unpaid reproduction provided the understructure for the devaluation of reproductive, caring labor and those who do it. These are gendered and racialized class practices that continue into the twenty-first century.

The Male/Masculine Conceptual World of Capitalist Organizing

Discourses of capitalist organizing emerged on the template of the gendered divisions of societal labor. In the historical development of capitalism, Dorothy Smith (1987) argues that forms of knowledge were produced that facilitated organizing large-scale production and markets and engaging in competitive battles. These forms of knowledge were created within spaces separate from the domestic activities maintaining daily life: Leading capitalists and their lieutenants were distanced from the daily exigencies of feeding, cleaning, and managing households and intimate family relations. This distancing was part of the social arrangements that allowed these men to focus their attention on making money and on the increasingly abstract processes of creating and managing production. As discussed in chapter 3, Smith (1987, 1990, 1999) analyzes these processes as extended social relations, or the relations of ruling, of capitalism. Her analysis illuminates the ways in which gender is deeply embedded in the conceptual and material processes that organize, coordinate, and control capitalist societies.

"Relations of ruling" refers to the vast complex of interconnected practices that organize, coordinate, and control production, finance, distribution, and other noneconomic processes such as education and other state functions. Relations of ruling articulate local places to each other and to extra-local places of power, that are at the same time, the places from which ruling is initiated. Nike, McDonalds restaurants, or the U.S. Post Office are examples. In each organization, procedures for doing the work are specified from outside the local unit and complex methods of communication, including such activities as advertising and accounting, link local places to regional and national centers. The lives of clients, customers, and taxpayers are linked into the lives of employees and managers as all participate in some way in the relations of ruling. The concept "relations of ruling" is not synonymous with class: It refers to the multitude of interconnected practices of managing and governing within which class, gender, race, and sexualities are constituted, usually simultaneously.

Certain forms of knowledge and consciousness are integral to the relations of ruling. Two forms of consciousness emerge historically, one located in the objectified, increasingly textually mediated relations of ruling and the other in the concrete activities of daily life (Smith 1987, 1999). The consciousness located in processes of ruling conceptualizes the world for the purposes of managing and organizing. Abstraction and generalization, which are usually gender- and race-obliterating ways of thinking, facilitate organizing.[24] Working people are turned into factors of production, such as the labor force. Business practices reduce or increase the labor force, but the lives of those who are reduced or increased are invisible on the company books. For example, "business process outsourcing" is a fairly recent term for relocating jobs such as accounting to Third World countries, leaving U.S. employees to find new work. Actual work of people producing their lives is turned into a mythical commodity, labor power, to be bought and sold, as Polanyi (1944) argues. The wage is represented theoretically as an abstract, gender-neutral process. (One might ask, "If the wage relation is an abstract, gender- and race-neutral process, how is it that one of the most persistent manifestations of gender and racial disadvantage arises through that relation?") People seeking financial assistance are cases; cases or clients are bureaucratic categories with no bodies, no gender or race, although a majority of people seeking aid are women from minority groups. People who stop getting welfare benefits are called "leavers," an administrative term that hides their ongoing financial need and the fact that most are single mothers and many don't "leave" (Morgen, Barry, and Acker 2003).

From a standpoint within the relations of ruling where those with power are mostly men and only a few women, the ongoing practical activities of keeping daily life going, mostly carried out by women, are invisible, simply assumed to exist. This aspect of social reality is peripheral, uninteresting from the standpoint of the practices and procedures of running production and government, unless it can somehow be organized to produce profit or it becomes an object of control. Making a similar point, Diane Elson argues that macro-economic policy, representing the interests and perspectives of production, implicitly assumes that "there is an unlimited supply of unpaid female labour, able to compensate for any adverse changes resulting from macro-economic policy, so as to continue to meet the basic needs of their families and communities and sustain them as social organizations" (Elson 1994, 42).

In sum, the invisibility of race, gender (of men and women), and everyday unpaid reproduction except as a source of demand for products from a standpoint within the ruling relations is written into the processes and procedures, including the conceptual practices, that organize our societies. The ostensibly rational, objective, calculative competitive practices of the financial and industrial corporate world operate in such a way that the needs of women, children, and most men are simply absent, as Smith (1999) puts it. I think this holds as a very general statement, although some corporations consider the need, or the demand, for social responsibility, and national politics, culture, and overall economic conditions produce much variability.

The entry of a majority of women in the wealthy countries into the paid labor force and the increasing success of a few white women and women and men of racial minority groups in gaining entrance to top corporate and government positions has not altered the abstract, textual practices of organizing. The bureaucratic abstractions of organizing that make gendered and racialized patterns of power and disadvantage invisible still exist. Most women as well as most men now face these abstractions and their practical applications as organizers of their lives, as they contend with seemingly disembodied processes that result in wage dependence and sometimes unemployment. The effects of apparently disembodied processes vary widely. Women and men negotiate the effects on their own and their families' lives by varying the time they spend at paid work on a daily, weekly, and lifetime basis (Moen 2003).

THE GENDERED AND RACIALIZED ORGANIZATION OF WORK

With the emerging dominance of waged work in large organizations in the nineteenth and early twentieth centuries, the gender-coded separation between production and reproduction became an underlying principle in the conceptual and actual physical and temporal organization of work. At the same time, race, along with gender, became a principle for allocating people within this total social organization of work (Glucksmann 1995). The separation also shaped the spatial and time relationships between home and paid work, bodily movements through time and space, the general organization of daily life, and the ways that groups and individuals constructed meaning and identities. For example, the rules and expectations of ordinary capitalist workplaces were and still are built on hidden assumptions about a gendered separation of production and reproduction (Acker 1990), within which is embedded the image of the worker as a man. Although in academic and managerial discourses "the worker" is represented as gender and race neutral as well as disembodied, this concept conceals the assumption that the disembodied worker is a white male and that "work" is organized on the basis of this assumption. Thus, work is organized on the assumption that reproduction concerns are left at home, that the worker has no other responsibilities that might interfere with total attention to tasks or projects assigned by the employer. Employees are expected to arrive at stated times, stay on the job except for toilet, coffee, and lunch breaks, accomplish certain amounts of work, and often work overtime. They are expected to show up day after day, no matter what is happening in the other parts of their lives. Enforcement of these assumptions is probably more stringent for working class employees, such as women in lower-level service and clerical jobs or men in manufacturing jobs, than for those in managerial or professional positions.

The lack of fit between work and the rest of life increases with long or irregular work hours. The lack of fit may also increase as the employee is more and more involved in coordinating and knitting together activities within workplaces and between workplaces (Acker 1998). Webs of social practices link and coordinate the work in one department with other departments in an organization, or the work in one organization with the work in many other organizations: Very few jobs exist in isolation, without demands from other places. Supervisors coordinate the flow of work across departments (in universities department secretaries do this kind of coordination), retail managers coordinate the ordering and choice of products, social workers coordinate services to clients across organizational borders. Maintaining these linkages, meeting the demands may be absolutely essential for the survival of the job and the activities. These linkages only complicate and intensify the lack of fit of paid work with the exigencies of the rest of life, making it more difficult to arrange work in flexible ways. Such difficulties exist even in countries that recognize the rights of employees to do caring work.

For example, in Sweden, many policies exist to facilitate the combination of parenting and paid work (Acker 1994b). Parents are guaranteed a certain number of months of paid leave—with the guarantee that they will not lose their jobs—upon the birth or adoption of a child. Parents of young children may reduce their working hours without fear of retaliation from employers. Parents who have children in daycare routinely leave work to pick up the children. Most do not work overtime. In my experience in Sweden, these rights to combine paid employment and parenting complicate the logistics of the workplace for managers and other workers. Replacements must be found for those on leave. Reduced hours may mean that tasks are undone or passed on to others. Picking up the children may require walking out of a meeting just when a decision is about to be made. Work that crosses the borders of organizations may be even more disrupted as people have to coordinate several schedules and time tables with the hours of day care centers and the potential absences of key employees (Acker 1998). Women are still much more likely than men to use the family-friendly measures (Leira 2002). Their lengthy leaves and reduced working hours contribute to different career patterns for women and men and the continuance of gender inequalities.

In sum, in Sweden as in the United States and Britain, the model worker, for whom work routines are designed, is still a man who does not have to stay at home with a sick child or do the ordinary tasks of keeping a household functioning. This gendered structure of work persists even though women are almost half the paid labor force in the United States and high proportions of mothers of young children are working for pay: Family life has been transformed to meet the needs of paid work, but paid work has not been transformed to meet family needs. Rosemary Crompton (2000) suggests that, as more men assume caring responsibilities, employers' provisions for child care resources may become a class issue as well as a gender issue. Moreover, "the debates over gender and class have brought into prominence significant sources of tension and conflict in the organization of market capitalism that have long been masked by the predominant gender division of labour" (Crompton 2000, 180). These are tensions over the contradictions between reproduction and production.

THE NONRESPONSIBILITY AND PRIVILEGING OF ORGANIZATIONS

The break between production and reproduction embedded in the emergence of capitalist societies is continually reconstituted through two additional processes: first, the ongoing efforts of capitalist corporations and their coordinating associations to make successful claims of nonresponsibility for human reproduction and the environment, and second, the privileging of economic organizations over other areas of life.[25] Both of these processes are particularly ascendant now in the United States, with the widespread acceptance of neoliberal economic ideas and the seeming rule of the "market." Claims of nonresponsibility are not always as successful as they have been at the end of the twentieth and beginning of the twenty-first centuries.

I define nonresponsibility as refusals or attempts to avoid contributions to meeting the needs of people, if these contributions do not directly enhance production or accumulation. Nonresponsibility may be focused on employees of a particular employer or on the community or society as a whole. Nonresponsibility includes practices that deny workers living wages, safe working conditions, reasonable hours, and job benefits, and refusal to support more general community welfare. It includes resistance to affirmative action and pay equity, as well as refusal to support the provision of day care and paid leave for family responsibilities. In addition, nonresponsibility includes refusal to take responsibility for environmental damage and damages to the health and safety of communities. It also includes unwillingness of business groups to support public programs such as various forms of income replacement, provision of medical care, public housing, or job creation. Economists classify some of these neglected needs as externalities, paid for by communities, families, or individuals. I prefer the notion of nonresponsibility because it includes more areas of action and suggests to me an active process in which claims for both responsibility and nonresponsibility are made and challenged. Capitalism's nonresponsibility has negative effects on men and women, but impacts are differentiated across gendered and racialized class processes. Nonresponsibility contributes to the marginalization and devaluation of caring and reproductive activities and those responsible for these activities, mostly women. Nonresponsibility consigns caring needs to areas outside or at least peripheral to the capitalist organization's interests and, thus, helps to maintain the image of the ideal, even adequate, employee as someone without such obligations. Thus, organizational policies and practices continue to encode this gendered notion of the employee in spite of lip service to the values of family and caring. In addition, business organizations and their political allies control societal resources and allocate them first to their own interests, not to caring and reproduction, particularly of low-income African-American, Hispanic, and other racial/ethnic families. The privileging of large organizations facilitates their nonresponsibility.[26]

Nonresponsibility is constituted through particular practices that are part of the continual organizing of capitalist societies, historically constituted, sometimes contested, and highly variable. These processes are linked into fundamental relations of capitalist societies: those that organize production toward profit and the accumulation of capital and not, in the first instance, toward provisioning the population or assuring human reproduction, as I discussed above. Thus, claims to nonresponsibility for both human beings and the environment are affirmations of the central aims of profit-making organizations. I think it is very important to see nonresponsibility as actively constructed through diverse organizational inventions and state actions, such as legislation in the nineteenth century that reformed the Poor Law in Britain (Polanyi 1944) and the United States, discussed above, or that created the rights of corporations to act in their own interests, as their leaders defined those interests (Perrow 2002).[27]

The establishment in the nineteenth century of *laissez-faire* ideology with rational economic man as the iconic figure supported denial of responsibility by economic organizations. Rational economic man acted purposively in his own interest, his decisions contributing to positive outcomes for the community and nation.[28] The worker, too, was to act in his own interest, defined as working for a wage. The needs of reproduction, to the extent that they were visible, would be provided for by wage labor and other positive economic outcomes. Polanyi (1944) argued, as I discussed above, that the establishment of labor as a commodity necessitated cutting the worker "free" from any supports, such as public assistance, that would allow him to exist without working for a wage. The reform of the Poor Law in Britain that abolished "outdoor relief" was an essential step in legislating free market ideology and a victory for nonresponsibility. The history of Anglo-American capitalism can be read as a series of ongoing battles between workers, reformers, and their social movements and employers and their associations over issues related to responsibility for reproduction and provisioning, such as the payment of starvation wages, the refusal to provide safe working conditions, insistence on long working hours, or the destruction of environments. In the late nineteenth and early twentieth centuries, factory acts to protect workers were passed, efforts were made to establish the ten-hour day, to regulate child labor, to provide workmen's compensation for injuries, and Mother's Pensions were established in some states.[29] Capitalist employers and their associations frequently claimed that protections were antithetical to the health of business and opposed them.

At the same time, it would be a mistake to see only a unified opposition by capitalist firms to any sort of intervention to support reproduction. Capitalist organizations and the men who lead them have historically (and still do today) sometimes paid attention to the needs of workers and of human reproduction in general. A distinction should be made between measures to support the reproductive needs of their own employees and measures to support the needs of the population in general. When firms are well-established in a particular place and dependent on a local labor supply they may be willing to support their own workers or employees in positions critical to the operation of the organization. They may provide a living wage, some parental leave, medical insurance, and on-site day care, while opposing tax-supported measures to give these protections to non-employees. At particular times, larger groups of employers may even push for reforms, as Polanyi (1944) argues. To secure an appropriate and committed labor force, to assure a community of consumers, to achieve legitimacy and civil order, large capitalist organizations have adapted to particular conditions of production or acceded to demands for reform from employees, labor unions, other social movements, and from governments responding to the politics of these movements.

Capitalist organizations have even reluctantly acquiesced to demands for new forms of distribution to ordinary people.[30] Responding to the crisis of reproduction brought on by the Depression in the 1930s, the United States passed the Social Security Act, a tremendous step toward social protection through new distribution programs, forcing employers to assume through tax payments some responsibility in the areas of support of the unemployed and the elderly. The Act also established income supports, or welfare, through Aid for Dependent Children, for children living with their single mothers. The further development of welfare states after World War II—especially in the rich Northern countries—diluted corporate power over workers by establishing job protections as well as state supports for reproduction and forcing firms to also take some responsibility (Esping-Andersen 1990). Although outcomes varied, welfare states were usually based on the assumption that women still provide the unpaid work of caring (O'Connor, Orloff, and Shaver 1999). In the same period in the United States, under pressures of the labor movement, large corporations negotiated higher wages, medical care, vacations, and other benefits with their workers, even as they may have still opposed national and state legislation for welfare programs. Thus, in the United States many work organizations took some responsibility, but primarily for their own employees, while in Europe, benefits tended to go to all workers, with highly variable supports for women doing unpaid caring work (see, for example, Esping-Andersen 1990; Williams 1990; O'Connor, Orloff, and Shaver 1999). Although many U.S. employers did begin to provide for some of the needs of their employees, particularly male employees, in the post–World War II period, they collectively began immediately after World War II to reduce the power of the labor movement, achieving the passage of the federal Taft-Hartley Act that undermined the protections labor had won with the Depression-era Wagner Act.[31] That legislation began a long campaign to weaken labor organization and protect the corporate claims to nonresponsibility.

No fundamental economic logic of capitalism exists that results in one way of managing the break between reproduction and production, or one pattern of organizational nonresponsibility. As Fred Block (1990) has argued, there are different strategies of accumulation and capitalism has prospered with different kinds of government policies. Similarly, capitalist states and organizations have prospered with different strategies of reproduction, different policies in regard to the reproductive needs of employees, and different stances toward communities and toward government supports for redistribution and reproduction in general. These differences are embedded in different histories and in different gendered and racialized class relations, and, in turn, help to recreate those relations. Charles Handy (2003), a British management expert, argues that the "current Anglo-American version of stock market capitalism" in which shareholder value is the primary criterion of success, "had no place for many of the things that Europeans take for granted as the benefits of citizenship—free health care and quality education for all, housing for the disadvantaged, and a guarantee of reasonable living standards in old age, sickness, or unemployment" (70). Handy notes that the American model started to take hold in Europe, but that many Europeans now believe that it went too far. European capitalism continues to live with welfare state supports for income and reproduction that far exceed those in the United States, in spite of some retrenchment. This is also the case in Scandinavia. For example, in Sweden, supports and protections for reproductive work have not been substantially reduced in spite of attacks on and some downsizing of the welfare state (Leira 2002). Employing organizations must pay attention to employees' reproduction needs because in many instances such attention is guaranteed by law. In spite of economic problems, Sweden and many European countries have successful capitalist economies.

Recent history is full of continuing corporate efforts to protect and restore nonresponsibility, with considerable success. U.S. corporations seem to have acted on the famous statement of Milton Friedman: "Few trends could so thoroughly undermine the very foundations of our free society as the acceptance by corporate officials of a social responsibility other than to make as much money for their stockholders as possible" (1982, 133; quoted in Nelson 2003, 82). The restoration of neoliberalism as the dominating economic discourse has provided legitimacy for reducing welfare state programs and restoring corporate nonresponsibility that was somewhat modified in the post–World War II period. (I discuss the cuts in welfare state programs in chapter 6.) While both corporate and state support for reproduction have decreased, some parts of reproductive services have moved into the capitalist economy, becoming available only to those able to pay, as well as becoming a source of profit. From opposition to worker efforts to raise wages to failure to support paid parental leave legislation, public day care, or universal medical care, corporations escalate their denial of responsibility for anything but the bottom line. Caring and nurturing, unless a source of profit, are not important, in spite of rhetoric to the contrary. As caring work is devalued, so are those who primarily do that work.

The transnational organization of production builds nonresponsibility into the structure of capitalist processes. As corporations such as Nike or Liz Claiborne contract production to firms in other countries, the corporation often has relatively few workers of its own, thus few who might demand responsibility. As Appelbaum and Gereffi (1990, 44) say, "Contracting means that the so-called manufacturer need not employ any production workers, run the risk of unionization or wages pressures, or be concerned with layoffs resulting from *changes* in product demand." Thus, nonresponsibility in the interest of accumulation underlies corporate decisions to continually move production to the location with the cheapest labor. Nonresponsibility is built into globalizing processes; indeed, the opportunities for production and gain without challenges to nonresponsibility probably constitute a major incentive for moving production from rich, capitalist countries to poorer, low-wage locations. At the same time, back in corporate headquarters in the United States or other rich countries, where design, marketing, and production decisions are made, a significant degree of gender and racial/ethnic equality may emerge as skilled professionals are hired to do this work.

Capitalist organizations have power and privileges that often result in victories in struggles over nonresponsibility for reproduction. The privileging of capitalist organizations is nothing new, but with the dominance of neoliberal market policies, it seems more obvious today than it was during the post–World War II years of building welfare states. For individuals, privileging of organizations means that the demands of work organizations usually must come first in the daily round of activities, as I argued above. Obviously, most of us have to go to work if we want to eat. Thus, we enter employing organizations, but not on our own terms. Privileging also means that large capitalist, state, and voluntary organizations, in pursuing their own ends, have disproportionate influence in defining the society as a whole, with the largest corporations in a determining position in the United States. While business organizations do not necessarily agree with each other on a range of issues, there is probably consensus among them on the proposition that what's good for capital in general is good for the country and the world. In this sense, economic organizations are privileged; they come first over the needs of women and men and their families and communities. Privilege is maintained by effective monopoly over the ways that production is created and coordinated and by the control of the bulk of the economic and political resources of the society, including the media. Thus, privilege is maintained and extended through concrete organizational practices, such as making political contributions and opposing organized labor. Many of these activities promote organizations' claims to nonresponsibility. In this process, the gender division of labor between caring and providing (Leira 1994) is continually recreated as the most powerful organizations, either by default or through intentional policy, create caring needs as peripheral, invisible, and someone else's (women's) responsibilities.

CONCLUSION

I have tried to demonstrate in this discussion that "A capitalist economy that operates through a gender division of labour is, necessarily, a gendered accumulation process" (Connell 2000, 25). I would add that an economy that operates through a racial division of labor is necessarily a racialized accumulation process. I have argued that the fundamental organization of capitalist production, including the transformation of human labor into a commodity, separates production and reproduction, creating tensions, even contradictions, between these two necessary social activities. These are gendered tensions, as women are historically assigned to caring work and subordinated in the world of paid work. This organization of production undergirds: 1) the devaluation of unpaid work and caring, 2) abstract conceptual practices that obscure unpaid work and caring, 3) a lack of fit between paid work and the rest of life, 4) corporate claims to nonresponsibility for human needs, and 5) efforts to create new forms of distribution to ordinary people. In the United States, this organization of production emerges within systems of slavery and racial/ethnic subordination, building in racial exclusion and discrimination from the beginning.

This sets the stage for more detailed examination of gendered and racialized class practices and relations in the next two chapters. I intend to leave open the question of whether or not fundamental changes can occur without basically altering capitalist practices. Certainly, tremendous positive changes have occurred in United States society in the last thirty to forty years in patterns of subordination and exclusion based on gender and race, while gendered and racialized class-linked increases in income and wealth inequality have soared. Gendered and racialized practices are not erased and new configurations of exploitation, domination, and inequality seem to be continually produced in the ongoing processes of global corporate expansion and organizational restructuring.

NOTES

1. Omi and Winant (1994) develop the notion of *project* to discuss racial formation. This is a helpful notion that I borrow to assist in thinking about capitalism and class, but use in a somewhat different way. To think about the development of capitalism as a project or as many projects brings actors' bodies and activities, as well as the cultural representation of those bodies and activities of actors, into a central place in "processes."

2. The male identity of the leaders of industrialization is obvious in every history of the process. See, for example, Gutman (1976) or Perrow (2002).

3. Chris Middleton (1983) argued that, in Britain, male heads of households in the emerging capitalist class appropriated the labor of members of the household, including wives and daughters. In the process, patriarchal power was reorganized and women in this class actually saw the range of their contributions to production shrink as they were excluded from various occupations and economic sectors.

4. There is a huge literature on the working lives of women, their history, and present configurations. See, for example, Kessler-Harris (1982), Amott and Matthaei (1996), Glenn (2002) for histories and Padavic and Reskin (2002) for a contemporary overview.

5. See Eric Williams (1944).

6. While race/ethnicity-based dominations of colonial peoples were built into capitalist development in Britain and European countries, these patterns of racial exploitation and oppression did not become integrated into gender and class processes within national boundaries until after World War II. Each country had a different history of colonialism, different labor force recruitment policies in the postwar period, and different policies in regard to immigration. All of these patterns result in different racial patterns, different problems today.

7. For example, Dolores Janiewski (1996) shows how preexisting race and gender ideologies, along with employers' commitments to maintaining the existing

sexual and racial order, shaped Southern managerial strategies in the textile and tobacco industries.

8. Many histories of labor struggles exist. See, for example, Foner (1947), Taylor (1992), Milton (1982). For examples of women's participation in labor struggles, see Frankel (1984) and Kessler-Harris (1982).

9. For interpretations of the processes and policies resulting in hierarchical segregation, horizontal segregation between occupations, and manual and non-manual work and the pay gap, see Reskin, McBrier, and Kmec (1999) and Kilbourne, England, and Beron (1994).

10. Connell (2000) defines masculinities as "configurations of practice within gender relations, a structure that includes large-scale institutions and economic relations as well as face-to-face relationships and sexuality" (29). The referent of "masculinities" is often ambiguous (Connell 1995). "Configurations of practice within gender relations" could refer to ideologies, images, ideals, myths, or behaviors and emotions of actual men. Moreover, masculinities are often changing, reproduced through organizational and institutional practices, social interaction, and through images, ideals, myths, or representations of behaviors and emotions. Jeff Hearn (2004) reviews the problems with the concept "hegemonic masculinity" and proposes that talking about "the hegemony of men" and dropping the notion of masculinity may solve some of these problems.

11. Although prescriptions for successful management have included in the last few years human relations skills and softer, more emotional and supportive approaches to supervision usually identified with femininity, these have not, it seems to me, disturbed the images of hegemonic masculinities. See Wacjman (1998).

12. Violence is another ambiguous term. Jeff Hearn and Wendy Parkin (2001) in *Gender, Sexuality and Violence in Organizations*, include sexual harassment and bullying along with physical violence and expand the concept to include "violation," which denotes a wide variety of actions that demean, coerce, and intimidate within work organizations.

13. Linda McDowell's (1997) study of merchant bankers in London describes another embodied hegemonic masculinity, a manly, heterosexual, class-based masculinity that dominates and disempowers many "others."

14. See Sandra Morgen (1990) for a useful discussion and summary of the debate on "reproduction" in socialist feminist theorizing.

15. Another recent retelling of this story is by Sue Ferguson (1999). Evelyn Glenn (2002) discusses the separation of production and reproduction in the history of U.S. industrial capitalism and the variations by gender and race in the impact of the separation.

16. Diane Elson (1994) describes the separation between production and reproduction in economic terms as a division between the monetary "productive" economy and the nonmonetary "reproductive" economy. "The ability of money to mobilize labour power for 'productive work' depends on the operation of some non-monetary set of social relations to mobilize labour power for 'reproductive work.' These non-monetary social relations are subordinate to money in the sense that they cannot function and sustain themselves without an input of money; and

they are reshaped in response to the power of money. Nevertheless, neither can the monetary economy sustain itself without an input of unpaid labour, an input shaped by the structures of gender relations" (Elson 1994, 40).

17. This may be a too simplistic model of capitalism and capitalist firms, as Julie Nelson (2003) argues. Nelson points out that arguments that shareholders are not the only stakeholders in corporations are not new, and that research shows that profit maximization is not the driving force in some of the most successful companies. Small businesses and large corporations are complex social processes, embedded in the societies in which they exist, as Nelson also argues. My argument is only that production is organized to achieve profit, not to support such things as caregiving. In addition, as I argue below, there are particular conditions under which corporations pay attention to human needs, but these do not always exist.

18. Efforts to reform the poor law in the early nineteenth-century United States varied greatly between states and localities, although the arguments against aid to the "able-bodied" were the same as those in Great Britain. See Coll (1969) and Mencher (1967).

19. This is a persistent theme in much of the literature on the emergence of the welfare state, such as Esping-Anderson's (1990) influential *The Three Worlds of Welfare Capitalism*.

20. Carole Pateman (1989) discusses the complexities and ambiguities of the distinctions between a public and private domain. She argues that the patriarchal character of the separation between public and private was "forgotten," and the separation between public and private became located within civil society, implicitly the sphere of men. Thus, the fact that "patriarchalism is a constitutive part of the theory and practice of liberalism" (123) becomes obscured and the domestic arena is seen as irrelevant to social and economic theory.

21. As discussed in chapter 2, feminist theorizing in the 1970s and 1980s sometimes suggested a functional relationship between production and reproduction: Reproduction has the function of reproducing the labor power necessary for capitalist production, or reproducing the ideology of hierarchy and subordination that is also necessary for the economy (for example, Hartmann 1981; Eisenstein 1979). Thus, women's unpaid work and their subordination are functionally necessary for the economy. Christine Delphy (1984) located reproductive activities within a family mode of production distinct from the capitalist mode of production, with women subordinated within both modes of production. The approach I suggest here is different from both of these. In addition to general problems with functional explanations, I see no functional necessity for unpaid work organized in a particular way. The notion that unpaid work occurs within a domestic mode of production may be useful for understanding some societies at particular historical moments, but is much less useful for understanding societies such as the contemporary United States in which a large majority of women are wage earners and many families consist of a single mother and children.

22. Lynet Uttal and Mary Tuominen (1999) make the valuable point that child care and housework are different forms of labor. Caregiving, when paid, is work exchanged for wages, but it also has value and meaning based on commitment to

valuing other human beings. Uttal and Tuominen analyze the complicated and often contradictory connections between these two principles in commodified caregiving.

23. Alice Kessler-Harris (1982, 270) reports that in 1940, one in every five female wage earners were domestic servants. Half of these were African Americans. As late as 1960, 39 percent of African-American women were working in domestic service (Amott and Mattaei 1996, 327). This was a large labor force, working in middle income as well as affluent households.

24. While feminists have extensively criticized many concepts that contain an implicit male referent and thus make women invisible, such concepts do play a part in organizing social life. Therefore, it seems to me that most feminists have an ambivalent relationship to these concepts: They need them, but understand their complicity in maintaining women's invisibility in so doing.

25. The following discussion is based, in part, on my 1998 article, "The Future of Gender and Organizations."

26. Nancy Folbre (2001) in *The Invisible Heart* has a similar analysis, arguing in chapter 8 that corporations avoid paying the costs of reproducing their workers, prefer childless workers, and search for the lowest paid labor regardless of the consequences.

27. Charles Perrow (2002) describes the historical process through which the particular U.S. corporate form was created in three Supreme Court decisions in 1819, removing much public control from private economic activities. As Perrow says, "The consequences were immense. For example, the ruling encourages the privatization of what, for other countries, was a public good under public control, the railroads" (42). I believe that the consequences were immense in other areas too, as I discuss in this section.

28. See Lourdes Benería (1999) for another analysis focusing on the development of market society.

29. See, for example Bremner (1956) and Piven and Cloward (1993).

30. Piven and Cloward (1993, 52–53) discuss a statement in 1932 by the U.S. Chamber of Commerce and the National Association of Manufacturers opposing federal aid to the unemployed and supporting private charity and state and local assistance.

31. Piven and Cloward (1993, 443).

5

Large Organizations and the Production of Gendered and Racialized Class

Gendered and racialized class relations are created, in part, by organizing practices that accomplish the practical goals of production and distribution. Managers and other corporate strategists, through their organizing, also continuously recreate the masculine model of the organization and the worker as unconnected to, and therefore not responsible for, the work of human reproduction. In other words, the gendering and racializing class practices that I outlined in chapters 3 and 4 actually happen, in the main, in organizations. Therefore, an examination of organizations is important in understanding gendering and racializing processes.

Feminist scholars have, since the mid-1980s, studied and theorized "gendered organizations," creating new understandings of work-based inequalities (Martin and Collinson 2002).[1] A large and growing number of studies show how gendered practices and assumptions are embedded in organizing processes, and scholars have argued that it is impossible to understand capitalist organizations without explicating how gender is involved in their history and their present practices (Acker 1990; Savage and Witz 1992; Ashcraft and Mumby 2004). In this chapter I expand this work[2] to include race and class, reviewing how actions of large organizations play a major role in the structuring of class relations, and arguing that the gendering and racialization of class occurs in organizing processes. I discuss those processes and practices and ask if they have changed with organizational restructuring, new technology, and increasing transnational economic organization. I develop the concept of regimes of inequality as a way of understanding the dynamics of gendered and racialized class relations within specific organizations. The idea of regimes of inequality may also be useful in analyzing complex stories of organizational conflict and change. I outline the components of inequality regimes and look at how changes in inequality regimes are resisted and/or accomplished.

Organizations are central to class processes in at least two ways.[3] First, the capitalist economy functions through organizations. The practices of work organizations are major elements in class processes in communities, nations, and across national boundaries. Large organizations in capitalist societies participate in producing large-scale gendered and racialized class inequalities as they organize production and distribution, centralize the control of wealth, and take little responsibility for reproduction, as I argued in chapter 4. Organizations shape class relations as they decide what to produce or what services to offer, as they decide to move production to China or Mexico, or to stay in the United States and try to drive down costs, or as they decide whom to employ and what wages and benefits to offer, shaping the prospects for a reasonable level of living for large groups of people. Transnational organizations such as the World Trade Organization and the World Bank shape national and transnational class relations through policies that, for example, force privatization of government companies or reductions in social welfare spending in debtor countries (e.g., Teichman 2001). This is one example of the many class-constituting processes that take place between organizations in both the public and private sectors. Organizations also shape class relations through their lobbying efforts that, combined with the power of their money, achieve political and legislative decisions friendly to their interests. Class relations are written into laws, regulatory practices, and union-management agreements that specify, support, and sometimes limit the power of organizations to control workers and organize production, as I argued in chapter 3.

Although organizational decision makers play a significant part in producing class and its inequalities, they and their organizations are not all alike. Organizations are historically, geographically, and politically located. Contemporary organizations in any one country vary in many ways: size, sector of the society, area of the country, the specific history of the organization and its location. They exist in different economic arenas with different problems and potentialities. Within sectors they also do different things and often have different interests; their competition and clash of interests often have profound impacts on class. For example, in the complicated saga of the decline of U.S. production of textiles and clothing, the retail apparel industry's competitive practices involved pressures on manufacturers to lower prices and to move production to low-wage countries, resulting in a large decline in employment that continued into 2004, increasing the ranks of the insecure female working class in the United States and creating new female working classes in other countries (Rosen 2002).

Organization size probably influences the ways in which gendered and racialized class relations are created in organizations. Small, local organizations may not reflect and reproduce overall class processes so thoroughly as large organizations. Small organizations have managers or owners who are not elites and who are often in much more unstable and insecure positions than Phil Knight of Nike or Bill Gates of Microsoft. Inequalities between owners, managers, and workers may not be as great as in the large corporations. At the same time, small establishments employ many workers; numerically they are important in class processes. An additional difference that may be important is the sectorial location of organizations. In the public sector, policies and practices are more open to examination and political pressures that, under favorable circumstances, can support affirmative action and pay equality. However, public sector organizations have much the same sorts of class-linked hierarchies and organizing practices as private sector firms.

The second way in which organizations and organizing are central to class is that essential organizing practices are, at the same time, essential elements of class practices. Class happens in work organizations, as people do the work, as managers pay them wages, and as management in private corporations eventually take their profits. Employment agreements and their implementation, outlined in chapter 3, are organizing processes. Exploitation and wage dependency, necessary for survival for all but the economic elite, are constructed in organizing practices. The organization of work and wage patterns take place, as I argued in chapter 4, in the context of a gendered and racialized substructure in which gender- and race-neutral images of "the worker" and organizing obscure underlying arrangements based on gendered and racialized assumptions. Class relations of distribution also begin in work organizations with wages, bonuses and stock options, and payments to the state such as income and social security taxes and unemployment insurance premiums. State distributions flow through various state organizations, all with their own practices that are implicated in class, and often differentiated on bases of race and gender.

Organizational hierarchies of power and reward are class hierarchies. These hierarchies are structured along lines of gender and race. White, mostly male, elites are in top positions. While the marauding male entrepreneur may build new capitalist projects, the rational, masculine CEO keeps the corporation expanding. Lower, less powerful levels of managers and employees are often less exclusively white and male. At the very bottom level, undocumented immigrant women are often cleaning the restrooms at night. Union organizing and employers' responses, class conflict and accommodation, take place in or around organizations. Gendered and racialized class identities, as well as consciousness or nonconsciousness of class, are also partly formed in experiences in work organizations. Those who are not employed in organizations are also affected by organizations in societies such as the United States in which waged work is so predominant. Organizations exclude some and set the conditions of survival for many other loosely connected contingent workers.

Class practices are not confined to organizing boundaries. Class-related cultural and consumption differences or differences in family relations and community lives, always mediated by gender and racial realities, happen in the spaces of everyday life outside organizations (Kessler-Harris 1993). But, life outside and inside organzations interpenetrate each other. The same bodies move between organizations and other spaces; individuals construct the links as they go about their daily business. The demands of work impinge on the demands of home, family, and community and, to some extent, vice versa. Class-linked identities formed at work travel with people into home and community. The growth of transnational corporations and other multinational or even global organizations complicates the question of boundaries. As all of these practices suggest, organizations cannot be seen as clearly bounded systems, for boundaries are shifting and porous. In spite of these objections to thinking about organizations as internal to certain boundaries, I will focus here on what happens in the confines of employing organizations, using the idea of inequality regimes to bring class, race, and gender into the same frame of analysis.

This discussion of organizations, like most such discussions, uses the abstract discourse of the relations of ruling within which sociological talk has developed. As a result, bodies in all their messy corporeality are more absent than they should be. But, bodies as images, imaginations, and physically present and active are the essential material conditions for the ongoing practices that we label as work and gendered and racialized class relations. Images of bodies, one's own and others', can be linked to complexly constructed class/gender/race identities, intersecting with and mediating the experience of work in organizations. The impact of work on bodies may be perceived differently, depending on gender and race identities of workers and the gendered and racialized class positions of observers. For example, caring work and clerical work are often seen as "light" (female) in contrast to "heavy" (male) physical labor. But, caring is physical as well as emotional labor and often results in exhausted and damaged bodies. Clerical work, particularly the use of computers, can also be physically damaging. Here, too, a great deal of variation and difference exists. Bodies are for sale because labor cannot be sold unless it is provided through a body. Bodies are also a way of selling. Bodies and sexuality are part of work relations; for example, young women workers in a Mexican border factory are "subjected to an ongoing evaluation in which desirability and productivity are indistinguishable" (Salzinger 2003, 67). Women's bodies may mark them as out of place in certain circumstances. Mothers' lactating bodies may be particularly out of place in work settings. In the following discussion of inequality regimes, I do not always specifically discuss bodies, but I assume that they are always there.

ORGANIZING INEQUALITY REGIMES

Looking at "inequality regimes" is a way to explore the second approach to organizing and class, discussed above: how organizing practices are, at the same time, gendered and racialized class practices. The term "inequality regimes"[4] stands for historically specific patterns of race, gender, and class relations within particular organizations (Acker 2000).[5] R. W. Connell (1987; see also Walby 1990) developed the idea of "gender regimes" to indicate particular, historically specific configurations of gender relations within institutions and organizations. I am indebted to his work, but elaborate the idea of regimes in a different way, focusing on organizing processes rather than on structures of power, cathexis, and labor as he does. "Regime" has been frequently used in recent scholarship, such as that on "welfare state regimes," as part of the construction of typologies, or ideal types. Critics point out that the term may imply more coherence than actually exists in particular groups of societies and that its use in making comparisons may obscure important differences. For example, categorizing welfare state regimes on the basis of employment-related state benefits (Esping-Andersen 1990) was inadequate for describing differences between states in providing maternity and child benefits and other programs supporting women (Lewis 1992, 1997; Orloff 1993). In addition, the construction of ideal types can lead to an analysis comparing concrete cases against the measuring rod of the typology, rather than looking for the historically situated practices and processes that constitute the concrete case. However, while I want to avoid using "regime" as the basis for constructing a typology, I have not been able to find another word that captures as well the sense of an ongoing identifiable set of processes and meanings that I have in mind. Thus, "inequality regime" specifies interconnecting organizational processes that produce and maintain racialized and gendered class relations.[6] Employment contracts, discussed in chapter 3, indicate where managers and employees are situated within inequality regimes.

Inequality is defined here as systematic disparities between groups of organizational participants in control over organizational goals and outcomes, work processes and decisions, in opportunities to enter and advance in particular job areas, in security of position and levels of pay, in intrinsic pleasures of the work, and in respect and freedom from harassment. Every organization has an inequality regime, as the almost universal presence of "leadership," hierarchies of power and authority, race and sex segregation of jobs and hierarchies, and accompanying large wage differences in organizations suggests. Inequality regimes vary widely in the severity of inequalities, but they exist even within organizations that intend to be egalitarian.[7] While variations exist, there are also common patterns found in most bureaucratic organizations in the rich industrial countries.[8] The restructuring of bureaucracies since the early 1980s means that we can no longer assume all organizations adhere to a static hierarchical model. At the same time, it is very difficult to estimate how general and how fundamental changes may be (see Cornfield, Campbell, and McCammon 2001). Any direction of changes toward more or less participation, more or less skill, is also difficult to determine. Thus, I see inequality regimes as fluid, not fixed, although the pace of change also varies. In looking at inequality regimes, I attempt to present an approach that can capture moving realities, complex interplays at particular moments of time.

To explore organizations from this perspective, I describe the components of inequality regimes and some of their variations. These include:

- bases for inequality
- organizing processes and practices that maintain and reproduce inequalities
- visibility of inequalities
- legitimacy of inequalities and ideologies and images on which legitimacy is based
- controls and compliance
- competing interests and organizing change

I do not discuss the types and severity of inequalities, such as wage inequality, in specific organizations because these have been documented in many studies (for example, Padavic and Reskin 2002; Tomaskovic-Devey 1993). These are also discussed using aggregate data in other chapters. Here, I focus only on other characteristics of inequality regimes outlined above.[9] The characteristics of inequality regimes I discuss here are the processes or mechanisms that create and maintain inequalities.[10] I assume that people in differing positions of power, interacting with each other and constructing their own notions of identity and efficacy, are also creating and recreating inequality regimes. I see identity formation and interaction patterns as embedded in, but not determined by, the processes of inequality regimes. I do not discuss these processes separately.

The Bases of Inequality

Organizational hierarchies are intrinsically class hierarchies, as I argued above. The other bases of inequality may differ: What constitutes differences that matter are historically and culturally defined. In contemporary organizations, difference and inequality are evident along lines of mutually constituting gender, race, and class, but disparities in power, autonomy, rewards, and rights based on ethnicity, religion, age, physical ability, and sexuality are also widely apparent. The category "race" contains different groups that may also be differentiated by culture or ethnicity.

The gendered and racialized class inequalities in work organizations are obvious, for example, in the relative scarcity of white women and people of color in most top level positions and the existence of large job categories filled almost entirely with low-wage women workers with little power and autonomy, as well as in the disproportionate segregation of African Americans and other minorities in low-level jobs.

Some organizations have primarily white male members, a few may have only white female participants or only participants with another particular racial or ethnic identification. The gender and racial/ethnic composition of organizations is a consequence of practices of exclusion and inclusion, both historical and contemporary. Patterns of inclusion and exclusion seem to be formed rapidly. For example, James N. Baron and his associates (2002) found that, in high-tech firms at least five years old, the proportion of women in professional positions was low. The founders' original "cultural organizational blueprints" reflected in early staff choices of women for key roles significantly affected later participation patterns of women.

The absence of one or more bases of inequality does not mean, of course, that gender, race, and class and other inequalities are not produced in and by these organizations. Large, white male organizations are often centers of symbolic affirmation of existing gender, race, and class inequalities and major arenas in which these relations are reproduced for broader areas of the society. Male-only, white-dominated organizations, for example, the U.S. military until very recently, are probably larger and more influential for relations of inequality in the society as a whole than those organizations that are not white-male-dominated. Those organizations in which participants are primarily white women or people from other racial/ethnic groups are apt to be subunits of larger organizations, such as nursing units in hospitals, or service organizations such as schools, day care centers, or hairdressers. Gender and race are also symbolically reproduced in these enterprises, both in their internal processes and in the images they present to their surrounding communities. Many work units, such as those in manufacturing or the skilled trades, are still predominantly of one gender or the other, even though considerable integration has occurred in the United States as a result of antidiscrimination laws, affirmative action, and vast changes in organizational and occupational structures.

Most organizations also operate on the assumption that participants are heterosexual, implicitly defining homosexuality as unacceptable, or at least undesirable, and a basis for inequality. Although the taboo on homosexuality in the United States may not be as great or as widespread today as it once was, it still exists as a public issue and a basis for discrimination. The most prominent example of an organization that is unable or unwilling to give equal treatment to homosexuals is the U.S. military, the bastion of heterosexual masculinity. Heterosexuality still shapes organizing practices, for example, in gendered bureaucratic roles that often assume a particular heterosexual imagery, in gender-loaded interaction expectations, in the sexualized culture of many workplaces (Alvesson 1993; Adkins 1995), or in the expectations that top executives will have wives to facilitate their careers.

Organizing Processes that Reproduce Inequality

Organizing processes that reproduce hierarchy and inequality include the conscious construction and deconstruction of hierarchies, jobs and work processes, recruitment and hiring, control and supervision, and wage determination. Some of these processes are relatively invisible and nonconscious. Bodies and sexuality are implicated in these processes. The processes are highly variable, as are the shape and degree of hierarchy and participation.

Organizing Work into Jobs and Hierarchies

Organizational structures differ, ranging from rigid, autocratic hierarchies to relatively flat, team-organized work processes. Most organizations, but especially large corporations, are authoritarian, nondemocratic institutions, usually put together as bureaucracies. Government bureaucracies may be equally hierarchical. Decisions about goals, locations, technologies, or investments are made at the top; participation in such decisions decreases at each lower level.

Class divisions of authority and control are given palpable form in the structure of jobs and hierarchies; race and gender divisions have shaped these processes in the past, and that past often shapes the present, at least to a degree. An obvious example is the defining of clerical work as the work of young white women and management as the work of white men. Anne Witz and Mike Savage (1992, 10) observe that "The modern organization came into being depending on cheap female labour, and in turn helped define women as subordinate workers to men within emergent white collar labour markets." In the United States, this white collar bureaucracy was, until fairly recently, a domain of white privilege into which no African Americans could enter, except at the lowest levels. Bureaucratic authority relations had gender and racial undercurrents: assumptions of legitimate power and control based in the superior power and control of white men in the powerful institutions such as the economy, the military, religion, government, and families. The legacy of that process is bureaucratic power still grounded in implicit assumptions about the legitimacy of male authority (Ferguson 1984), and organizations still divided along lines of gender and race, although less so than in the past, with white men still monopolizing top positions.[11] White women, African Americans, Latinas, and many "others" are increasingly in management and professional positions, as I noted in chapter 3, and the management of diversity is now an important task of human resources managers (Thomas and Ely 1996). However, the historical absence of African Americans in the bureaucratic form in the United States is still marked by their extreme visibility to white participants when they enter organizations that were formerly all white, and their continuing situations as outsiders (Collins 1990). The exclusion of African Americans, in a society divided by race, defined bureaucratic work organizations in racial as well as gender terms. Other groups marked as racially and ethnically different from whites were also integrated into organizations in particular ways. The organizing of manufacturing work has been similarly patterned along racial and gender divides, with accompanying identity and ideological differences. Racial and gender divisions of organizational class processes have not disappeared.

Defining jobs as bundles of tasks that fit into class-related hierarchies also involves gender and race, with hidden assumptions about what is appropriate work for particular socially constructed categories of people. This process often divides gendered and raced categories within particular class configurations. For example, fish processing, assembly work in electronic production, or other "light" industrial employment, has been defined as women's work, while more "skilled" and "heavier" work, such as moving materials and boxes or doing heavy industrial production, has been defined as masculine. These gender and often racial definitions of suitable work began with industrialization as white and then immigrant women were recruited into some jobs and men into others. Gendered and racialized recruitment are documented in studies in many countries and are still prevalent (e.g., Acker and Van Houten 1974; Hossfeld 1994; Collins 2000; Salzinger 2003). At the same time, what is suitable now in one organization may not be in the future or even in another organization today.

Bureaucratic systems of job design, job evaluation, and organizing accountability build gendered class assumptions into hierarchical relations (Acker 1989a). For example, job classification schemes that define tasks and hierarchies of positions often contain gendered assumptions about skill and responsibility levels of different jobs, categorizing female-dominated jobs as less skilled and less responsible than many male-dominated jobs, a judgment challenged by pay equity studies (for example, Acker 1989a). As I have already argued, the very idea of skill is gendered (Phillips and Taylor 1980), produced in struggles of white male workers to increase their wages and to differentiate themselves from the unskilled, other men, and all women (Cockburn 1983, 1985). This history is embedded in organizing practices and the implicit assumptions on which they are often based. Organizations don't always use job classification schemes: This is only an example to illustrate that the bureaucratic, rationalized aspects of organizing produce inequalities, indeed, are designed to produce inequalities. Although such bureaucratic schemes appear as disembodied abstractions, they are put together and implemented by embodied people working within the discursive frames of managerial practice that assume class, gender, and often race relations.

Inequality regimes differ in the ways in which job requirements and expectations, such as work hours, promptness of arrival, attention to the work while at the job, or working overtime are modeled on the image of a white male worker/breadwinner who has no responsibilities for children or other aspects of family life (Acker 1990). This is a manifestation of the gendered substructure of class relations that I outlined in chapter 4. Some organizations seem to use two models of the ideal worker, one the full-time, skilled male; the other, the part-time, unskilled female (Benschop and Doorewaard 1998). Some organizations, or units within organizations, are much more "family friendly" than others. However, women as well as men are expected to comply with the gendered discipline of the job and the organization.

Degrees of hierarchy and different organizing practices may have an effect on the gendering of inequalities. For example, flat, collegial organizations may contain fewer gender inequalities than more traditional bureaucracies. Elin Kvande and Bente Rasmussen (1994) found that women engineers had more opportunities to excel and advance in team-organized settings than in bureaucracies. However, "team" was a masculine construct implying total time commitment to the group and the task: The women in these flat organizations had to model their work behaviors on masculine expectations, creating difficulties in combining their work with their family lives. The equalizing effects of flat organization may occur more often for professional and highly specialized technical workers than for other workers. On the other hand, other evidence suggests that new and less obvious forms of inequality and work differentiation develop in relatively flat professional organizations. For example, Jennifer Pierce's (1995) study of law firms in the United States shows a significant degree of gender and racial inequality in those professional settings.[12]

Nonhierarchical organization and an emphasis on participation does not guarantee the elimination of class and racial inequality and conflict, as the history of feminist health collectives and other feminist organizations in the United States shows (Ferree and Martin 1995). These organizations were committed to cross-race and cross-class inclusiveness and democratic process, but turning commitment into reality was very difficult (Morgen 2002; Scott 2000). Organizational structure, often dictated by outside funding bodies, involved bureaucratic and professional controls by middle class white women over working class and sometimes racial/ethnic women. The different groups brought different resources of knowledge and experience to common projects. At the same time, white, middle class women had difficulty seeing and acknowledging their own privileges and how these interfered with democratic goals.

Recruitment and Hiring

Recruitment and hiring are processes in which managers sift and sort applicants to find those with the right fit for the job. Along with pre-recruitment (education, networks, family connections) and promotion (see Brown et al. 2003 on race), recruitment and hiring are additional ways in which inequality regimes are produced and ways in which they vary. The existing gender and racial composition of the job is often significant in perceptions of qualities needed for selecting those with the right fit. Karen Hossfeld (1994) describes this process in high-tech manufacturing firms in Silicon Valley. Asian immigrant women were the preferred labor force for assembly jobs in the organizations she studied. Such women were stereotyped as better workers and as better able to work for very low pay than other workers. They were also attractive employees because, as immigrants, they were less likely than Americans to join unions. White Americans and African Americans were not seen as suitable for the entry-level jobs, but for different reasons. White Americans, employers believed, would find the jobs uninteresting. African Americans, particularly men, were unsuitable because employers considered them unreliable and troublemakers. Racist stereotyping was part of the process of excluding blacks from these jobs. Excluding whites tended to preserve the racial/class divides in these organizations in which all of the managers and office staff were white. In this case, racist stereotyping and economic gain together produced a gendered and racialized organizational class structure.

Hiring from networks of family and friends of managers and workers tends to replicate the existing gendered and racialized class compositions. Related informal processes that are part of the increasing flexibility of organizing can contribute to such outcomes. For example, in a study of a local college, Donald Van Houten and I found that full-time hiring was restricted because of budget cuts and part-time instructors were hired on a temporary basis to fill in. Department heads could make these hires without advertising or going through any formal search, and they often hired people through personal networks. Since most department heads were white men, their networks were among people like themselves and their hires were most often white men. When the rare full-time slot became available, it usually went to a person who had been part-time, because part-timers were given preference in the evaluation of candidates on the grounds that they had demonstrated their commitment to the organization. Such procedures seemed fair to the part-timers, but the result was continuation of the almost all-white, heavily male faculty, except in traditionally female disciplines such as nursing.[13] In another example, the lack of personal networks that facilitate training and job placement, along with racism, was a major reason that young black men did much less well than young white men in finding good working class jobs (Royster 2003).

The gendering and racializing of class relations that occur in workplace practices, such as hiring, is through the lens of bodies. Gendered bodies, along with the hierarchical positions of those involved, act as cues in face-to-face interactions, influencing ways in which employers, supervisors and coworkers make workplace decisions, including hiring (Reskin 2002; Fenstermaker and West 2002). A prospective employee must have the proper gendered and racialized body to be considered for employment in certain positions, even though such decision practices may be used to include the previously excluded as a result of equal opportunity laws and diversity programs. Images of appropriate bodies and assumptions about how desired worker characteristics are associated with particular bodies are held by employers and by employees themselves (Gottfried 2003). These images appear in the media and in self-help books and articles instructing job seekers about how to present themselves. For example, a successful female entrepreneur's body can be identified in pictures in *Fortune* or *Business Week*. That successful female body is probably young, but not too young, slender, and usually white. It contrasts with the successful male body that is larger, may be older, but still white, and is, of course, dressed quite differently. The images may have little connection to the actually existing linkages between bodies and worker abilities. Leslie Salzinger (2003) provides a particularly interesting example in her study of Mexican border factories. Maquiladora managers believed that young women were ideal workers, obedient, compliant, and cheap. Therefore, they hired young women. Many of these young women became less obedient and compliant with dropping real wages, poor working conditions, and emerging job alternatives. However, many managers refused to change their notions about the ideal worker, even as they were forced to hire men in order to fill their jobs.

Bodies enter into the negotiation of work agreements in other ways. For example, employers may still want reassurance that a female employee will not become pregnant, although asking directly in an interview is, in the United States, defined as sex discrimination. White bodies privilege both women and men in regard to many jobs in many places. Women's bodies are implicitly appropriate for some kinds of work, men's bodies for others, although the gender assignment of appropriate bodies to particular work can change over time (Reskin and Roos 1990). Jobs are also often racialized in the sense that jobs may be created with the knowledge that workers with particular racial, and usually gender, identities are available to fill the jobs. Such patterns also are time and place specific.

Wage-Setting Practices and Supervisory Relations

These practices and relations also reproduce gendered and racialized class inequality (Acker 1989a, 1990). Wage-setting practices differ, including bureaucratized systems with pay grades linked to job classifications, collectively bargained pay (that may be linked to a bureaucratic wage system), and individualized wage setting in which the employee bargains directly with the employer. Different systems contribute to different pay discrepancies between white men and women, women of color, and men from other than white groups (Acker 1991). Trade union bargaining seems to produce more equal wage levels than the other methods, although male-dominated unions have been known to bargain away gains for women in favor of gains for men (Acker 1991). Seniority-based pay penalizes new labor force entrants, with a disproportionate impact on white women and people of color. Moreover, unions have sometimes agreed to dual pay scales, one for present workers and a low scale for new hires. Although the systems vary, the type of system and the ways that differential evaluations are built into the fine print of the system are important in understanding the everyday production of inequality.

Other ordinary processes, such as working on a production team, interacting with colleagues, going to staff meetings, and planning and carrying out daily work, are sites in which the doing of gender and race occurs (Martin 2003). Some workplace practices that contribute to inequality are difficult to identify and speak about because they consist of often unspoken messages transmitted in ordinary interactions (Reskin 2000). These practices often result in gendered and racialized inequalities within class-defined groupings. For example, Jennifer Pierce (1995) describes the contradictory, but unarticulated, expectations that interfere with the success of women trial lawyers: If they behave as aggressively as their male colleagues, those colleagues see them as overly masculine; if they are not so aggressive, they are seen as too feminine. Their behaviors can never qualify them as fully accepted members of the male-defined groups that control their law firms. Academic women face even more subtle barriers with real, material outcomes. Although in the United States women earn about 44 percent of PhDs, they hold about 33 percent of faculty appointments, and they earn less than men with comparable achievements (Krefting 2003). "In the micropolitics of academic life, women remain on the margin trying to prove they have the skills to 'play the game at all' while men realistically presume support and focus on strategizing reputation" (Gersick et al. 2000, quoted in Krefting 2003, 260). Small incidents of exclusion and lack of respect, each too trivial to justify a response, add up to patterned disadvantage. Academic women also face contradictory stereotypes: If they are likeable, they are seen as not competent; if they are competent, they are seen as too aggressive, not likeable (Krefting 2003).

THE VISIBILITY OF INEQUALITIES

Visibility, the degree to which organizational members are aware of existing inequality, is a component of inequality regimes. Visibility varies in different organizations and over time, with variations influenced by organizational politics. The visibility of inequality often differs on the basis of organizational position or position in the structures of inequality. Managers often fail to be aware of, or they take for granted, inequalities that subordinates find oppressive. One of the privileges of the privileged, it has been observed, is to not see one's own privilege. White and male privileges, sometimes interlinked with class privilege, are ubiquitous in the United States, but white privilege is particularly invisible to white people (Smith 1995); this invisibility is a major problem in eradicating race privilege in organizations.

In two studies in which I have participated in the last few years,[14] white employees could not see any racial discrimination, although people of color in the organizations were painfully aware of discriminatory policies and behaviors. In one of these organizations, a college with 250 faculty members and administrators, there were only two African Americans on staff. One was the first affirmative action director the college had ever hired. After a year on the job, she had not been able to get the college administration to put an affirmative action plan into effect. She had not been included in hiring processes in spite of her insistence that this should be done. Money set aside for an instructor in race relations had been used for other purposes. No minority teaching staff had been hired. These and other issues had brought complaints from the African-American community. Yet, white staff whom we interviewed saw no problem of racism; instead some thought that the African-American staff had difficult personalities.

Similarly, men often find it difficult to see evidence of gender-differentiating processes that result in inequalities that are plain to women. Often, inequality is so much taken for granted, as commonsense understanding of the way things are, that invisibility is enhanced. This is a form of "hegemonic gender regulation" (Benschop and Doorewaard 1998; Gottfried 1998).

The problem of visibility is widespread and complicated. In several studies done in different countries (Czarniawska-Joerges 1994; Ely and Meyerson 2000; Korvajärvi 2003), researchers report that evidence of gender seems to disappear in contexts in which organizational participants believe that there is gender neutrality. For example, in research on clerical organizations in Finland, although there were clear gender hierarchies, "the debate on issues concerning work seems to be silent on gender issues, maintaining a culture of gender neutrality" (Korvajärvi 2003, 120). In this and other studies, gender neutrality is accompanied by a "naturalized heterosexuality." Gender inequalities are seen by both women and men in most, but not all, of these studies as existing at a distance and abstractly in other organizations or "in society." There is also a commonsense view of racism in which nonwhite people disappear in white interpretations of organizations and in white organizational studies. The unequal power, privilege, and rewards of organizational class structures are more visible, I believe, but that does not mean that these inequalities are objects of demands for change, as I discuss below.

THE LEGITIMACY OF INEQUALITIES

Organizations are locations in which the legitimacy of inequality, which I discussed in chapter 3, is created and sometimes challenged. People in organizations, my own research suggests, often see visible inequalities as perfectly legitimate, acceptable, and justifiable. Lower-level employees may recognize and dislike class-based inequalities, such as wage and wealth disparities or managerial irrationality and unfairness, but still see the underlying class processes as legitimate, or at least inevitable. The socialist movements that questioned the legitimacy of class, and other social movements in the 1970s that campaigned for work democracy and worker-controlled participatory decision making, are long forgotten. The legitimacy of class is constantly affirmed in the media, law, and in the unquestioning acceptance by workers, employers, and the society as a whole of the inevitability of the wage relation and the naturalness of organizational hierarchy, leadership, and wage disparities. As Kathy Ferguson (1994) pointed out, "discrimination on the basis of class is an oxymoron, or perhaps a tautology; class *is* the basis upon which organizational discriminations are conducted" (95–96).

Obvious gender and race inequalities, although these are frequently simultaneously reproduced with class, have less legal or formal legitimacy than class in contemporary U.S. organizations.[15] The civil rights and women's movements achieved legal proscriptions against discrimination, opened opportunities for white women and people of different racial and ethnic groups, and raised the visibility of these bases for inequality while questioning their legitimacy. The attack on gender and race inequality has been, on the whole, defined as an attack on overt intentional discrimination, leaving unchallenged and still invisible to many members of organizations significant components of inequality processes (Brown et al. 2003). For example, although equality advocates in organizations have challenged wage, hiring, and promotion discrimination based on race or gender, they have rarely questioned the gendered and racialized definitions of jobs and hierarchies.[16] In spite of equal opportunity and antidiscrimination laws, neither gender nor racial inequality has been thoroughly delegitimated, as attacks on affirmative action show (Brown et al. 2003). Judicial decisions have undermined equality legislation, preserving old patterns of systematic disadvantage. For example, Robert L. Nelson and William P. Bridges (1999, 14) conclude that in court decisions against women's pay equity efforts, "The judges deployed the authority of law to legitimate institutionalized forms of gender inequality in the workplace."

Ideologies that explain why a particular ordering of advantage is natural or desirable often support the legitimacy of inequalities. For example, low pay scales for many service and clerical jobs done primarily by women or by men of color are justified by claims that those jobs require low levels of skill (Acker 1989a), as I discussed above. The attributions of low skill levels to low-wage work have retained their legitimacy in spite of the research on gender and skill and in spite of other research showing that at least some skill-level attributions are affected by the organizational level of the job (Acker 1989a).

Appeals to "the market" and to the necessity for coordination, efficiency, and productivity often legitimate inequality regimes. Economic success may be best achieved through a hierarchical ordering of responsibilities and divisions of labor, it is claimed. Low wages and wage reductions for some and high wages for others are also justified as necessary in a competitive market climate. Race, gender, and class are invisible in these appeals; the object of discussion is an abstract organization going about achieving its abstract goals. But, race, gender, and class are involved, as the legitimacy of inequalities is assumed. The dominance of market ideology displaces other ways in which discussions of wages are framed. Arguments for basing wages on notions of justice or levels that provide a "decent living" are taken up only by labor unions and other social movements, not by corporate advocates (Figart et al. 2002; Kessler-Harris 1990). The market argument in regard to wage setting is important in maintaining corporate nonresponsibility for reproduction and adequate provisioning. Managerial and consultant discussions of the necessity of empowering employees, increasing participation in decision making, and reducing hierarchy in organizations (for example, Hammer and Champy 1993), can also function as ideological screens behind which the same old structures of inequality keep functioning.

Beliefs about gender and race differences may buttress class inequalities that are, at the same time, gender and race inequalities. For example, managers and employees may see gender inequalities at work as legitimate because women bear children and thus have a special obligation to do unpaid caring work rather than focusing all their attention on paid work. Employers' beliefs that African Americans or Latinos are deficient in some way, even if these beliefs are unarticulated and unrecognized (Reskin 2003; Brown et al. 2003), may contribute to the legitimacy of processes excluding many African Americans or Latinos from desirable jobs. However, white people often openly express such beliefs in the United States, supporting these ideas with arguments that blacks and Hispanics get preferential treatment and whites suffer from reverse racism (for example, Royster 2003).

Gendered and racialized images of the organization and its managers reinforce the legitimacy of inequality. However, white feminist analyses often fail to see the racialized nature of these images. As Rosabeth Moss Kanter (1977) argued, managers and organizations are often represented with masculine images as strong, competitive, aggressive, assertive in taking and using power and control. The skilled industrial worker is also masculine, tough, strong, fearless, assured. These are, of course, different images, but masculinity cuts across class and, perhaps, racial lines to exclude women as inappropriate for certain positions, thus legitimating gendered stratifications both vertically and horizontally. Different forms of organizational masculinity exist in different times and places (Burris 1996; Collinson and Hearn 1996), but gender as a legitimating basis for differential opportunities tends to be reproduced in organizations. Many women have entered managerial ranks in the last twenty-five years, creating the possibility that images of masculinity may be losing potency as supports to organizing class inequality. New images of managers as passionate and skilled at relationships seem to bring feminine characteristics into the legitimation of hierarchy (Hatcher 2003), but these more feminine images may be easily incorporated into a business masculinity and do little to undermine the legitimacy of inequalities (Wacjman 1998).

Thus, in spite of laws prohibiting gender and racial discrimination and in spite of entry of some representatives of formerly excluded groups into the work worlds of white men, many of the actual practices contributing to inequality remain in place and continue to be legitimate and largely invisible. Visibility does not necessarily lead to action to remove inequalities: Those with greater power or privilege may be convinced that their power and privilege are richly deserved. Legitimacy and visibility are linked, but may be combined in different ways, affecting the stability of the regime. The most stable combination is probably high legitimacy of inequality and low visibility, the most unstable is probably low legitimacy and high visibility. As I argued above, inequalities may be more visible from some organizational positions than from others; similarly, legitimacy may depend on the eyes of the beholders. Legitimacy and visibility are also linked to the interests of organization members, which I discuss below.

CONTROL AND COMPLIANCE

Control, domination, and compliance have long been major topics in conventional organizational theory and research. Beginning with Max Weber (1947; see also Bendix 1962) organizational theorists have discussed domination, coercion (or illegitimate power), and authority (or legitimate power). Other distinctions are also useful in understanding inequality regimes: Controls may be obvious or unobtrusive and direct or indirect. Direct controls are built into bureaucratic texts that specify authority lines, tasks, and procedures. Middle managers and supervisors implement these texts in daily interactions that often contain gendered, sexualized, and racialized meanings and implications (Reskin 2000; Ridgeway 1997; Martin 1996). Direct controls include coercion and implicit threats of dismissal. Sexual harassment may be a form of coercion. When wages are the only source of money necessary for survival, the wage relation itself is coercive, the fear of its loss leading to compliance (Perrow 1991, 2002). Ultimately, work organizations may fall back on violence as a means of control, for example, forcibly removing noncompliant employees from the premises or using private security forces or the police to control strike activities (Hearn and Parkin 2001). Less obvious forms of violence that I have called "normal violence" (Acker 1998, 2000) are also effective controls. These are implicit or explicit threats and other intimidating behaviors of people in powerful positions. Temper tantrums, shouting, throwing objects, and threats of dismissal or demotion are not uncommon. Although organizational participants may see such acts as individual and psychological, normal violence is made possible by the structure of power and control that protects people in high, managerial positions from controls that limit such behaviors in others.

Technologies that drive and monitor work (Edwards 1979) embed unobtrusive forms of control. Computer monitoring technologies increase the possibilities for unobtrusive controls. Perrow (1986) demonstrates the power of even more unobtrusive controls embedded in information flows, decision-making premises set by professionalization and selective recruitment of decision makers. Selective recruitment of particularly powerless people, such as immigrant or rural women, to routine production and service jobs is another form of unobtrusive control. This is a long existing mechanism of control, documented in early textile production (Perrow 2002), in the Hawthorne studies of the 1920s (Acker and Van Houten 1974), in IT in Silicon Valley in the 1980s (Hossfeld 1994), and world wide in many studies of globalized production. Workers may participate in constructing their own controls as, in their interactions, they produce tolerable ways of experiencing their work (Burawoy 1979). In other forms of control, workers are expected to internalize the mandates of the workplace, effectively exerting control over themselves. This has always been a form of control in professional work organizations, but now with new forms of organization such as team-organized production, internalized controls are attempted in other sorts of organizations. Gendered and racialized expectations may also be internalized forms of control, as female workers in particular, must often monitor their behaviors to comply with gendered expectations of bosses (e.g., Pierce 1995).

The perceived legitimacy of the subordination, fear and intimidation, or processes of calculated self-interest maintain conscious compliance with inequality regimes. Research evidence on whether compliance is calculated or based on a belief in the legitimacy of subordination can be found in a number of studies of women and work. For example, Lisa Adkins (1995) examines the compliance of female hospitality industry workers to demands for sexual attractiveness, an often unwelcome requirement of the work that makes the women vulnerable to unwanted approaches by male customers and colleagues. Jennifer Pierce (1995) describes how female paralegals and secretaries comply reluctantly to demands in law firms that they play a mothering role toward male lawyers, demands that also confirm their subordination. In both cases, compliance appears to be based more on calculated self-interest than on belief in the legitimacy of subordination. This is what they have to do to keep their jobs.

Compliance linked to perceived legitimacy of the organization was evident in my study of female workers in Swedish banks (Acker 1991). Some of the older employees believed strongly in the banks' mission to serve Swedish society and did not want to admit that problems such as a gender wage gap or limits on women's promotion existed. Other younger employees, however, did not share this view, suggesting that the legitimacy of inequality is fragile when challenged, in this case by feminists in the labor unions. Perceptions of the possibility of effective action may, in this and other cases, influence compliance. Compliance is also maintained by self-interest combined with positive feelings of accomplishment. Many jobs are intrinsically interesting. Many more are increasingly interesting with the restructuring of work in recent years that has decentralized decision making and enlarged job content (Acker 1994a).[17] Arlie Hochschild's (1997) study of a large corporation suggests that many people find social support, approval, and accomplishment at work. Such feelings of satisfaction are probably the most effective controls. How widespread satisfaction or even pleasure in work may be is another question, although Hochschild reports this finding for both professional and production line workers.

COMPETING INTERESTS AND ORGANIZING CHANGE

Multiple interests compete to both maintain and challenge regimes of inequality. Management may have unrestrained rights to maintain inequalities through coercion, dismissal, and selective rewards, or these rights may be limited by the state or by collective bargaining. On the other hand, managements may mitigate inequalities in the interest of maintaining commitment of the workforce and high productivity. The relatively powerless may maneuver individually and/or collectively to fight back, or at least to resist efforts to increase inequality. Thus, employee or union efforts to decrease inequality in the name of fairness and equity and management efforts to decrease inequality in the name of more efficient use of labor resources are different efforts to organize change. Both these types of efforts confront competing and contradictory interests, not only between management and workers, but within both of these groups. Here I comment on two change efforts—affirmative action/pay equity and management efforts to restructure for greater worker participation. Did these efforts reduce gender and race inequality in organizations? Is there any consensus on outcomes?

Efforts to Reduce Gender and Race Inequality

Challenges to inequalities are emergent in inequality regimes. The potential for resistance and change originating among the relatively powerless in organizations probably differs depending on the forms and efficacy of controls. High levels of legitimacy can limit challenges, as can high levels of fear of retaliation. In addition, cynicism about any possibility of greater equality, a sentiment I have encountered in a number of organizational studies, can also limit challenges.

Challenges are often instituted outside the organization in other political and policy-making organizations, then are, or are not, implemented (or imposed), and finally reverberate back into the wider society. Affirmative action, for example, was a challenge to organizational inequality for white women and people of color. Some observers conclude that the success of that challenge is difficult to document with certainty (Badgett and Lim 2001; Reskin 1998), others conclude that gains are clear (Brown et al. 2003, 186–87) and that affirmative action opened opportunities for white women, blacks, Latinos, and Native Americans. Affirmative action increased the visibility of both gender- and race-based exclusions from organizations. Where affirmative action was legally mandated, it created the conditions for people inside particular organizations to push for hiring those who had been previously excluded. I believe that this is what occurred in the 1970s and early 1980s; U.S. universities had many more white women and people of color on their faculties in 2004 than thirty years earlier. Affirmative action did not, however, bring equality and equity to academia; women still are disadvantaged in pay and promotion, even when controlling for relevant variables such as productivity (Bailyn 2003; Krefting 2003), as I pointed out in chapter 4. A strong reaction against affirmative action, on the grounds that it discriminated against white men in particular, had, by the beginning of the twenty-first century, greatly reduced its use and its enforcement.

Pay equity projects mushroomed in the 1980s in public sector organizations, bringing modest wage gains, with the support of unions, for low-wage female and minority male workers in many places (Figart et al. 2002). But, the movement died as public services were privatized and as labor union influence was undermined. Support for pay equity was often controversial among workers: White male workers often saw pay equity efforts by white women and people of color as undermining their own claims to superior skills and higher pay based on those skills (Acker 1989a). Other projects to increase gender equity in organizations illustrate conflicting interests that do not always coincide with bureaucratic hierarchies. Cynthia Cockburn (1991) found, for instance, that the sponsorship of the CEO of a corporation did not guarantee success in such a project, as male managers down the line saw their own control possibly eroding with more equity for women. These managers then mobilized opposition to change.

Employees may defend forms of masculinity and femininity that are embedded in organizational practices that also help to secure and legitimate inequality regimes (Collinson and Hearn 1996). An account of a gender equity action research project that had limited success provides a dramatic example (Ely and Meyerson 2000). The researchers teamed with top management of a well-known corporation to attempt to remedy high turnover and low representation among senior women. The researchers found that at the top there were constantly changing priorities, unclear performance criteria and authority lines, and constant crises. Employees had a number of strategies to handle these situations. The most valued was the "heroic" masculine problem-solving performance. Heroes got quick results and promoted themselves, but success was short-lived, and heroics led to neglect of less dramatic but essential organization building. Men were usually the heroes, while women did the backstage organizational maintenance. Women were rarely heroes; they were branded as too aggressive when they tried to take this role. This work culture was inefficient and it led to the attrition of women. There were, thus, links between gender inequality and inefficient practices in the top management group. In spite of demonstrating the inefficiencies of these processes, both female and male managers were so invested in this way of proceeding, and by implication in their gendered identities linked to their differentiated managerial roles, that no change resulted from the project.

Inequality regimes embedded in gendered identities may persist, even when the issues at hand are couched as reorganizing for efficiency rather than greater equality (Ely and Meyerson 2000). In sum, although masculinity and femininity as ideological constructions and as actions and identities of men and women vary tremendously, one constant seems to be that some form of (hegemonic, white) masculinity almost always holds the most class power in Euro-American organizations.

Managerial Efforts to Restructure, Create Teams, and Empower Workers

Restructuring of hierarchies, departments, and divisions of tasks, facilitated by new technology and stimulated by calls for flexibility in a competitive world, have been taking place in many organizations at least since the beginning of the 1980s. Politics of inequality are endemic to processes of change, such as organizational restructuring and work reorganization. Intentional change efforts such as total quality management and process redesign have been only minimally successful (Denison 1997; Hammer and Champy 1993; Knights and McCabe 1998). Other innovations that involve reducing bureaucratic oversight and relocating some supervisory functions in teams of multiskilled workers also seem to be only minimally successful (Vallas 2003). Team-structured work, in the abstract, seems to hold the possibility of overcoming some of the problems of inequality regimes by dissolving gender, and perhaps racial, divisions of tasks and distributing decision-making responsibilities throughout the group. Therefore, understanding why success has been minimal and occasional may further illuminate how racialized and gendered class relations are maintained in inequality regimes. I use some case studies to illustrate different processes and outcomes, not to provide an overall assessment.

Team self-management may result in more coercive supervision by colleagues than by previous supervisors (Barker 1993), causing particular difficulties for women with children who may be late or absent because of family crises. In industrial workplaces that have had a gendered division of labor, team organization often introduces task rotation so that both men and women are supposed to be doing the same tasks. Several studies show that gender divisions are not abandoned, but are reorganized with the introduction of team-organized work (Vallas 2003; Greene, Ackers, and Black 2002; Newsome 2003; Ollilainen and Rothschild 2001). A frequent reason is that male workers are unwilling to give up their advantages in the workplace, including their exclusive right to the more highly skilled tasks (Vallas 2003; Metcalfe and Linstead 2003). This is a matter of masculine identity and pride, as well as the higher pay that goes to jobs socially constructed as skilled. In some cases, women are also reluctant to challenge the gendered culture of the workplace by taking on male tasks, partly because this could mean giving up the compensations this gendered culture had for them, such as the conviviality of working only with other women who were friends. Racial divisions also may be barriers to instituting work reorganization (Vallas 2003).

Some efforts to construct teams and redistribute responsibilities and tasks are successful. The gender structure of the workplace may influence the success of restructuring and equalizing efforts in work organization. For example, in a study of Swedish bank offices, I found that the most successful effort to build teams with collaborative and egalitarian work relations was in an almost entirely female branch (Acker 1994a). In other branch offices, men were reluctant or entirely unwilling to give up their dominant, male-identified, positions in the interests of egalitarian, and theoretically more efficient, reorganization. Another example of partially successful restructuring and work reorganization in a predominantly female organization comes from a recent study on organizational change in welfare offices (Acker and Morgen 2001). My colleagues and I found that in two welfare offices, supervisory positions had been eliminated and workers had been empowered to make decisions they could not previously make. Workers experienced this change as very positive, improving their ability to make decisions on their own, to participate, and to influence their organization. But, top management reinstituted bureaucratic controls when a budget crisis occurred and workers were again disempowered, revealing to some disillusioned employees that the locus of power had not changed. Many factors influence the ways in which gender, and sometimes race, are implicated in what amounts to the reorganization of class relations in work organizations (for example, Rasmussen 2004). On the whole, it appears that the male advantages and the gender and racial ordering of work are not significantly altered in most reorganization and team-based restructuring.

Restructuring does not usually unsettle inequality regimes partly because the gendered substructure of organization remains intact or is strengthened in the process of reorganizing. The basic structuring of work and the workplace on the model of a worker who has no other obligations is not disturbed. The ideal team-based worker is implicitly as masculine as the ideal worker in a bureaucratic or Tayloristic organization, although their specific characteristics vary (Benschop and Doorewaard 1998). The ideal bureaucratic worker puts paid work first, works hard and full-time, is career-oriented, rational, and skilled. If he is an industrial worker, his work may be deskilled, but is still more valuable than the work assigned to women. The team player also puts paid work first, is highly motivated, is committed to the team and to the organization, is full-time or more than full-time, is interested in advancing a career, and is entrepreneurial (see also Metcalfe and Linstead 2003). Organizations in the computer sector provide examples of highly effective team-based work that epitomizes the masculinity of the ideal worker, of team processes, and of the organizational culture. In interviews with high-level female executives in a leading hardware and software development company Joanne Martin and Debra Meyerson (1998) found that these successful women, mostly young and childless, invented different ways of coping with a masculine work culture with which they were uncomfortable. This was a culture of self-promotion, extreme competition between teams, and controlled anger and aggression (see also Cooper 2002). For the male majority, this was just the taken-for-granted way that work got done; men saw these practices as gender-neutral. The few women were insiders as highly skilled professionals in responsible jobs, but they were also outsiders, as "not men" who could not totally fit into this culture.

One conclusion from this brief review of changes in organizing practices and their implications for inequality regimes is that the underlying processes of gendered and racialized class inequality are usually preserved. Under some circumstances an organization's inequality regime may be shaken. This may happen when the visibility of inequality is high, legitimacy is low, controls are weak, and the political/economic environment encourages dissent. For example, during the late 1960s and early 1970s, the inequality regimes in some U.S. universities and colleges were severely challenged, as students began to demand not only reductions of inequality for minorities and white women students but also drastic changes in organizational class structures. Some students argued implicitly that they were as much a part of the organization as were the faculty, suggesting that clients, patients, and customers be seen as organizational members. At the University of Oregon, for example, graduate students in some departments demanded participation in decision making about curriculum and other matters that faculty, as relatively higher in the education class structure, had controlled. Caught in the contradictions between their proclaimed beliefs in democracy and their real dictatorial control, some faculties gave in to the demands. However, as soon as the student movements subsided, faculty once more took control. Similar processes occurred in other public sector organizations in the United States in the 1960s and early 1970s. For example, organized welfare recipients very briefly exerted some influence over certain welfare programs, affecting program rules (Piven and Cloward 1993). In spite of these brief forays into organizational democracy, most inequality regimes, most of the time, seem to me to be relatively stable, held in place by all the mechanisms I have discussed above, but most centrally by gendered and racialized substructures of organizing and by wage dependence, the economic imperative that forces most people to work in order to survive (Perrow 1991, 2002).

THE EXPANDING BOUNDARIES OF INEQUALITY REGIMES

Organizations and their inequality regimes are becoming extended and segmented with relatively new forms of organizing production and distribution in our globalizing world. Managements move production to countries with low wages and many eager young female potential workers. They use existing gender, class, and race inequalities to maximize control and minimize costs in production and distribution. The most familiar examples are organizations in the clothing industry, in which almost all production is now located outside the northern industrial countries, often in factories not owned by the core corporation, but contracting exclusively with it and manufacturing to its specifications. Such a tight coupling between organizations raises questions about where one organization ends and the other begins. Under some circumstances, production may return to the United States in the form of sweatshops employing immigrant workers, but still producing for large companies (Bonacich and Appelbaum 2000). Organizations also establish directly owned manufacturing plants, offices, and operations outside national boundaries. Thus, the organizational form and the locations of parts of the organizing may vary, but in all these forms, aspects of an inequality regime may be externalized and the boundaries of an organization's inequality regime may extend beyond national and even organizational boundaries. For example, Nike may externalize most of the organization's wage inequality by locating the lowest-paid workers in foreign countries, working for foreign-owned firms. Nike can then claim that it has little responsibility for working conditions and levels of pay. Gendered and racialized class inequality has probably increased in these transnational organizing forms, but the inequality is externalized to other countries and outside the formal organization boundaries to other organizations and to communities. Management controls and methods of exploitation that might be illegal within the rich industrial countries can be used with impunity in countries without strong protective labor laws. These class practices were also invisible in the wealthy countries until they became the focus of criticism in the antisweatshop and antiglobalization movements.

Gendered and racialized class relations, rooted in organizing processes, are also changing in the white collar and technical fields as globalizing organizations change their practices. Particular clerical and service tasks are outsourced to companies in other countries, attracted by the low wage levels in some poor countries and facilitated by satellite and other technologies. Data processing or telephone customer services are examples. Technical and professional jobs, such as computer programming, accounting, banking, and some medical specialties are also being relocated to low-wage countries. I discuss this further in chapter 6. The characteristics of inequality regimes may change in these cases: Most obviously, whites do not have the clear advantage in access to good jobs because these jobs are offshored to countries whose racial/ethnic profiles are not white dominated. The ways in which class is structured through gender and race/ethnicity become more complex. This process of expansion and mutating forms of inequality regimes involves the nonresponsibility of capitalist organizations that make use of and reproduce gendered and racialized exploitation and subordination.

Organizational decisions to export certain processes and functions to take advantage of low wages in less affluent countries have impacts on the inequality regimes of organizations in affluent countries and in these societies in general. The disappearance of well-paying jobs increases disparities in income and wealth in affluent countries and is related to the widely documented increasing inequality in the northern wealthy nations, especially the United States. I discuss this further in chapter 6. The additional points I emphasize here are that increasing inequality is an outcome of identifiable decisions that alter the inequality regimes of organizations and that to understand the ongoing development of inequality regimes, our analysis must move outside conventional notions of organizational boundaries.

CONCLUSION

All organizations have inequality regimes in which class relations are created and recreated in the ordinary processes of getting the work done. These class relations are gendered and racialized. Indeed, what looks like class from one conceptual point of view may look like gender and/or race from another point of view. The gendering and racialization of capitalism as an economic system occurs through inequality regimes, as managers organize work on an implicit male model, as both managers and employees take actions that reproduce gender and race segregation, as images of aggressive, hegemonic masculinity are confirmed, and as corporations claim and even fight for their nonresponsibility.

Inequality regimes are complex and highly various. While any organization as a whole is built on systematic inequalities, particular subunits may be fairly egalitarian. At the same time, inequality regimes are not infinitely various, for they are formed in accordance with surrounding laws, social conventions, and markets. They are also ongoing and changing over time as leadership and external conditions change, or as internal conflicts generate change. Understanding particular inequality regimes could be useful for charting strategies for changing organizations toward less hierarchical and unequal relations. Many change efforts have been unsuccessful, I believe, partly because those who attempted to achieve change did not comprehend the deeply embedded obstacles, and complicated, active oppositions they would meet. Indeed, I first started to think about inequality regimes as I was trying to understand why change projects in which I was involved so often had disappointing results.

Inequality regimes may be particularly subject to changes as employers develop strategies to deal with and take advantage of the increasing pace of globalization of production, markets, and competition. Those who control companies and public entities decide to shed workers, outsource production and services, hire part-time and contract workers, eliminate layers of middle management, transfer previous management functions down the hierarchical line or into computers, and increase the pace of work for employees who remain. All these decisions, and many more, affect racialized and gendered class processes both within and outside organizations. In the next chapter, I look at contemporary changes in the society-wide organization of production and distribution, in gendered and racialized class configurations, in the adequacy of people's efforts at provisioning, and at the ways in which people are attempting to accommodate production and reproduction in their daily lives. I also ask whether it is still possible to contend that there is a gendered and racialized substructure to capitalist processes.

NOTES

1. A large literature exists on the gendering of organizations. The following discussion draws on that literature. See, for example, in Britain, Jeff Hearn, David Collinson, Anne Witz, David Morgan, David Knights, Deborah Kerfoots; in the United States Rosabeth Moss Kanter, Marta Calás, Linda Smircich, Patricia Y. Martin. Australians Robert Connell and Judy Wajcman are also important in this endeavor. Research and theorizing on gendered organizations usually does not explicitly situate itself within discourses on class or race. Class is usually implicit, but unremarked, a silence that suggests that class domination and exploitation are seen as inevitable components of work organizations.

2. Studies of gender inequality are often implicitly about organizations and organizing processes (for example, Reskin and Roos 1990; Nelson and Bridges 1999). Labor process studies beginning with the work of Harry Braverman (1974) and continuing since then, have explored the ways in which class is socially produced, accommodated to, and contested within workplaces (e.g., Willis 1977; Burawoy 1979; Edwards 1979). Almost all of these studies have been about male-dominated workplaces. Feminist ethnographies, such as those by Robin Leidner (1993), Jennifer Pierce (1995), and Leslie Salzinger (2003), have provided separate studies of the production of gender and class.

3. Donald Van Houten and Paul Goldman (1977) argued for a Marxist analysis of bureaucracy as a way to understand how organizations are essential to class practices and capitalism. Charles Perrow (2002) in *Organizing America* makes a persuasive argument for the centrality of large organizations in the development of class and corporate capitalism. Robert Perrucci and Earl Wysong (2003) also argue for the importance of organizations in the production of class as well as gender and racial inequalities.

4. Donald Van Houten coauthored the first effort to develop the idea of

inequality regimes, bringing his expertise on organizations to the project. I have expanded the analysis, but much of his work is still present.

5. Robert Nelson and William Bridges (1999), in *Legalizing Gender Inequality*, develop an organizational theory of the gender pay gap based on a careful study of a series of pay equity cases. They acknowledge their decision not to include race in their study, observing that race inequities are produced through different processes than gender inequities, and that to include both gender and race would result in a project too cumbersome to handle.

6. There are some similarities between the idea of "inequality regimes" and Charles Tilly's analysis of inequality processes in *Durable Inequality* (1998). Tilly builds a comprehensive theory of inequality. That is not my intent. I only aspire to identifying some of the organizing practices that result in inequalities in work organizations.

7. This includes feminist organizations committed to flat structures and consensus decision making. See, for example, Morgen (2002).

8. Similarities between various countries in inequality patterns are quite striking in spite of differences arising from different ways of regulating labor, different union densities, different political traditions and ideologies. For example, Sweden and the United States have great differences in these areas, yet the inequality regimes in work organizations appear to be quite similar, at least to this observer.

9. Amy Wharton (1994) provides a useful overview and critique of research and theory on the connections between organizations and stratification structures and processes.

10. Barbara Reskin (2000, 2003) makes the argument that researchers have amply proved the existence of gender and racial inequalities and that what is needed is more study of the mechanisms that produce inequalities. She does not discuss class.

11. In 2002, women held 15.7 percent of corporate officer positions in Fortune 500 corporations, up from 8.7 percent in 1995. Only six of these corporations had a female CEO in 2002. See Catalyst (2002).

12. Frances Conley (1998), for example, describes patterns of gender discrimination within the elite group of neurosurgeons at Stanford University.

13. Hiring temporary workers may be less bureaucratic and more rapid than hiring permanent workers and thus more compatible with flexibility in adding and subtracting workers. Vicki Smith (2001a) provides an interesting example of this process.

14. One is an unpublished study in the 1990s with Donald Van Houten of restructuring in a college, the other is a study of welfare restructuring with Sandra Morgen (2001).

15. Attacks in the late 1990s on affirmative action and other equality measures seek to restore the legitimacy of race and gender discrimination. However, class discrimination and oppression remains the form that is almost never challenged in the United States.

16. The structure of jobs, including the composition of tasks, was challenged by feminists in the late 1960s and 1970s, when the movement was in its early and radical stages. Elimination of hierarchy and divisions of labor, democratization of

decision making, and shared leadership were goals of experimentation and principles of practice in feminist organizations. These efforts did not, on the whole, survive the bureaucratization and co-optation of feminist organizations. See Ferree and Martin (1995) for accounts of this experience.

17. This positive outcome of restructuring is often accompanied by increased stress and pace of work that may dilute the feeling that work has improved. For summaries of research on restructuring, see Cornfield, Campbell, and McCammon (2001) and Smith (1997).

6

Changes in Gendered and Racialized Class

By the end of the twentieth and the beginning of the twenty-first centuries, gendered and racialized class processes had been changing as part of pervasive changes in the U.S. and global economies that began in the 1970s. In this chapter, I return to the discussions in chapters 3 and 4 of gendered and racialized class processes to examine in more depth the changes that are altering the diverse ways in which Americans are embedded in class practices and experience the effects of these practices. First, I discuss large-scale changes in the organization of production, the decline of manufacturing jobs and the increase in service sector jobs, and their gendered and racialized impacts. Second, I look at changing work practices: Work became less secure and wage inequalities both increased and decreased in gendered and racialized class patterns. I also look at increasing wealth inequality and changes in state distributions in which African Americans and Hispanics were affected more seriously than whites. I discuss changes in personal relations of distribution and efforts to bridge family and work demands. Finally, I briefly examine the class implications of recent employer-initiated changes, offshoring of technical and professional jobs, and the emergence of the Wal-Mart model. Both could result in further, serious alterations in gendered and racialized class configurations in the United States. In these discussions, I emphasize that the gendering and racializing practices that I outlined in chapter 3 are still integral elements in the ongoing creation of class inequalities. I also argue that many of these changes are rooted in processes reminiscent of the emergence of nineteenth-century gendered and racialized industrial capitalism. The nonresponsibility for human welfare of capitalist organizations in the pursuit of profit still dominates twenty-first-century capitalism and shapes class practices and inequalities.

CHANGING CLASS PRACTICES AND CLASS EFFECTS

Changes in Class Practices

During the last thirty years of the twentieth century, vast changes took place in the U.S. and global economies, facilitated by new technologies and fueled by the unceasing quest for competitive success and profit.[1] In the wealthy capitalist nations, manufacturing jobs decreased, undermining the "good" jobs of the past, and service sector jobs exploded, providing many new jobs, some "good" and some "bad."[2] Change processes include decentralization, reorganization, relocation, subcontracting, and outsourcing and offshoring of production. Deregulation, under the banner of "free marketization," reduced or eliminated government controls on various industries, leading to greater competition and employers' search for lower costs and increased productivity.[3] Employers sought more flexibility in employment agreements, giving them more leeway in expanding and reducing their labor forces, and they used downsizing to save on labor costs.[4] In the United States, other types of controls were further weakened, such as effective rights to organize unions.[5] At the same time, beginning in the 1950s, the civil rights movement and the women's movement achieved new protections to improve the economic and social status of women and to reduce racial discrimination and exclusion. In the early years of the twenty-first century, the laws that prohibit racial and gender discrimination and aim to increase employment equality are still on the books, but these laws have also been undermined and enforcement agencies are also weak.[6] Privatization of government functions and reductions in welfare state supports are also ongoing. In addition, new leading sectors of global capitalism based on technological innovations emerged, such as computer and information technology, global finance, and biotechnological innovation. All of the above changes are interrelated. They are guided and justified by neoliberal thought that argues for the "free market," opening up the opportunities for corporate competition as the only avenue to economic growth and well-being.

Changes in the Composition of Paid Work

The two major changes in the composition of paid work in the second half of the twentieth century, the decline of manufacturing and the rise of service employment, resulted in significant shifts in access to and control over the means of provisioning, unsettling old gendered and racialized class relations. The reduction of manufacturing employment began in the 1970s, as corporations began transferring production from the rich nations to lower-wage locations, looking for greater production "flexibility," including reduction of protections for labor, and lower costs.[7] Much of the job loss came as a result of specific managerial decisions to move production and/or to decrease the workforce. Other reasons for job loss included the import of cheap manufactured goods,[8] and technological change leading to increased productivity. Reducing wage costs was, and continues to be, a goal in these processes. A detailed study (Baumol, Blinder, and Wolff 2003) of manufacturing downsizing in the late 1980s and early 1990s concludes, with some caution, "downsizing in U.S. manufacturing appears to have been largely a way to squeeze labor" (26). These strategies were linked to a business-led "war on labor" that began after World War II to attempt to reduce the power of labor unions, including their power in wage bargaining, as I noted in chapter 4 (Goldman and Van Houten 1980; Piven and Cloward 1993; Piven 2002; Logan 2003).

Immigration, legal and illegal, is another way employers used to switch to low-wage labor. This is not a new strategy, but a way in which the racialization of class processes has often been renewed. Large numbers of both legal and illegal immigrants are entering the United States from many countries to take low-wage, low-skilled jobs and, with special visas discussed later in this chapter, to take highly skilled IT jobs. As Alejandro Portes (2000, 275) points out, immigrants now "add to all economically active classes—from elite workers to petty entrepreneurs." In regard to low-wage jobs, employers argue that there are not enough Americans willing to do such work. Critics respond that immigrants are willing to take these jobs at very low wage rates and that employers prefer them to displaced American workers who often have a history of union membership and action. Illegal immigrants, in particular, are powerless and easily exploited (Human Rights Watch 2005). Immigration thus becomes a source of tension and a focus of hostility for downsized manufacturing workers and potentially for Americans who have lost well-paying technical and professional jobs as well.

In the United States, manufacturing employment declined from 23.4 percent of all employment in 1979 to 11.2 percent in 2003, amounting to a loss of about 4.9 million jobs (Mishel, Bernstein, and Allegretto 2005, 173–75). The loss of these jobs slowed in the boom years from 1995 to 2000, then picked up again and continued into 2004. These are the "good," often unionized jobs that have substantial health, vacation, and retirement benefits as well as adequate wages. The loss of these jobs was a primary cause of declining male wages in the bottom 60 percent of the wage distribution between 1979 and 1995. In 2003, the median male wage was still 3.3 percent below its level in 1979, in spite of wage increases from 1995 to 2000 (Mishel, Bernstein, and Allegretto 2005, 123). African Americans lost more than white workers in jobs and wages because African-American men, in particular, were more concentrated in manufacturing jobs. Discrimination and declining enforcement of antidiscrimination laws made it difficult for them to get new, well-paying employment (Brown et al. 2003, 80–85). These changes have eroded the traditional male working class, although women workers were also affected in industries such as textiles and apparel. These relatively well-paying blue collar jobs were replaced primarily by low-wage jobs in the service sector, although some downsized, white, male industrial workers were able to get other manufacturing jobs (Spalter-Roth and Deitch 1999).

Women, to a large extent, filled the expanding service sector jobs. White women's entry into the paid labor force was a major change in the gendering of U.S. class processes.[9] Married white women, both middle and working class, went out to work in increasing numbers; African-American women, many of whom had already been in paid jobs, had opportunities to move from domestic service and manufacturing into other kinds of jobs. Hispanic and Asian female workers, as well as women from other countries, also entered the female labor force in the United States in increasing numbers, as immigration increased. Service-producing employment increased from 70.5 percent of all employment in 1979 to 83.2 percent in 2003 (Mishel, Bernstein, and Boushey 2003, 171–78). Most of the job growth in the U.S. economy between 1988 and 2000 was in this sector; a large share of that growth was in two areas, health care and business services (Goodman and Steadman 2002). New high-wage service sector jobs were created, although the majority of the new jobs were low wage. Established service sector occupations, such as retail clerks, food workers, teachers, social workers, and managers, also expanded, providing increased opportunities for women. The service sector contains two tiers; women are employed in both, but in segregated jobs at lower wages than men in both tiers (Appelbaum and Albin 1990). Both tiers are also segregated by race, with African American and Hispanic workers disproportionately in the low-paying jobs.

White women in increasing numbers entered middle and upper middle class professional and managerial jobs as these areas of employment expanded, so that by 2002 women were one-half of those employed in these occupations. Women entered established high-status, male-predominant occupations as well as new high-wage jobs in finance, media, and technology fields, and they filled the ranks of expanding traditional fields such as nursing. Hispanic women were very underrepresented among managers and professionals. African-American women were also underrepresented except in a few female-predominant occupations such as social worker and recreation worker and in public sector management jobs (U.S. Census Bureau 2003). Racial barriers changed, but were not eliminated, in the corporate management world. Blacks, for example, were often channeled into "racialized jobs" dealing with race issues, such as personnel or public relations, but not into line jobs that could lead to the top (Collins 1997). White women did better in large corporations, but the percentage of female managers declines at each higher organizational level. Only six women held the position of CEO in Fortune 500 companies in 2002 (Catalyst 2002). In the managerial ranks, white women also filled staff rather than line jobs. In 2002, women held only 9.9 percent of line corporate officer posistions (Catalyst 2002). White female doctors, lawyers, and university professors, once a rarity, have become commonplace, although white women do not reach the highest professional levels as often as men. In 2002, women were about 30 percent of doctors and 29 percent of lawyers and judges (U.S. Census Bureau 2003). National Science Foundation data show that women were only 15 percent of full professors in colleges and universities in 2001. Organizations that restructure work processes often create new gendered positions and new patterns of segregation (Skuratowicz and Hunter 2004). New occupational areas can become gender- or race-stereotyped and segregated. The most obvious example is "computer systems analysts and scientists," a relatively new occupational category. Although it emerged after laws prohibiting discrimination were passed and white women were achieving education equal to that of men, it is segregated by both gender and race.[10]

Although all of this indicates declining inequality between women and men in the ability to earn independent incomes, it does not mean the end of the gendering of middle and working class occupations. In spite of the opening of many occupations to women, gender segregation remains high. Gender segregation of jobs declined somewhat between 1970 and 1990, but remained stable over the 1990s with an Index of Dissimilarity of about fifty-three (Padavic and Reskin 2002, 73).[11] This index is based on the jobs held by women and men at one point in time. Looking at gender segregation over time gives a picture of even greater segregation. A recent analysis shows that only about 15 percent of women continuously employed over a fifteen-year period worked in male-dominated occupational sectors and that only 8 percent of continuously employed men worked in female-dominated sectors (Rose and Hartmann 2004, 14).[12] I think it is safe to conclude that, in spite of the influx of women into all occupations, many of the old gendering processes still operate. Gendered and racialized images and expectations on the part of both employers and employees still influence selection of new job entrants and their experiences on the job (Pierce 1995; Brown et al. 2003; Browne and Kennelly 1999), as well as their opportunities for advancement (Maume 1999).

Restructuring of Work Processes and Employment Contracts

Restructuring of work processes, reductions in job stability, and fewer promotion possibilities, along with revisions of employment contracts, have accompanied the restructuring of production and employment. The general trajectory for the last twenty years in class practices has been a weakening of standard employment and an increase in nonstandard employment (e.g., Cornfield, Campbell, and McCammon 2001).[13] Work has become less secure, a more risky and less predictable source of provisioning for many in the United States.[14] Here I look at these trends, how they may be shaped by gendered and racialized processes, and whether they are having effects on racial/ethnic and gender inequalities.

The majority of standard work contracts produce "good jobs" and most nonstandard work contracts produce "bad jobs," as discussed in chapter 3. Good jobs have above-poverty wages, health insurance, and retirement plans (Kalleberg, Reskin, and Hudson 2000). Nonstandard jobs are, by definition, not regular, full-time jobs and are less secure than standard jobs. Most are bad jobs with low wages, no health insurance, and no retirement plans. High-wage professionals, usually white men, who are individual contractors are an exception, as I pointed out in chapter 3. Their contracts are nonstandard, but lucrative, and they can afford to pay for their own health insurance.

Nonstandard jobs are a substantial proportion of all jobs in the U.S. economy, held by 31 percent of female workers and 23 percent of male workers in 2001 (Mishel, Bernstein, and Boushey 2003, 251). These proportions were somewhat below the proportions in 1995, but no data exist for earlier years, making impossible any statements about long-term trends. However, case studies suggest that nonstandard, bad jobs are increasing (Smith 2001b; Appelbaum, Bernhardt, and Murnane 2003).

Some employers have transformed standard jobs into nonstandard jobs in order to save money on wages and benefits (Smith 2001a) or to achieve greater flexibility to hire when the work load is heavy and to fire when demand goes down. Tasks that used to be done by formally employed persons are now being done by independent contractors who assume the costs of medical insurance and future pensions, if they have these protections at all. Our Oregon study of women leaving welfare (Acker and Morgen 2001) provides an example of low-wage contract work done disproportionately by minority women. Some of our respondents were employed as caregivers for the elderly by the state of Oregon. They had employment agreements as individual contract workers, with low wages and no health insurance or sick leave, as well as no right to join a union, benefits and rights that were available to regular state employees.[15] Almost all these workers at the bottom were women—white, black, or Hispanic. Their employers or supervisors were also usually women; class relations may be negotiated, along with race relations, in daily interactions between women.[16]

Jobs with standard contracts are becoming less secure for many workers. For example, as work organizations restructure, possibilities for promotion decrease as internal job ladders disappear (Grimshaw et al. 2001), and unemployment due to downsizing or reorganization increases (Spalter-Roth and Deitch 1999). In addition, health insurance becomes increasingly costly and scarce for many workers, as soaring medical insurance costs lead employers to cut costs by transferring these costs to employees (Gould 2004).[17] All of these pressures are characteristic of many nonstandard jobs, but they are also eroding the standards of "good jobs."

These problems are not confined to white women and people from racial/ethnic groups, but available research suggests that white men have some privileged resources that may buffer them to a degree. For example, among the millions of workers who lost jobs due to downsizing in the mid-1990s, white men were more likely than other gender/racial groups to be reemployed in the next year and to escape the 20 percent wage loss that other groups suffered (Spalter-Roth and Deitch 1999, 465). White men also had the highest rate of return to skilled blue collar jobs and the lowest downward mobility from managerial and professional jobs. Spalter-Roth and Deitch (1999) show that gender and race shaped the effects of downsizing, to some extent protecting white men, both middle class and working class, and disadvantaging African-American men and women across classes. Similarly, whites and men continued to be more likely to have employer-provided health insurance than other categories of workers (Gould 2004, 4).

Jobs with evening, night, or weekend working hours are another form of less-than-satisfactory work for many. Although the largest numbers of workers with nonstandard hours are in the low-paid service sector, many other Americans have such work schedules. As Harriet Presser (2003, 1) points out, "two-fifths of all employed Americans work mostly at nonstandard times." Work schedules affect family life. Child care is particularly difficult to arrange at night and on weekends. Family time together is often lacking. The most serious impact is on single mothers in low-wage jobs (Presser 2003). Thus, nonstandard working hours increase gendered and racialized class disparities.

The effects of these pervasive changes differ at various hierarchical levels and in different employment sectors. Higher-level, more powerful positions carry with them better benefits, retirement pay, and severance pay than lower-level jobs. This hierarchy contributes greatly to inequalities in the United States. Retail, food service, motel and hotel housekeeping, and other such low-wage service sector jobs often have flexible and unpredictable hours, as well as low wages and few benefits.[18] For example, in our study of Oregon welfare leavers, many of the single mothers we interviewed had highly variable work hours and schedules, subject to demand by managers in the retail and motel businesses or in nursing homes, with the result that they had great difficulty coordinating their paid work and caring for their own children. Since they were usually paid by the hour, they could not count on a certain amount of income.

Nonstandard work is shaped, to a degree, by the needs and vulnerabilities of particular groups of workers, as well as by the preferences of employers. Unemployed workers may turn to temp agencies when they can't find a permanent job. After the recession of 2000, job growth from 2001 to 2004 in the temporary service agency field was much more rapid than job growth in the economy as a whole, 18.6 percent compared to .9 percent (Economic Policy Institute 2004b). Other workers had difficulties finding jobs take nonstandard employment: African Americans and Hispanics were disproportionately in the lower-wage nonstandard jobs, temp and on-call work (Mishel, Bernstein, and Boushey 2003, 252). Part-time work accounts for about two-thirds of women's nonstandard work arrangements. Most female part-timers take such jobs because they need to combine paid work and family unpaid work. Students also take part-time work. However, substantial proportions of part-time workers and those with other kinds of nonstandard jobs would prefer to have standard employment (Mishel, Bernstein, and Boushey 2003, 259).

Many standard jobs have disappeared with the decline of manufacturing employment that was highly unionized. Unions, which protect standard employment contracts, have seen their memberships decline as jobs have declined. The reduction of union jobs means that workers have a declining possibility of finding standard employment. This is especially the case for low-wage workers. An example again comes from our study of the experiences of women who left the welfare system at the end of the 1990s (Acker and Morgen 2001). Most entered service and clerical jobs. Only 12 percent found unionized jobs, but those who did had lower poverty rates, higher rates of employer-provided health care, more full-time work, and higher rates of satisfaction with their prospects for pay increases and promotion than those who were not in unionized jobs.[19]

In summary, employment contracts and conditions are changing significantly with changes in the organization of work, new technology, and employers' efforts to cut costs. Changes cut across gendered and racialized class configurations. Middle-class professional and managerial employees may go through downsizing or reorganizations that lower their earnings and increase their sense of insecurity, but sometimes increase their earnings, responsibilities, and feelings of accomplishment. The negative effects are felt most keenly by working-class people, those who have lost their well-paying jobs, and those who are already in low-wage, insecure jobs, disproportionately women and men from racial/ethnic minorities.

Declining security, stability, and predictability of employment, together with the disappearance of millions of family-wage jobs and the undermining of labor unions, contribute to the recommodification of labor, the partial return to nineteenth-century relations in which labor was treated primarily as a commodity for which employers would pay the lowest possible price. Employers' ability to find lower-cost labor outside the United States, or to employ very low-wage immigrant labor, also contributes to recommodification, as does the dismantling of welfare state protections that I discuss in more detail below. Current corporate reorganization processes, including downsizing, elimination of high-wage jobs, and wage and salary cuts, can also be interpreted as expanding the range of organizational nonresponsibility. Of course, while the United States may be returning to nineteenth-century economic relations, nineteenth-century conditions of life have not yet returned, except for the most desperate of the homeless.

Changes in Class Effects—Growing Inequality in Distribution

Growing Income Inequality

The restructuring and relocation of jobs, the changes in employment agreements, and other employer strategies to lower wages, discussed above, affect the levels and the stability of incomes, as well as the disparity between incomes, shaping gendered and racialized class inequalities in access to the means of provisioning.[20] At the beginning of the twenty-first century, the United States had a highly unequal gendered and racialized class structure in which differences in income and wealth had been increasing since the late 1970s, except for the boom years of 1995 to 2000 when inequalities temporarily declined.[21] The increasing inequalities and the low incomes for a substantial proportion of the population, especially single white women and African-American and Hispanic women and men, are linked to the practices that disempower and decommodify labor that I discussed above.

The distance between the highest and the lowest incomes increased between the late 1970s and the early twenty-first century. Top corporate managers' levels of pay soared: In 2000, the average (almost always white male) CEO's pay was 310 times the pay of the average worker, compared with a ratio of 26 to 1 in 1965 (Mishel, Bernstein, and Boushey 2003, 7). Underlying these extreme differences is the way that the total returns to production are divided. The division of the postrecession economic pie between profits and wages was very unequal, with returns to capital up by 32 percent between 2001 and 2004 and returns to wages and salaries up by only 1.2 percent (Mishel, Bernstein, and Allegretto 2005, 32–33).

In general, over the longer period from the late 1970s to the present, men's average wages declined and women's average wages increased, reducing the gender wage gap as it is usually defined. Averages can hide important variations. In this case, men who were high earners saw their wages increase, as did women in high salary brackets. The losers in relative terms were men with midlevel wages: In 2000 their median wages were still below their level in 1979, as I pointed out above. In absolute terms, white men still had higher wages than any other gender/racial group. The U.S. gender wage gap declined during the 1980s and 1990s. In 2003, full-time, year-round employed women had a median wage that was 76.6 percent of the median wages of men, an all-time high, but then women's median dropped in 2003 to 75.5 percent of that of men (Institute for Women's Policy Research 2004). Different measures of income produce different estimates of the gender gap. I discuss this issue further below, showing that the wage gap may actually be higher. The decline in the gap was due to dropping male wages in service and blue collar occupations, slightly rising wages of low-wage, high school educated women, although wages declined for the lowest-wage women, and the more substantial raises for college-educated, high-income women (Mishel, Bernstein, and Boushey 2003, 167). These patterns were part of the long-term changes I discussed above, the expansion of working class women's jobs, the feminization of middle class professional and managerial occupations, and the decline of good male working-class jobs. The cause of the recent increase in the gap is not clear. On the whole, gendered class income inequality decreased and the patterns of that inequality changed. Below I discuss the implications of these changes for the claim that the male provider family model is a thing of the past.

The patterns of gendered racial/ethnic class income inequality changed little, although some men and women from these groups achieved middle and upper middle class incomes. African Americans, Native Americans, and Hispanics had lower wages than whites. For example, in 2001, the hourly wage of African-American men was 74 percent of that of white men,[22] while Hispanic men earned only 65 percent of the earnings of white men. The earnings of African-American and Hispanic women were even lower. Wage disparities are linked to segregation, which continues to exist. Racial and gender segregation of economic sectors, occupations, jobs, and work organizations are deeply embedded aspects of gendered and racialized capitalism, as I argued in chapter 4.

Consistent with individual inequalities, inequality between households increased: The poorest families became poorer and the most affluent became more affluent.[23] Black family income was 62 percent of the incomes of white families in 2001, while Hispanic family income reached 64 percent of white family income (Mishel, Bernstein, and Boushey 2003,

41). Racial/ethnic families were hit harder than white families.by the economic downturn in the United States from 2000 to 2002. Household incomes declined by 1.6 percent for white families, but by 6.3 percent for African Americans and 4.4 percent for Hispanics (Bernstein and Chapman 2003). Two earners are now a necessity for many families, as many men's incomes do not even keep up with inflation.

The two-income family is now the most frequent form: Married couples with the wife in the paid labor force increased as a proportion of all families from 40.6 percent in 1979 to 47.7 percent in 2000, while those with the wife not in the paid labor force decreased from 41.9 percent in 1979 to 29.1 percent in 2000.[24] Single female-headed families increased over the same period, from 15 percent in 1979 to 17 percent of all families in 2000 (Mishel, Bernstein, and Boushey 2003, 49). At the same time, the family income gap between these types of families increased. For example, in 1979, families in which the wife did not work had incomes that were 70 percent of the incomes of two-earner families, while single female-headed families had incomes 40 percent as high as the incomes of the two-earner family. By 2001, those gaps increased: Family income of full-time homemaker families was only 57 percent of the income of families in which the wife worked, while single female-headed households had slipped further to 36 percent of the incomes of two-earner families.[25]

Inequality increased between dual-earner, husband-provider, and single mother families, primarily because of the rapid income increases of women in high-paid jobs.[26] At the same time, low-wage dual-earner families were often saved from poverty by the income contributions of women (Mishel, Bernstein, and Boushey 2003, 111). The increase in wives' paid work may hide from general view the economic impacts on working and middle class families of men's declining incomes.

Estimating the proportion of workers earning poverty-level wages or less is another way of measuring inequality and the numbers of bad jobs in the economy. With this measure both gender and racial differences are stark. Blacks and Hispanics have poverty-level wages in much higher proportions than whites, and women in all racial groups are much more likely to have poverty-level jobs than men.[27] Income inequality and poverty can also be measured with a "poverty rate," the proportion of all people who live in families with incomes below a poverty standard. In 2001, the poverty rate was at the same level recorded in 1979, 11.7 percent of all Americans (Mishel, Bernstein, and Boushey 2003, 315). White Americans had a poverty rate of 9.9 percent, while blacks and Hispanics had much higher rates, 22.7 percent and 21.4 percent, respectively. Single-parent female-headed families had a poverty rate of 33.6 percent in 2001 (Mishel, Bernstein, and Boushey 2003, 318). By 2002, the official poverty rate rose to 12.1 percent and household incomes declined, with African Americans and Hispanic Americans experiencing the greatest declines in income and increases in poverty (Bernstein and Chapman 2003).

The poverty measure in the United States underestimates the extent of economic inadequacy of U.S. incomes for providing access to provisioning.[28] Several researchers have constructed "family budgets" or "self-sufficiency standards"[29] that itemize necessary expenditures such as housing, food, daycare, and medical expenses, based on family composition and area of the country in which the family lives. The proportion of families living below this "health and decency" level can be estimated for particular states or regions. These studies show reasonable family budgets that are about twice the official poverty levels. Increasingly, researchers are using the "twice poverty rate" (those with incomes below 200 percent of the poverty line) as a measure of "low income."[30] Using this measure, more than 9.2 million families in the United States were low-income in 2002, 27.4 percent of all working families, and 40 percent of working families of color (Waldron, Roberts, and Reamer 2004, ii). Mishel, Bernstein, and Allegretto (2005, 325) report that 35 percent of prime-age families (household head age twenty-five to fifty-four) with children had incomes under twice the poverty line. And these poor families made major work efforts.

Children live in poverty at higher rates than adults in the United States. Using the official poverty measures, child poverty rates for all children under the age of eighteen declined in the late 1990s, but rose again from 2000 to 2003 to 17.2 percent (DeNavas-Walt et al. 2004). Children under six living with their single mothers were the poorest, with a poverty rate of 52.9 percent in 2003 (DeNavas-Walt et al. 2004, 19). Some of the increase in child poverty is due to welfare reform, which I discuss below. After this reform there was a sharp decline in the proportion of poor children receiving cash assistance (Lyter et al. 2004). In the United States, almost the entire responsibility for the support of children is on the parents, through personal relations of distribution. As low-wage jobs persist or increase as a proportion of all jobs, family distribution weakens, and child poverty is apt to increase. This is what has happened, primarily in working class families. A reasonable conclusion is that distribution to children through personal relations is ineffective as a way of ensuring adequate provisioning for all children. In the middle class, income is often ample for supporting children and personal distribution functions well. Many children have more than enough material goods and excellent educational opportunities, while children in poor communities may lack enough food and good schools.

Growing income inequality contributes to anxiety, feelings of powerlessness, and very material difficulties in managing from day to day. Low wages also bolster business profits. In a labor market with frequent downsizing and layoffs, they demonstrate to workers that it may be prudent to go along with the boss and keep the job they have, for the next one may be even more poorly paid. Gender and race still shape income inequality, although white men have lost some of their advantage over women.

The Declining Social Safety Net

Attacks on the Poor Law, the nineteenth-century social safety net, were critical steps in establishing labor as a commodity in early industrializing capitalism, according to Polanyi (1944).[31] Similar attacks in the United States have left middle- and low-income people without an effective social safety net today, more and more exposed to the vagaries of the labor market. The welfare state has been under successful attack in the United States and, to a lesser degree, elsewhere for at least the last twenty years, as part of the neoliberal, business-supported, drive to transfer many economic functions to the market and privatize and downsize government (Piven 2002). This has been a cumulative victory for the nonresponsibility of capitalist organizations, as welfare state focus has moved away from the survival and caring needs of the people to enforcing the values of the market. The U.S. welfare "reform" law is a primary recent example. Of course, corporations were not the only supporters of the restructuring of welfare, but conservative think tanks and policy intellectuals, generously supported by some corporations, developed the arguments against social spending that helped prepare the public approval and the political will to pass this legislation (Piven 1999, 97).[32]

The major welfare restructuring law, the Personal Responsibility and Work Opportunity Reconciliation Act, ended Aid to Families with Dependent Children (AFDC), that allowed poor parents to stay at home to care for their children, and established Temporary Assistance to Needy Families (TANF), linking benefits to paid work (Boris 1999). Passed by the U.S. Congress in 1996, this act ended entitlement to cash assistance even for children, established a lifetime limit of five years for the receipt of public aid, established stringent eligibility rules, including measures to enforce paid work as an eligibility requirement, reduced food stamp aid, and ended benefits for most noncitizens. The law also aimed to reduce illegitimacy and promote marriage, and much of the argument in favor of restructuring focused on changing the behavior of unmarried mothers. The scarcely concealed subtext was that black mothers are the ones to be reformed (Roberts 1999). The law marks a long-developing and fundamental change in women's responsibilities for reproduction that have accompanied increases in women's paid labor: Women are now expected to be wage earners as well as carers, and are only entitled to give full-time care to children if they have a nongovernmental source of income, such as a husband. Employment opportunities were ample when this new law was implemented at the end of the 1990s and many welfare clients got jobs. However, a large proportion remained in poverty, although working (e.g., Acker and Morgen et al. 2001). With the economic downturn at the beginning of the twenty-first century, their situations are getting worse and now there is almost no safety net available (Chapman and Bernstein 2003). Most noncitizens, primarily people from Third World countries, were left with no safety net at all.

Other aspects of the social safety net have been undermined. Unemployment insurance has also been severely eroded with changes in eligibility rules that exclude many workers, particularly low-income workers who are disproportionately white women and women and men from racial/ethnic minorities.[33] In 2003, only about 40 percent of the unemployed received unemployment insurance (Economic Policy Institute 2004d). In addition, the state-federal Medicaid program, medical assistance to low-income people, has been cut in many states during the recession as states struggle with budget deficits. The economic downturn beginning in 2000 increased both unemployment and poverty, as detailed above, but federal welfare distributions were not increased to meet this need. In the United States, only Social Security, the old age pension system, has remained relatively untouched, but is under attack in 2005 by the Republican administration that hopes to privatize the program. These developments illustrate how much these economic distribution programs are the product of political processes in which class, gender, and race are implicated, and thus, how economic arrangements are also embedded in politics. These politics also illustrate the nonresponsibility of corporations that pursue their own interests, paying no attention to the inability of communities, states, and the nation to meet the provisioning needs of a substantial proportion of the population. Few corporations are demanding better welfare support and more effective unemployment insurance.

Growing Wealth Inequality

Unequal distribution of wealth adds to the unequal income distribution to further undermine economic safety nets. Savings and other sources of wealth can carry families and individuals across times of crisis when earnings disappear. In the United States, wealth distribution is highly unequal, as discussed in chapter 3.[34] "The wealthiest 1 percent of all households controls about 38 percent of national wealth, while the bottom 80 percent hold only 17 percent" (Mishel, Bernstein, and Boushey 2003, 277). The distribution of stock ownership is even more unequal. Households in the lowest one-fifth of the wealth distribution in 1998 had a negative wealth or net worth of −$8,900: They owed more than they owned. In the same year, the average wealth of the wealthiest one-fifth was $1,126,700 (Mishel, Bernstein, and Boushey 2003, 281). African-American households have very little wealth compared with whites, with a median net worth in 1998 of $10,000, about 12 percent of the median net worth of white households. Families in the lowest one-fifth of the U.S. gendered and racialized class structure have practically no family safety net. With unstable employment and an inadequate public safety net, they are vulnerable to economic disaster, as the growth of homelessness and of demands on community food banks attest. Extreme concentrations of wealth are the effects of the practices of "private" ownership and control of production and finance as these are politically constructed and reconstructed. Great wealth increases opportunities to influence those political processes under the U.S. electoral system. The lack of any wealth, together with a weak or missing social safety net, is another factor forcing those low in the wage hierarchy to continue to accept their low wages: They have no alternative.

Safety net programs are also undermined by tax reductions for corporations and wealthy individuals that reduce the funding available for programs for low-income people. These are state distributions that go to the nonpoor in the form of tax expenditures, which I discussed in chapter 3. Tax expenditures are another form of nonresponsibility, as they redistribute earnings and wealth from middle- and low-incomes to the affluent. State distributions to wealthy individuals and corporations increased in the early years of the twenty-first century. Cuts in federal taxes, including the income tax, between 2001 and 2003 resulted in much larger reductions for the top 1 percent of income earners than for any other group. For this top group, cuts averaged $66,601 per year, while for the bottom 20 percent of income earners the cuts averaged $61 per year (Mishel, Bernstein, and Allegretto 2005, 85, table 1.20). This is a massive new federal redistribution. Federal corporate taxes were also cut from 2001 to 2003. During this period, corporate profits rose by 26 percent, while corporate income taxes dropped by 21 percent (McIntyre and Nguyen 2004). "According to Citizens for Tax Justice director Dr. Robert McIntyre, in 2000 business tax reductions were estimated to total at least $195 billion" (Morgen 2004). In the state of Oregon, corporate tax reductions have disproportionately shifted the tax burden from large corporations to individual tax payers.[35] This shift of resources reduces money available for safety net programs, ultimately increasing pressures on workers to accept low wages and difficult working conditions.

In summary, the corporate ruling class and top-level professionals and managers in the private sector are getting richer while the less affluent middle class ranks and the working class are getting poorer. Two incomes make some families rich, help some to hang onto middle class consumption standards, and save others from absolute poverty. Single-mother families are apt to be at the bottom of the income hierarchy. African-American and Hispanic families in each category have lower incomes than white families. Thus, family structure has a gendered and racialized impact on class. Gendered and racialized class patterns, or class effects, seem to have become more complex and more polarized. These effects show clearly that class and capitalism continue to be gendered and racialized, although gender and race patterns change in sometimes unexpected ways as the organization of capitalist production changes, with the "globalizing" processes of the last thirty years.[36] These effects are concrete manifestations of the gap between the aims of capital to produce profit and the aims of individuals, families, and communities to provide secure and satisfying levels of living. To some considerable degree, these inequalities result from multiple actions by representatives of business and by politicians convinced by neoliberal economic arguments and campaign contributions to support the interests of nonresponsible corporations.

CHANGES IN RELATIONS OF DISTRIBUTION AND GENDER DIVISIONS OF UNPAID LABOR

As production was restructured, with the decline of manufacturing and the growth of service employment that brought millions of women into paid work, class practices that affect women and men differently also began to change. The changes were probably not as great for African Americans as for white women, because African Americans had a longer history of paid employment (Bound and Dresser 1999, 62). White women often became breadwinners along with men, changing old power patterns. Women and their families had to reorganize daily life to accommodate responsibilities at paid work. People began to cope with the incompatibilities between the organization of paid work and the rhythms of embodied caring needs. Private problems (and joys) increasingly become public issues. These changes in gender arrangements were effects of changing class practices, particularly the demand for service and clerical workers, but also in the commodification of much household production. The changes also made more visible how unpaid labor is part of gendered and racialized class practices. Here I discuss three interrelated issues involving gender, race, class, and unpaid labor. They are: 1) Is the male breadwinner model of the family a relic of history? 2) Has the gender division of unpaid household labor changed so that women are no longer disadvantaged economically by the division? 3) Does the unpaid labor of linking paid work and the rest of life contribute to the gendering and racializing of class effects or outcomes?

Is the Male Breadwinner Model a Relic of History?

Questions about distribution to women through marriage and whether the male family provider model has died a timely death are complicated; there is no simple "yes or no" answer. Increasing numbers of women no longer rely on their relations with men in marriage or partnership for their only or major source of support, and dual-income families are becoming the norm. To assess the argument that the male provider model is on its way to extinction, it is necessary to look again at the evidence on women's paid work and earnings. Women in the twenty-first-century United States work for pay at almost as high a rate as men and the gender wage gap has declined, as discussed above. However, the usual gender pay gap measures underestimate the gap between women's and men's actual earnings. The gender gap is usually calculated by comparing median or average hourly wage rates or the median or average earnings of full-time, year-round workers. Both measures fail to include the actual earnings of all who are employed, including part-time and part-year workers. These measures are also based on cross-sectional data that give a picture at one moment in time, rather than revealing earnings over a longer period. An alternative approach analyzes long-term earnings by looking at the paid work careers of prime age (twenty-six to fifty-nine) women and men (Rose and Hartmann 2004; Gottfried et al. 2004). Rose and Hartmann's (2004) analysis shows that "Women workers in the prime working ages of 26 to 59 make only 38 percent of what prime-age men earn across the 15 years of the study" (iii). Women with at least some earnings in every year averaged just 56 percent of the earnings of men, while women working full-time in every year took home 64 percent of the earnings of similar men (Rose and Hartmann 2004, 22). The primary reasons for the earnings disparities were differences in the hours worked and years out of the labor force. An unexplained gap remained—women still earned only 72 percent of men's earnings after accounting for hours and years of working.[37]

The male provider model is not dead, these studies suggest, because, over time, a high proportion of women do not earn enough to support families. But, the old model has been transformed into a "woman as junior partner" model. Other models coexist as well. Although women are now coproviders, and some women earn more than their husbands, they are much more often junior partners where money is concerned. Men, in every racial group and in every occupation, still earn more than women. Thus, their economic contributions to the household tend to be higher. Women still reduce their working hours or drop out of the labor force for periods of time when family and child care work is too demanding. As I argued in chapter 3, doing unpaid caring work has a negative impact on women's abilities to earn a money income and thus to have access to and control over the means of provisioning. Taking time off in this way assumes another source of support, usually a husband. Thus, most married woman workers, especially those with children, still probably need someone else's income to survive comfortably. In middle- and lower-income families both incomes are definitely needed; there may be no choice but work for pay for both partners. The low incomes and high poverty rates of families headed by single women confirm this conclusion.

Patterns of personal distribution are complex and highly varied, affected by race, community, and family composition as well as by general economic conditions, availability of well-paying jobs, and the particular needs of family members at particular times. African-American women have historically had less possibility than white women of living primarily from distributions from their husbands while spending their energies on unpaid family work. Changes in this form of distribution, resulting from more job opportunities for women and worsening job situations for men, affect the intimate relations that are the local, immediate practices of distribution. Women who earn a wage are potentially in a more equal position in the gender power structure of intimate life than the full-time housewife. But women's lower earnings and their junior partner status may still allow many men to think of themselves as the family's provider and thus to preserve notions of masculinity and male identity based on the male provider role.

Has the Gender Division of Unpaid Household Labor Changed?

Although men now do somewhat more of the housework and child care than they did in the past, unpaid reproductive work is still primarily the responsibility of women (Gerstel, Clawson, and Zussman 2002; Jacobs and Gerson 2004). Class-related factors affect the gender gap in household work, as Harriet Presser (2003, 133–135) shows for families in which workers have nonstandard schedules. The gap narrows when the income and age gap between wife and husband narrows. Professional and managerial employment also narrows the gap, as does the gender ideology of both wife and husband. The more egalitarian the couple, the greater the man's share of unpaid work. But egalitarian beliefs do not increase his hours of family work, they only decrease the hours his wife does unpaid work. The wife's gender egalitarian beliefs do reduce the hours both she and her husband put into work in the home. Presser's findings indicate that there are slow and small class-related changes in the inequality of the distribution of unpaid family work, raising the possibility that gender inequality in general may decline in the affluent middle class as women gain more equality in paid employment.

Does the Unpaid Work of Linking Paid Work and the Rest of Life Contribute to the Gendering and Racializing of Class?

Linking the demands of paid and unpaid labor is an often invisible aspect of unpaid labor (see chapter 3) that has only become visible to white social scientists and human resources managers as white women have entered the labor force in such large numbers. It is work necessary to deal with the lack of fit between the organization and time demands of production and reproduction (see chapter 4). This work is left to individuals, most often women, to manage. The work includes preparing bodies (food, clothes, baths) and transporting them to work and other destinations such as schools, planning and scheduling family activities, finding child care, making sure that children go where they are expected. This work may involve negotiating the requirements of other institutions as well. Schools, doctors, hospitals, grocery stores, clothing stores all have their routines and schedules that must be noticed and allowed for in arranging a day or a week in which the main demand on adults is to get to work and pay attention to the tasks there. Women are the primary household "managers" as feminists pointed out and research confirms (Orrange, Firebaugh, and Heck 2003).

The connections between gendered and racialized class and the necessary work of articulation are multiple, but these connections also vary. Some jobs are more stressful and insecure than others; some have very long working hours, while others do not. Variations in time demands and other pressures on the job result in variations in difficulties in articulating work and the rest of life. As work becomes more stressful and insecure, individuals may feel more pressures to conform to employer expectations that are still based on the model of the worker as devoted single-mindedly to the job and unencumbered by family responsibilities. With no wife to assume such responsibilities, women with children, single mothers in particular, cope alone with conflicting demands of work and family.[38] Increased working hours reduce the hours available to life outside of work and can increase difficulties in combining work and family. As Jacobs and Gerson (2004) find, professionals and managers are more likely than others to have long working hours, although workers in other sorts of jobs are the majority of those who work overtime.[39] Professionals and managers may be expected to work long hours partly because employers do not have to pay for these overtime hours because these high-level workers are exempt from the requirements of the Fair Labor Standards Act (Jacobs and Gerson 2004). Jacobs and Gerson argue that time issues are felt most keenly in two-earner families and in single-parent families, and that the increases in these family forms are the main source of Americans' sense of being overwhelmed with demands for which there is little time.

Conditions at work facilitate family-work articulation, and these may vary by gender, occupation, and position in the work hierarchy. Flexibility in the use of time, the ability to move about on the job, and freedom from constant supervision may facilitate this work of knitting paid and unpaid obligations. Routine jobs usually done by women have been more heavily supervised and tied to one spot than other tasks, usually done by men (Acker and Van Houten 1974). Such routine jobs also have little flexibility in scheduling. Upper-level white collar employees are better able than lower-level employees to control their own schedules, but men seem to have this possibility more often than women (Jacobs and Gerson 2004). As Jacobs and Gerson (2004, 100–107) show, those most likely to need flexibility are the least likely to get it. In their study, these are women professionals with young children (106). Single mothers, in general, have less possibility of determining their own working hours than any other category of working family (Mishel, Bernstein, and Boushey 2003, 249.)

Resources other than time to accomplish the knitting together differ by racialized class situations. For example, parents' search for adequate day care is often limited by lack of money. In addition, getting children to day care or to other activities often requires a car. But, low-income mothers often do not have their own cars, making transportation a major problem for some, as we found in our study of welfare clients in Oregon (Acker and Morgen 2001). More affluent workers can hire others to do some of their coordination work (Blair-Loy 2003), but this is impossible for those with low or even middle incomes.

One of the solutions to the problems of managing complex work-family connections is to just eliminate the problems by quitting work. This is a widespread solution that women use, as the data on years out of the labor force, discussed above, show. Only 40 percent of married women with children under fifteen worked for pay full-time year-round in 2000 (Padavic and Reskin 2002, 163). Studying working time and earnings over a fifteen-year period, 1983 to 1998, Stephen Rose and Heidi I. Hartmann (2004) found that just under half of adult women had earnings in every year, while this was true for 84 percent of the men.[40] Women who worked in every year still worked fewer hours than men. Years without paid work lowered the annual incomes of these women even during working years. Men who had time out of the labor force also had lower earnings, but the penalty they suffered still left them with earnings almost twice as high as those of women (Rose and Hartmann 2004). Many women do not want or cannot afford this solution. Some of them opt for part-time work, but working part-time has costs to career prospects and income increases (Blair-Loy 2003). Employers' family-friendly policies may help to negotiate this invisible and difficult terrain. Many employees now have limited rights to time off for care emergencies, they may have flexible schedules, and some people may be able to do some of their work at home, but these changes do not necessarily mean that work expectations accommodate to family needs for most people, or that the accommodations are adequate when they exist.[41]

Considerable research on the availability and use of family-friendly policies such as flexible hours, reduced working time, job sharing, child care, and parental leaves indicates that where such policies are available, a considerable proportion of employees use them (Jacobs and Gerson 2004; Hochschild 1997; Blair-Loy and Wharton 2004; Glass 2004; Moen 2003). However, many upper-level employees do not use family-friendly policies even when they exist because of competitive job pressures (Hochschild 1997), or because they fear that they could not cope with heavy work demands while using policies such as flexible working hours (Blair-Loy and Wharton 2004). Professional and managerial workplace culture often prescribes long hours and a great deal of "face time" at work as signs of dedication. Failure to demonstrate this commitment is construed as negative for career advancement. "Women and men alike thus tend to perceive that family-friendly workplace policies come with costly strings attached" (Jacobs and Gerson 2004, 114). Some research supports this perception: Jennifer Glass (2004), for example, found that use of family-friendly policies had negative effects on wage growth.

Family-friendly privileges and flexibilities are more likely to be available to upper-level than to lower-level employees, and to professionals rather than managers (Crompton 2000). Lower-level service, clerical, and manufacturing workers are less frequently offered family-friendly work programs (Rosenfeld 2001). Workers of color are more likely to have lower-level jobs and, thus, to also be more exposed to rigid work expectations. Single-mother-headed families also have the lowest median incomes of any type of family; many are in lower-level jobs, as discussed above. They may also experience pressures not to use these family-friendly provisions, if such provisions exist for them. For example, in a recent study of women who had received welfare (Acker and Morgen 2001), my colleagues and I found that many of these women with very low-wage jobs were afraid of being fired if they took any time off to care for their sick children, even when workplace policies allowed such leave. All of this suggests that a substantial proportion of single mothers, those who most need flexible, family-friendly policies are those least likely to have them; those least likely to need such policies are, on the other hand, most likely to have them. These are racialized and gendered class practices that add to the accumulation of practices that create a widening gulf between the conditions of provisioning among the already advantaged and the already disadvantaged.

Family-friendly policies as they exist in the early years of the twenty-first century do not seem to be the solution to the problems of knitting together the demands of paid work and unpaid work. The language of the "family-friendly workplace" reveals the limitations of this approach. The workplace and employer are encouraged to make certain adaptations to the particular needs of a subset of employees, those who are mothers and, sometimes, fathers. Everything else goes on as usual: The standard employment contract remains the same. The timing, scheduling, pace, place, duration of work spells, and other aspects of organization are not expected to change. As individual men share more family work with women, they too are subject to the increased stresses that come from the lack of fit between reproductive responsibilities and work expectations. Grounded in the gender-coded separations of production and reproduction, of life and work, the lack of fit is incorporated into bureaucratic organization and becomes a set of apparently gender-neutral constraints.

The organization of work and production, along with the nonresponsibility of capitalist organizations, continually functions to ignore the demands of caring, confirming and entrenching the subordinate place of reproduction and women. Some fundamental reorganization of work would probably be necessary to have a thoroughly family-friendly workplace and eliminate the lack of fit between work and life.[42]

EMERGING CHANGES IN PRODUCTION—IMPLICATIONS FOR GENDERED AND RACIALIZED CLASS

At the beginning of this chapter, I discussed two long-run changes in the U.S. economy, the feminization of middle class and working class service work and the decline of manufacturing, both of which were gendered and racialized in processes and effects. In the 1990s and the early 2000s, two other changes suggest new transformations in racialized and gendered class patterns. These are the offshoring of white collar work, including high-wage, often male-dominated, professional jobs, and the spectacular success of the low-wage, low-price Wal-Mart retail model. Both of these changes are part of globalizing processes, in which corporations have abandoned any responsibilities to interests other than their own economic gain. The changes are made possible by the development of computer technology, the deregulation of markets and employment, and the availability and accessibility of skilled workers in low-wage economies. The offshoring of administrative support, technical, and professional jobs could potentially undermine the incomes of middle class men, as well as women who have entered many of these occupations. The spread of the Wal-Mart model may have already eroded the incomes of working class women and men in retailing. Both changes could greatly expand the distance between the upper reaches and the lower levels of class processes, increasing disparities in control and access to the means of provisioning.

Information technology (IT) was the growth sector of the 1990s. As manufacturing jobs became scarcer and the work world less predictable, young people were advised to get higher education in order to survive in the new economy. IT was the most promising and the most exciting field. New jobs existed not only in software and computer manufacturing firms but almost everywhere as work processes from manufacturing to retailing were using the new technology. The most skilled IT jobs, requiring computer science and computer engineering training, were male-predominant fields almost from the beginning. Women as a proportion of computer/mathematical scientists (this includes all those employed regardless of their academic degrees) seem to have hit a high point in 1990 when they were 36.5 percent of those employed in the field (National Science Foundation 2000). By 2002, their proportion had dropped to 30.8 percent (U.S. Census Bureau 2003). Women are a much smaller proportion of those employed as electrical and electronic engineers, having expanded their representation from 8.7 percent to 10.3 percent of these categories in the period between 1990 and 2002 (National Science Foundation 2000; U.S. Census Bureau 2003).

IT work organizations had highly masculine cultures (e.g., Martin and Meyerson 1998) and small numbers of women in professional positions, as case studies also show (Baron et al. 2002). Thus, the collapse of the dot-com bubble in 2000 disproportionately hit male professionals. Unemployment in IT occupations, which had been very low in 2000, rose, and by 2004 the unemployment rate for computer programmers was 7.6 percent, compared with white collar unemployment of 4.1 percent (Mishel, Bernstein, and Allegretto 2005, 236–37). By 2004, investment in computer software had recovered and exceeded its 2000 peak, but jobs were lagging behind (Mishel, Bernstein and Allegretto 2005, 185). One of the reasons was offshoring, moving the work to low-wage countries with highly educated workers, such as India and China, following the pattern for blue collar jobs and, more recently, routine white collar jobs such as call center work.

Estimates vary in regard to the numbers of jobs lost and future trends. The Economic Policy Institute (2004c) estimates, using Bureau of Labor Statistics data, that U.S. software occupations, such as programmer and software engineer, declined by 198,000 jobs between 2000 and 2004. At the same time, Indian software exports to the United States increased rapidly (Economic Policy Institute 2004c). Other estimates are that perhaps 100,000 service sector jobs per year have been offshored since 2000 (e.g., Garner 2004). Other technical and professional jobs, such as stock analysis, architecture, engineering and design, and back office functions of various kinds are being relocated as well as programming and software engineering. A recent study at the University of California, Berkeley argues that any job can be offshored that does not demand face-to-face contact and that can be done through computer technology. This study estimates that 11 percent of all jobs, or 14 million U.S. jobs, could be vulnerable to offshoring (Bardhan and Kroll 2003). Some economists and professors in business schools think that the draining of good American jobs could total between 3.4 and 6 million between 2005 and 2015 (Garner 2004, 10). But, changes could be even more severe and faster than these predictions. Jeffrey Garten, dean of the Yale School of Management, argues that the wide availability of broadband will make the process of moving professional services much faster than was the process of moving manufacturing production and that this will result in "wrenching adjustments for the American workforce" (Garten 2004). Others argue that, although some workers will be hurt, the economy as a whole will benefit with accelerated growth of trade. Less-skilled jobs will be done in countries with large unskilled labor forces and new higher-skilled jobs will be created here as innovation blossoms in a prosperous economy (Garner 2004). This has been the accepted wisdom among economists for decades. But this received wisdom is being challenged as high-skill jobs are leaving.[43]

Another process that reduces the supply of well-paying computer industry jobs, mostly for white males, is the creation of special visas, H-1Bs and L-1s, that allow employers to bring foreign computer professionals into the United States (Matloff 2003). This visa program was established in 1990 and later expanded. Arguing that there was a shortage of computer professionals, the industry lobbied for this program. Opponents say there is no shortage, but that the companies want to pay lower wages than those going to U.S. workers. H-1B employees may accept lower wages as part of an implicit trade-off for employer sponsorship in application for a green card that allows the foreign worker to remain legally in the United States (Matloff 2003). In 2000, 28 percent of IT hires into positions requiring a B.A. degree were H-1B visa holders (Matloff 2003, 16). American workers have been fired, with foreign workers hired for their jobs. Layoffs and foreign replacements have generated a great deal of hostility and fear among American professionals affected, to judge by reactions expressed in industry journals and on websites (e.g., Besser and Ratner 2004).

The reasons for offshoring, and also for importing foreign workers particularly for IT jobs, are profits and competitiveness. Technology and the reduction of trade barriers are necessary conditions, but lower wages are the primary motivation, almost all experts agree (e.g., Garner 2004; Bardhan and Kroll 2003). Tremendous savings in wage costs are possible, although how high those savings might be is a matter of dispute. According to one study, the average American computer programmer is paid between $60,000 and $80,000, while the average computer programmer in India is paid between $5,880 and $11,000 (Bardhan and Kroll 2003, 4). A commentator in *Forbes*, a leading business magazine, observed, "The sober truth is that cutting costs is the only route to profits salvation these days. Most costs, directly or indirectly, are labor. And that means more layoffs" (Shilling 2003, 224). This comment was about downsizing in general, but it also applies to offshoring. Business consultants are advising their clients to "take advantage of the multiplying opportunities overseas" (Uchitelle 2003). Businesses are also being advised that if their competitors are taking such steps, they will be disadvantaged if they do not do the same. Venture capitalist firms are urging startup firms to lower their costs by using offshore workers (*San Francisco Chronicle*, Business Section, 1, March 7, 2004).

The global restructuring of employment is accomplished through concerted practices such as these, in extended social relations linking businesses in the United States and other countries, management consulting firms, venture capital firms, the U.S. Congress, academic economists, computer science departments in universities, and workers themselves. The process is another instance of corporate nonresponsibility. The business press has reflected the conviction that corporations that move jobs have no responsibility to their workers or to the United States as a whole. As John Thompson, chairman and CEO of Symantec Corporation said recently, echoing Milton Friedman (1982), "U.S. corporations' first responsibility is to their shareholders. You cannot say, 'I'm going to put national interests ahead of shareholder interests'" (*San Francisco Chronicle*, Business Section, 12, March 7, 2004). Recently, some of the business press has raised alarms about the possible consequences of offshoring (Garten 2004; Bernstein 2004), to which I now turn.

The possible consequences of offshoring are, first, the loss of good jobs and second, downward pressures on the wages of the remaining good jobs to meet the competition of equally qualified workers who work for much lower wages.[44] The impact on earnings depends on how many kinds of jobs are affected. Offshoring of manufacturing jobs will probably continue. If, in addition, a very large group of white collar jobs are also lost, the downward pressure on wages could affect most white collar, middle-class workers (Garten 2004). If that happened, some commentators say, the gains to consumers from lower prices generated by lower production costs would not make up for lost income. Those gains would go only to companies and shareholders—to capital (e.g., Bernstein 2004). Even more dire consequences are possible: With the growth of the pool of highly educated scientists and technicians in many other countries, the United States might lose its lead in innovation and in the creation of new high-wage jobs to replace those lost (Bardhan and Kroll 2003). A much more positive scenario does exist, in which "innovation would lead to a continuing stream of new service and manufacturing activities, and hence new jobs and occupations" (Bardhan and Kroll 2003, 12).[45]

The disappearance of good professional jobs and lower white collar jobs could have an effect on gender and racial configurations of class. Offshoring of IT jobs has had a gendered and racialized impact, because, as I pointed out above, programmers and computer scientists and engineers are disproportionately white men. If offshoring continues to expand as many predict, sending overseas the jobs of engineers, stock analysts, accountants, radiologists, architects, and many more, a general decrease in earnings could lead to a declining American standard of living and greater inequality between high-income earners and middle- and lower-income earners, between CEOs, top managers, and ordinary employees, and between owners of stocks and bonds and everyone else. Indeed, the middle could disappear, as some argue has already happened.[46] African Americans and Hispanics would probably suffer the greatest declines in earnings and opportunities, as they have in every economic downturn. White male professionals and managers could see their organizational and income advantages decline, as happened to working class men, and many women, with the loss of manufacturing jobs. But women in the newly feminized upper-level positions could also see their incomes, privileges, and prestige threatened. And all this could lead to greater equality among the disadvantaged majority. White, middle-class women who previously would have spent a few years at home with their young children might not be able to give up a job because their incomes would be even more essential to family provisioning. Working-class women might find that they have new competitors for their jobs, the middle-class women whose jobs are gone.

On the other hand, those with gender and racial privilege could maintain their privilege in reorganized class processes. The processes of gender and racial segregation have not disappeared. The very fact that new occupations, such as computer science and engineering, emerged as both gendered and racialized testifies to the persistence of ideologies, assumptions, and established practices that preserve gender and race over time and over significant technical and economic changes. White aggressive masculinity is still projected in images of leadership (whether in the military, politics, or business), as resolute, risk-taking, strong, no sympathy for "weaklings," and aggressive. These images could help to again propel white men to the most advantaged positions, even in a dramatically downscaled job world.

The other significant development, the Wal-Mart model, has implications for paid employment and class similar to those of offshoring, but working class rather than middle class workers feel its direct effects. Wal-Mart is a low-wage, low-skills, low-benefits, high-turnover model (Lichtenstein 2004). This integrated business model is highly successful in holding down other costs and prices (Bianco and Zellner 2003). Labor historian Nelson Lichtenstein (2004), argues that Wal-Mart is to early twenty-first-century capitalism what General Motors was to post–World War II capitalism: the template that all must follow. Wal-Mart is almost the antithesis of General Motors, which was the model high-wage employer, dedicated to training and retaining its highly skilled work force. At Wal-Mart, according to Lichtenstein, skill goes into the technology and management, not into the workforce. Wal-Mart is very efficient, using technology to integrate its entire supply chain, with a computerized tracking system for every item that makes it possible to respond almost immediately to demand. Wal-Mart is really a manufacturer as well as a retailer (Lichtenstein 2004), as it dictates and controls production as well as distribution. China, where costs can be energetically controlled, is the location of much of its production. The company also maintains low prices as it relentlessly forces down the wages paid to Third World workers who produce the products it sells (Goldman and Cleeland 2003).

A leader in low wages, Wal-Mart pays its retail clerks an average wage that is below the poverty line and 20 percent lower than unionized supermarkets (Bianco and Zellner 2003, 102–103). Female cashiers earned, on average, $13,831 per year in 2001 (Drogin 2003). In that year, the official poverty threshold for a three-person family with two children was $14,269 (U.S. Census Bureau 2004). Wal-Mart has been charged in lawsuits with cutting wage costs in many ways, such as requiring unpaid overtime. There is also evidence that Wal-Mart employees often depend on public resources such as Medicaid and food stamps (Featherstone 2004, 144–49). Wal-Mart is accused of sex discrimination in pay and promotion in the largest class action suit ever certified in U.S. courts (Featherstone 2004). An analysis of pay data (Drogin 2003) showed that women earn less than men in every job category. For example, in 2001, the average hourly pay rate for female cashiers was $8.03; male cashiers earned $8.33 per hour. The difference became much larger at each higher job level. The suit, still in the initial stages, potentially covers 1.6 million female workers. The stories of gender discrimination told by some of the women complainants in the suit reveal that Wal-Mart managers in many different locations excluded, denigrated, stereotyped, and sexualized women workers and favored men in wage setting (Featherstone 2004). Gendering practices are alive and well at Wal-Mart. Wal-Mart is solidly antiunion, and its low-wage policies are putting much pressure on the relatively good wages and benefits that unionized workers in this sector enjoy. As the world's largest and arguably most successful retail corporation, Wal-Mart has a huge effect on wages and management practices in general. Some observers believe that Wal-Mart is an important force holding down wages and inflation in general in the economy (Lichtenstein 2004).

The Wal-Mart model does not support "good" jobs, builds gender discrimination into operating practices, and seems to rely on public safety net programs as a hidden subsidy. At the same time, it is very attractive to consumers, particularly those with low incomes. It establishes a negative circuit in which low-wage workers in other countries produce cheap goods for low-wage (and other) workers in the United States, who have lost manufacturing jobs to Third World countries and whose wages are further threatened by the influence of Wal-Mart's brutal cost-cutting policies that ripple throughout the economy. The profits from this strategy are very high. The company is so successful that the four Waltons, children of the founder, are among *Forbes* magazine's ten most wealthy Americans. Wal-Mart is a prime example of corporate nonresponsibility and of the present campaign to turn workers into lowest cost, easily replaceable, factors of production.

CONCLUSION

Corporate strategies, leading to the decline of good manufacturing jobs and the creation of both good and bad service sector jobs, resulted in many changes in gendered and racialized class patterns over the last years of the twentieth century and the beginning of the twenty-first century. Almost all women became wage earners for significant periods of their lives, and white women's incomes became essential for many families, as had been the case for African-American families for generations. Working-class men found fewer and fewer good jobs and their earnings either dropped or remained stagnant over the entire period, with the exception of the economic boom years of 1995 to 2000. Both trends led to small reductions in gender inequalities, but racial disparities remained. The inequality of income and wealth increased substantially. As more and more white women went into middle-class jobs, the problems of combining paid work and family obligations became socially visible, but few in the public debates questioned why unpaid but necessary family work, still done primarily by women, should be so marginalized and devalued. A few relatively weak initiatives to ease the combination of paid and unpaid work appeared, such as "family-friendly" corporate programs and the federal Family and Medical Leave Act, but these were more accessible to high-income than to low-income workers.

At the same time, corporations focused on cost reduction through reorganization, downsizing, and relocation of production to low-wage areas, as well as on efforts to destroy labor unions or to prevent new unionization. The old post–World War II supports guaranteed by employers, such as implicit or contractual lifetime employment, regular wage increases, sick leave, health insurance, and pensions, were also being whittled away as "standard" employment gradually became less standard. Corporations also supported, through think tanks, lobbying, and political contributions, a neoliberal war on government provision, resulting in the weakening of the social safety net, including unemployment insurance, disability insurance, and welfare to families with children (TANF).

This period in the United States and in the transnational economy invites comparisons with the nineteenth-century emergence of industrial capitalism analyzed by Polanyi (1944), as I suggested earlier. Capitalist institutions and organizations have made strenuous efforts to "free" labor and its costs by dismantling as many as possible of the protections for labor against the inherent dangers of the labor market. As Polanyi (1944) argued, to create labor as a commodity, it was necessary to free its price from protections that kept the price from varying with supply and demand (see chapter 4). The creation of labor unions, and the welfare state benefits that unions and other reformers favored, led to various protections from market processes for workers and their wages. With only a few, and weak, protections, U.S. workers must confront wage competition from very low-wage areas of the world. Offshoring of middle class technical and professional jobs and the Wal-Mart low-wage/low-price/high-tech model are only the latest examples in 2005 of these strategies to "recommodify" labor. The Wal-Mart template of organization includes nonunionized, low-wage, easily replaceable labor. In this model, labor is again, or still, treated by employers as a freely traded commodity, bought in the market when there is a demand, but left on the shelf when demand drops, without much consideration of what happens to the bodies of workers or their families.

One consequence of recommodification is increasing earnings inequality, a large proportion of jobs that do not pay a living wage, an equally large proportion that pay enough to get by if there are no family emergencies, and a smaller proportion that pay much, much more. The main burden of this process still falls on low-wage workers, disproportionately women and people of color, who also have the least protection from the tattered public and corporate safety net. This underlying recommodification is difficult to see from some locations in the society because it occurs along side tremendous affluence and high levels of material and cultural consumption. And, of course, some work organizations do not, even implicitly, deal with workers as simply factors of production. But the main trend is now toward more exposure of workers and their wages to competition in global markets in which labor is just another commodity.

Recommodification of labor is linked to corporate organizations' claims to nonresponsibility for reproduction. Pushing down the cost of labor through recommodification is a way of reducing corporate contributions to reproduction, such as payments for medical insurance or family leave or taxes for unemployment insurance, and increasing the share of profit that goes to the corporation, its shareholders, and its executives. Recommodification provides symbolic as well as material gains for large corporations, as it confirms that the responsibility of the corporation is to its shareholders and not to the society at large. Measures that increase those returns are justified by this ideology. Nonresponsibility is both a right and a necessity.

In the next and final chapter, I summarize my argument and present some possible avenues toward solutions to the problems generated by our gendered and racialized class relations.

NOTES

1. There are huge literatures on globalization and economic restructuring. On globalization, see, for example, Giddens 1999; Bauman 1998; Beck 2000; Sen 2002; Wallerstein 1974; Hardt and Negri 2000.

2. See Standing (1999) for an overview and discussion of changes in employment and conditions of work. See also Vicki Smith (1997, 2001a, 2001b).

3. For a useful recent summary and critical discussion of research and theories on changes in organizing capitalism see Paul Thompson (2003).

4. See Appelbaum, Bernhardt, and Murnane (2003), *Low-Wage America*, for studies showing varieties of employers' responses to competitive pressures to reduce costs, including wages.

5. See Human Rights Watch (2000), cited in Appelbaum, Bernhardt, and Murnane (2003).

6. See Brown et al. (2003) for a discussion of racial inequality based on racism and long-standing disinvestments in racial minority communities. Civil rights

laws are only part of needed remedies that must include more fundamental institutional changes. See Reskin (2002) for an assessment of remedies to employment discrimination. See Nelson and Bridges (1999) on efforts to achieve pay equity for women.

7. This discussion of the decline of manufacturing jobs is based on Mishel, Bernstein, and Boushey 2003, 176–88.

8. Mishel, Bernstein, and Boushey (2003, 181–87) discuss the role of international trade and investment on the U.S. wage structure, including the loss of high-paying manufacturing jobs. They note that this is a new area of investigation and that "it is beset with considerable controversy and confusion" (182).

9. Rosemary Crompton (2001) calls this increase in female paid work the "feminization" of the middle classes. I don't use this terminology, even though it has its attractions, because it implies that class refers only to relations of paid work and ignores the importance of distribution in the shaping of class relations and situations.

10. In 2002, women were 27.8 percent and African Americans were 6.9 percent of "computer systems analysts and scientists" (National Science Foundation 2004).

11. The Index of Dissimilarity is a rough measure of unequal distribution. It means that to achieve an equal distribution of women and men, 53 percent of either women or men would have to change to other jobs in which a majority of the other sex are now employed. Other researchers get other estimates. Maria Charles and David B. Grusky (2004) examine vertical and horizontal gender segregation by occupation and industry, showing in great quantitative detail how these patterns persist. Using the Index of Dissimilarity, they show that disaggregate sex segregation declined from an index of 61.4 in 1970 to 48.2 in 1990. They also report another estimate for 2000, based on a smaller number of occupations, of 39.6 (144–45). Previous research (Baron and Bielby 1985) has shown that segregation across job categories within organizations is higher than occupational segregation. Therefore, indexes based on census occupational categories are apt to underestimate the degree of segregation.

12. In this study, occupations were considered to be male- or female-dominated if 65 percent or more of employees with these jobs were of one sex or the other.

13. While this statement seems accurate, little comparable data exists prior to 1995 when the Bureau of Labor Statistics began surveys on contingent and alternative work (Mishel, Bernstein, and Boushey 2003, 251).

14. Vicki Smith (2001b, 7) argues that "uncertainty, and unpredictability, and to varying degrees personal risk, have diffused into a broad range of postindustrial workplaces, service and production alike." Among many other studies documenting these trends, see Appelbaum, Bernhardt, and Murname 2003, Presser 2003, Spalter-Roth and Deitch 1999, Osterman 1996, Kalleberg, Reskin, and Hudson 2000.

15. The proportions of workers with paid sick leave are also declining (Lovell 2004), and the United States has no paid parental leave benefits.

16. Subsequent to our study, the union organizing most state workers negoti-

ated successfully to change the status of these workers to employees rather than independent contractors.

17. In 2003, health care insurance was provided by approximately 60 percent of employers (Gould 2004) and employer-provided retirement funds covered about 50 percent of workers in 2000 (Mishel, Bernstein, and Boushey 2003, 144–45).

18. For a series of excellent, nuanced studies of low-wage jobs in a wide range of sectors, see *Low-Wage America: How Employers are Reshaping Opportunity in the Workplace* (Appelbaum, Bernhardt, and Murnane 2003).

19. Unpublished data from Acker and Morgen (2001).

20. Guy Standing in *Global Labour Flexibility* provides an insightful analysis of the consequences for workers of "globalization" and related developments. Building on the work of Polanyi (1944) he argues that the post–World War II period of stability in which distributive justice was a central goal has broken down and new forms of distribution are needed to ensure the sustainability of the system.

21. The following analysis is based on the considerably more complex statistical picture in Mishel, Bernstein, and Boushey (2003).

22. This is almost the same as the gender gap between white women and men.

23. In 1979, the 20 percent of households with the lowest incomes received 5.4 percent of all income. By 2001, the bottom 20 percent received less, 4.2 percent of all income. The highest income 20 percent, in contrast, received 41.4 percent of all income in 1979 and by 2001 they were taking home 47.7 percent of all income (Mishel, Bernstein, and Boushey 2003, 54).

24. The data on family structure and income are from Mishel, Bernstein, and Boushey (2003).

25. My calculations are based on data in Mishel, Bernstein, and Boushey (2003), 49.

26. Suggested also by Esping-Andersen (1993), as Rosemary Crompton (2001) notes.

27. For example, in 2001, 25.7 percent of black men had poverty-level wages compared with 14.5 percent of white men; 35.6 percent of black women had poverty-level wages compared with 26.2 percent of white women. Hispanic workers were even more disadvantaged: 35.9 percent of men and 46.6 percent of women were paid at or below the poverty level in 2001 (Mishel, Bernstein, and Boushey 2003, 137–39).

28. The poverty measure used in the United States was invented in the 1960s and its inadequacies have been documented almost from that time. Alternative measures have been proposed, but not adopted. Mishel, Bernstein, and Boushey (2003, 319–29) discuss the issues involved.

29. Pearce 2001; Northwest Policy Center 2001; Bernstein, Brocht, and Spade-Aguilar 2000. Diana Pearce has developed comprehensive standards for many states in the United States. Her measurement is described in the article "The Statistical Measure of Poverty," (2004).

30. For example, the Economic Policy Institute's research rigorously examining family budgets shows that twice the poverty rate is a much more realistic measure

of a family's ability to meet its basic needs, and many others now report data using this measure (Bernstein, Brocht, and Spade-Aguilar 2000).

31. See Piven and Cloward (1993), chapter 11 for a very similar, and more exhaustive, analysis.

32. For example, the Heritage Foundation, a think tank funded by conservative foundations, has several researchers who specialize in welfare state issues. These include Robert E. Rector, Senior Research Fellow, who has written numerous papers and books on welfare reform. According to his website he had a leading role in advocating for the 1996 welfare legislation. Lawrence Mead, a political scientist at NYU, wrote two influential books (1986; 1992) that helped shape the reform. He has been funded by the Smith Richardson Foundation and by the John M. Olin foundation, both conservative, corporate-linked foundations.

33. See Piven and Cloward (1993, 358–62), on measures to reduce coverage and benefits of social programs beginning in the 1970s, but escalating after 1980.

34. The statistics in this section all come from Mishel, Bernstein, and Boushey (2003).

35. In the 2005–2007 budget cycle in the state of Oregon, corporations paid 5 percent of all income taxes, households paid the other 95 percent. In 1973–1975, corporations paid 18 percent and households paid the balance. If corporations were paying at the same level in 2005 that they paid in 1973, the state budget deficit would be erased and many cuts to the safety net could be restored. This analysis was done by a private think tank, the Oregon Center for Public Policy. (Sheketoff 2005).

36. Another set of economic practices, those having to do with credit cards and banking, increase inequality. In our increasingly electronic-based money economy, lack of access to these services exacerbates disadvantage. For example, people without bank accounts must pay to cash checks at check cashing stores. Lack of a credit card makes it impossible to rent a car or to do other kinds of transactions. Sociologists are only beginning to study the multiple ways that money affects the ability to function in society, over and above what money can buy. See Geoffrey Ingham (2004), Jan Pahl (2000), and Viviana Zelizer (2002).

37. A similar study done by the General Accounting Office found that if the earnings of all women and men are compared, women's earnings fall to 44 percent of those of men rather than the 76 to 78 percent in gender gap measures (General Accounting Office 2003). Much of this difference is explained by women's fewer hours worked or time out of the labor force, although other factors are also involved, such as the effects of low-paying, sex-segregated jobs.

38. Jacobs and Gerson (2004) find that large proportions of men also experience work-family conflict, but men are not the ones who usually alter their work time to do unpaid family tasks.

39. See also Hochschild (1997).

40. See the study by the General Accounting Office (2003), *Women's Earnings: Work Patterns Partially Explain Difference Between Men's and Women's Earnings* for similar findings.

41. A study by the Families and Work Institute (Galinsky and Bond 1998) of work-family programs in firms with over 100 employees found that 88 percent of

the firms allowed employees paid time off to go to their children's school or day care functions, 66 percent permitted flextime arrangements, but only 9 percent provided child care at or near the work site while 5 percent subsidized the cost of child care. Higher representation of women and minority men in top positions correlated with more work-life supports.

42. The analyses in *It's About Time: Couples and Careers*, edited by Phyllis Moen (2003), also indicate employer family-friendly programs are not sufficient to facilitate the combination of family and work, and that reorganization of work itself will probably be necessary to achieve the balance so many seek.

43. An article by Paul Samuelson, the eminent economist, in the *Journal of Economic Perspectives* in June 2004 expressed some concern about theories, including his own, that predicted positive outcomes, for all involved, from trade.

44. See Aaron Bernstein's (2004) article in *Business Week* for quotes from a number of economists on the likely wage consequences of offshoring.

45. Laura Tyson, dean of the London Business School, also takes a more positive view, as do some other U.S. economists.

46. See, for example, Perrucci and Wysong (2003).

7

Conclusion—Some Optimistic Proposals

In this book I have proposed a way to think about class that incorporates gender and race/ethnicity as integral to capitalism and class relations, historically and in the present. I think that feminist sociologists have not given enough explicit attention to class issues for some time, although a great deal of feminist theory and research exists that is essential to understanding class. In focusing on class as gendered and racialized, I am suggesting one way to further the analysis of intersectionality, the mutual constitution of race, gender, and class structures of power and economic inequalities. The idea of "intersectionality" is important in pushing forward our comprehension of complex inequalities. However, the broad categories, "gender," "race," and "class," represent incredibly diverse lived realities that scholars have attempted to understand separately, in different research traditions and discourses. Putting them together conceptually is difficult, even when the focus is primarily on one category, class. Thus, I make no claims to have the only or best way of doing this.

In this conclusion, I summarize my argument and examine some policy proposals for changes in the organization of work/production, distribution, and the linkages between paid work and the rest of life that may reduce the negative and polarizing effects of present practices and create a more just, equal, and stable society. Finally, I briefly look at the prospects for achieving such changes within the present context of neoliberal ascendancy, political control by business interests, and extraordinary nonresponsibility of capitalist corporations.

RACIALIZED AND GENDERED CLASS—A SUMMARY

Class is conventionally understood as based in economic inequality that results from different positions in employment and/or control of production and accumulation. Class inequalities arise as some groups have power over production in the money economy and others work for them for a wage. Feminists have argued that such theories do not include all the productive labor necessary to keep a society going; some labor is unpaid, usually in the home, and is done primarily by women. A gendered theory of class would have to include women and their unpaid labor. Class theories also often assume a generic "worker" and "manager" who, it turns out, is not so generic for he is white and male. A racialized theory of class would have to take account of the historically differing experiences of diverse racial/ethnic groups, which, of course, include women and men, or gender. I argue that the notion of the "economy" must be broadened so that women's unpaid work can be included. Drawing on the work of economist Julie Nelson, I define the "economy" as the activities of provisioning human life or providing the material goods and processes for provisioning and survival. Class in this view consists of the practices and relations that provide differential control over and access to the means of provisioning. Provisioning is accomplished through many different relations: in paid and unpaid production processes, and in distribution of the fruits of production through wages, profit, the family, the state, and financial institutions. The highly varied activities necessary to link paid work and the rest of life are a third aspect of provisioning that becomes visible as more and more women become paid workers. These three components of provisioning are interdependent. Any particular individual is enmeshed in nodes of interconnecting practices.

Gender and race affect access to provisioning. Gendering and racializing processes are always situated within a history that influences present actions and practices. For example, selection processes that exclude most women from the skilled trades take place in a culture and history that defines cabinetmaking or plumbing as masculine activities. Gendering and racializing processes include: (1) The pursuit of material interests by employers and workers. Employers may, for example, keep down costs by hiring people with particular gender and racial identities who are believed to be willing to work for low wages. (2) The organizing of work and the construction of rules on the model of a male worker who has no responsibilities other than to the job. This creates difficulties for those with care responsibilities and tends to devalue caring work and women. This model is also implicitly a white model. (3) Producing and using gender and racial images, stereotypes, and ideologies to guide, justify, and legitimate various decisions. (4) Interacting on the basis of conscious or nonconscious, gendered and racialized images and expectations. (5) Constructing and reconstructing identities as gendered and racialized. These processes are integral to each other: Empirical examples involve actions based on interests, assumptions about organization, images and ideologies shaping interactions and identities. Women and men negotiate their paths through paid and unpaid production, distribution, and linking activities that are already structured by gender and racial/ethnic practices. They innovate, dealing with obstacles and opportunities, and sometimes change the gendered and racialized class practices.

Class inequalities are, of course, outcomes of capitalist economic and political processes. Gender and racial subordinations were integral to the emergence of industrial capitalism in the United States in the nineteenth century, a process dominated by white men and ideologically marked as masculine. Slavery, war against native peoples, conquest of Mexican lands, and the importation of many different racial/ethnic groups as laborers were part of that development. The legal subordination of white women to white men provided unpaid labor in the household that was essential to the sustenance of working class men. The contemporary labor force still carries the legacy of these patterns in gender and racial segregation and stereotyping of jobs, and gender- and race-based gaps in pay between white men and all others. These patterns continue, although they are modified, and white women and people of color are now present to some extent in top power positions, professions, and managerial roles.

Basic capitalist processes are built on gendered divisions. The capitalist economy is organized to produce profit, while the daily lives of most people, especially women who do unpaid caring work, are organized to support and care for themselves, their families, and their communities. Thus, a basic disconnect exists between production and what has been called "reproduction." This was a gendered disconnect: It created a gendered division of labor between reproduction and production, and located economic power in a domain controlled by white men and defined as masculine. At the same time, capitalist production and human reproduction, in its broadest sense, are dependent upon each other. Wage setting is a manifestation of the conflict between capitalist production and reproduction. Labor is necessary for production, and employers attempt to set pay in terms of price in a market, as a commodity, rather than in terms of providing a living for a family (Figart, Mutari, and Power 2002). And the focus on "price" contributes to the consequent devaluing of caring work: It has no price, or its price is very low, therefore, it's not worth much. But, payment for labor is necessary for sustenance, and ever more necessary as other avenues for making a living decline. Workers' movements, middle class reformers, women's and civil rights movements have had some success in protecting wages from market processes, and in providing for those without wages, such as single mothers, the elderly, or the unemployed. Capitalist organizations have gone along with welfare state provisions such as these, and during some periods have provided their own programs for workers. But, the long-term trajectory, particularly in the United States, is that capitalist organizations individually and collectively deny that they have any responsibility for the welfare of their workers, communities, the environment, or the society at large. Nonresponsibility is a goal energetically pursued by those who control the capitalist economy. At the beginning of the twenty-first century, efforts to enforce this goal are particularly lively and successful.

Capitalist organizations are central to the ongoing production of racialized and gendered class patterns and divisions. The leaders of large capitalist organizations are the decision makers at national and transnational levels. Their decisions, and sometimes the unanticipated consequences of those decisions, shape national and transnational class relations and patterns of inequality. They affect, but do not determine, local organizing practices. Internal organizational processes are gendered and racialized, as I outlined above. I describe organizations as inequality regimes in which the ordinary, ongoing activities of doing the work also reproduce complex inequalities. Hierarchical authority structures are class structures, differentiated along lines of race and gender. Inequality regimes vary along a number of dimensions, including the degree to which inequalities are visible and legitimate. I argue that class disparities tend to be more legitimate than racial or gender disparities, but the observer's location in the organization heavily influences what is seen and what is legitimate. Those who benefit from subordinations tend not to see them. Efforts to change organizations toward greater equality, whether by workers, outside reformers, or management, have had mixed success, partly because very complex interests are usually challenged in these efforts. With globalization of production, the boundaries of inequality regimes become more difficult to discern. Some organizations send their lowest-wage work to other countries, externalizing the greatest inequalities. Inequality regimes are in flux, particularly in large corporations, as managers restructure, relocate production, and change production processes and staffing patterns.

At the beginning of the twenty-first century, gendered and racialized class patterns are not the same as they were thirty-five years ago. The decline of good male manufacturing jobs and the rapid increase of service sector jobs bringing millions of women into the paid labor force have both resulted in changes in gendered and racial class patterns. Fewer men are family breadwinners, while more women have autonomy as earners. The economic situation of working-class men has deteriorated, but more severely for African Americans and Hispanics than for whites. Women's paid work is necessary for the survival of many middle-class and working-class families. Professional and managerial women, married to similar men, add their high pay to that of their husbands. The result is greater class inequalities between families. However, gender and race inequalities in pay and the race and sex segregation of jobs have not declined substantially, indicating that racializing and gendering practices are ongoing in work organizations. Women still do most of the unpaid family work, including the work of managing the linkages between workplace and family. To accomplish their family responsibilities, high proportions of women decide to stay out of the labor force for periods of time during their working lives. This reduces women's pay levels and their independent access to money for provisioning. Married women thus have economic reasons to continue to do the unpaid household and caring work: Their husbands earn more, so it is rational that the men put in more time at paid work. Thus, the male breadwinner is not totally gone, he just has more help from his wife than in the somewhat mythical post–World War II period. Moreover, white men are still at the top at every level of class structure, although many are also struggling to stay afloat economically.

Employment for many workers is less secure, with downsizing, offshoring, and organizational restructuring. The social safety net is inadequate or completely lacking for many people. The old standard employment contract is eroding, with pensions, health insurance, paid sick leave, parental leave, and other benefits declining for many. Nonstandard employment, with few of these benefits in the United States, may be increasing. Some employers have demanded wage reductions or two-tier wage systems, while pay levels have remained stagnant for many, except during the boom of the late 1990s. These insecurities have a heavier impact on middle- and working-class people than on those in the upper levels, who benefit from high incomes, lavish tax advantages, and increasing financial wealth. Single mothers and their families, disproportionately from racial/ethnic groups other than white, are the big losers, absolutely at the bottom on all measures of inequality, with the most inadequate social supports of any other group. Managing the linkages between paid work and family care is also more difficult at the bottom. Of course, these are averages. Some single mothers have good jobs and manage very well.

These changes in gendered and racialized class practices result from changes initiated by capitalist organizations, as they organize production and finance on a global basis, as they successfully attack state regulations they do not want, as they pursue privatization of government, and as they succeed in their war on labor. Capitalist organizations strive aggressively for nonresponsibility with greater success in the United States than elsewhere, recommodifying labor by destroying job stability and protections for working people in the name of competition, economic viability, and shareholder value. This has been the great success of neoliberal ideology and control of politics and the economy by capitalist organizations and wealthy individuals. Present offshoring of skilled and even professional white collar jobs to areas of low-cost labor and the outstanding success of Wal-Mart, the low-cost, low-wage, high-turnover, high-technology model, suggest that downward pressures on wages and increasing insecurities of employment will grow, with undetermined consequences for gendered and racialized class.

But that is not a certain outcome; perhaps new interventions will alter these trajectories. If we follow Karl Polanyi's (1944) analysis, we should expect to see measures to, in a sense, save capitalism from itself. While neoliberals and corporate leaders have not yet attempted to save capitalism from itself in the twenty-first century, there are many proposals for reform coming from social movements, politicians, and academics. These reforms would reduce racialized class inequality and promote employment security, deal with the disadvantages accruing to women because of their unpaid work and sex discrimination, and ease the problems of combining paid employment and family work. I turn to these proposals next.

RECONSTRUCTING CLASS RELATIONS: WORK ORGANIZATION, DISTRIBUTION, AND CARING WORK

Justice, individual freedom, equality, and income security[1] are the goals of the policies I outline here for reconstructing gendered and racialized class relations. Achieving these goals could begin to alter or at least reduce the effects of the gendered understructures of capitalism: the dominance of the aims of capitalist production and their disconnection from the aims of reproduction, the construction of work organizations and expectations on the model of a male worker unencumbered by any other demands, and the nonresponsibility of capitalist organizations for reproduction of human beings, communities, or the environment. Concrete goals include: 1) organizing child care and rewarding unpaid and paid caring work so that those who do it are not penalized and devalued; 2) reorganizing paid workplaces to allow flexibility and choice in the combination of family and work; 3) promoting equality, including equality of opportunity and freedom from race and gender discrimination; 4) increasing income equality and income security; 5) assuring representation or a voice for all people, for without democratization of paid work, none of the other policies have much chance of being enacted or maintained (Standing 1999). In several of these policy areas, implementing change would require dealing with the often invisible processes of gendering and racializing within work organizations and between organizations. Assumptions of white, male, and class privileges built into the actions and practices of those with the privileges should erode as those privileges erode.

Policy proposals are grounded in assumptions about possibilities. Many proposals seem to be based on the assumptions that distribution is primarily through earnings, everybody works, and that welfare state programs can take care of the insecurities of the system.[2] An opposing view is that these assumptions are no longer viable, because globalization and flexibility have undermined the possibility of secure lifetime employment and the welfare state that was built on that type of employment regime (e.g., Standing 1999). Welfare states continue to function in Europe, although they are under stress. Nevertheless, these economies are still vital and in many, citizens are much more protected from the vicissitudes of downsizing, restructuring, and offshoring than are Americans. The United States is an example of the decline of secure employment and meager welfare state protections, but as I have argued, this may be a result of conscious policy to undermine such protections rather than a fundamental inability of welfare states to function in the old way under these new conditions. I think it is possible to support welfare state provisions while recognizing that innovative approaches are also necessary.

Policy proposals usually deal with arrangements within national boundaries, but class relations are obviously global now. The question, then, is can we have equality and security in one country or must the solutions be global? The solutions probably must be global, but equalization can be upward rather than downward. Maintaining and improving justice, equality, and security in the wealthy industrialized countries may contribute to a race upward rather than to a race to the bottom. Obviously, the following policy suggestions do not deal with all the extraordinarily complex questions raised by this perspective.

Valuing, Supporting, and Organizing Caring Work

Publicly supported, high-quality child care should be available for all who want it, with flexible hours that allow for full-time care. Child care workers should be paid at least a living wage. Child care centers should be located either close to residences or workplaces.[3] The age of the children cared for in centers is an issue. Jacobs and Gerson (2004) report that there are few daycare places for children under three years of age in the United States. Care for young children could be expanded. In addition, paid parental leave would give support for parents providing care for young children. The Family and Medical Leave Act (FMLA) could be expanded into paid leave of sufficient duration to cover some of the care of infants and very young children. Most industrial countries have some form of paid parental leave. In most countries it is the mother who takes most of the time off. As a consequence, this may solidify women's disadvantages in the labor market. After-school programs for older children are another form of care that will facilitate gender equality and benefit children. Cash payments for child care, primarily used by mothers, have been instituted in Norway and Finland (Leira 2002), with high take-up rates. This policy also may solidify gender inequality in both family and work. At the same time, it is public recognition of the value of caring work. Care policies, such as the FMLA, also apply to care for adults who cannot care for themselves.

Short-term leave should be available for caring for children with temporary illnesses, taking them for doctors' visits, or for parent-teacher conferences. This type of leave is available for some workers, but often not for low-wage jobs. Finally, "care must become a dimension of citizenship with rights equal to those received from employment" (Standing 1999, 349). What this means in practice must be elaborated in different contexts. Transforming care into a right of citizenship, for both the care provider and the one receiving care, raises highly political issues that are not easily resolved.

Organizing Work to Support the Combination of Work and Family

Numerous proposals for reorganizing work to make it more family friendly are in the literature on work-family connections and the family-friendly firm. Many of these proposals are now policy, especially in large firms (Jacobs and Gerson 2004; Moen 2003; Galinsky and Bond 1998). These include flexibility, control, and autonomy in scheduling and work hours, flexibility in location of work, job sharing, temporary or permanent shorter work weeks, and child care and other parental supports listed above. Where the policies exist, the problem is that workplace culture and managers' expectations discourage use of the policies (Jacobs and Gerson 2004). Professionals and managers are often faced with a choice between moving upward in their careers by showing complete dedication to their work or giving up expectations of much career mobility by taking advantage of family-friendly policies. This is partly due to management expectations of long working hours for these employees. Jacobs and Gerson (2004, 180–181) suggest that structural factors contribute to these expectations.[4] Employers have an incentive to demand overtime from managers and professionals. Employees at this level are not entitled to payment for hours worked over forty hours per week under the Fair Labor Standards Act. Thus, a sixty-hour week costs the employer no more than a forty-hour week. In addition, benefits costs do not rise with longer working hours, saving the employer even more money. Those who work part-time, on the other hand, are not entitled to benefits or to other job protections. As a result, U.S. employers have incentives to construct a divided work force—long hours for full-time employees and part-timers on the periphery. Either way the employer saves. These incentives could be removed by amending the Fair Labor Standards Act to include professionals and managers, and basing benefits on time worked, so that those who work overtime would receive extra benefits and part-time workers would receive benefits proportional to their working time. These changes would remove the incentives to divide the workforce and to expect overtime from full-time workers. It might change the culture of the workplace so that those eligible for family-friendly benefits could use them. Limiting mandatory overtime and reducing the standard work week to thirty-five hours would also help to make the workplace more family friendly. These measures would begin to change the image of the ideal worker as unencumbered and male.

These proposals cover only a portion of working women and men. Working class jobs, whether in manufacturing, service, retail, or clerical work, do not usually have a menu of family-friendly options. If paid family leave and paid sick leave were extended to all workers, working class employees would be covered. How to arrange autonomy and flexibility in scheduling and place of work are more difficult to imagine, with the exception of computerized clerical work. Of course, this is the type of work most likely to be offshored. Some of these jobs are routinely organized as part-time partly because employers do not want to pay benefits, or they may be organized as contract work in which benefits are scanty.

Equality of Opportunity and Freedom from Discrimination

Equal opportunity laws could be expanded to recognize that equal opportunity is undermined when parents are penalized for taking time off or refusing overtime work to care for children. Equal opportunity in hiring and promotion, such as that encoded in affirmative action programs, could be revived. Residential segregation and racial exclusion can inhibit equal opportunity for members of some groups. Gender and racial segregation of jobs still channel workers into positions with wages and opportunities that are lower than those open to white men. In addition, workplace discrimination, including practices that are subtle or difficult to document, is still rampant. Immigrants, particularly undocumented immigrants, have additional difficulties because they do not have the protections that other workers still have. In addition, immigrants may be afraid to ask for those protections because they risk exposure to the authorities and deportation from the country. "Diversity" initiatives that address cultural and attitudinal issues may be of some use as a policy option, but these programs arose as responses to Reagan-era decline in enforcement of affirmative action and opposition to affirmative action by white males. "Diversity management" developed as an acceptable substitute, but one that lacks proactive measures, such as recruitment targets and training programs (Kelly and Dobbin 1998).

Equality of access to medical care should be established through a universal, single-payer system. Lack of adequate health insurance, or any health insurance at all, is now a major source of inequality in the United States. In 2002, 57 percent of those employed in the private sector had health care benefits, down from 69 percent in 1979 (Mishel, Bernstein, and Allegretto 2005, 138). Health care coverage was the lowest for those with the lowest pay. In addition, the amounts employees are required to contribute to the payment for insurance has increased in many cases. Many low-wage workers cannot afford this insurance even if the employer offers it. When a job is lost, coverage is usually lost. Medical emergencies occurring during a period of no coverage can result in financial catastrophe. Even with coverage, copayments and uncovered costs lead to bankruptcy for many people (Himmelstein et al. 2005). The problem of high medical costs and lack of insurance affects middle class as well as working class people. A single-payer system, by some calculations, would not be more costly than the present health care payment system and would erase this source of inequality. In addition, experts contend that one of the reasons for the slow growth of jobs since 2001 is that employers are reluctant to take on more costs for health care. Transferring this obligation to the government would remove this structural barrier to hiring.

Achieving Income Equality and Income Security

Measures to increase income equality, such as the minimum wage, already exist, but that minimum is often below the poverty threshold. Raising the federal minimum wage, which has been below the poverty threshold for a family of three since the 1980s (Figart et al. 2002, 184), would raise the lowest wages and push up other wages close to the minimum. However, wage inequalities are so large that this would be only a small move in the right direction. Some state minimum wages are considerably above the federal minimum, but are still not high enough to eradicate poverty among full-time workers.

Comparable worth, comparing the wages of jobs with comparable levels of skill and responsibility, is still a possible approach to gender- and race-based wage inequalities. I think that comparable worth faded away as a policy tool partly because it implied fundamental rethinking of the value of jobs that, in turn, implied large potential costs. Employers resisted the loss of control as well as the possible financial implications, in spite of the minor costs of completed projects (Acker 1989a; Nelson and Bridges 1999). The other reason for its demise was that it was introduced at the time that employers were beginning efforts to reduce male wages, in the early 1980s. In addition, unions, which had supported comparable worth, were declining in the public sector where most projects were located (Figart et al. 2002). However, to the extent that wages are still set through compensation plans that link certain levels of jobs to certain levels of pay, it may still be a tool for equity.

Establishing a living wage through local ordinances is a strategy that began in the 1990s. This strategy seems to have more possibilities than comparable worth, but the impact is very local. Its greatest value may be in stimulating thinking about the problem of low wages and how it might be approached (Figart et al. 2002).

Income equality could also be furthered by reversing legislation that has transferred wealth upward to the already wealthy and to corporations. In the United States, this massive redistribution of the society's income and wealth has withdrawn resources from government programs that, to a small degree, redress class imbalances. Rescinding tax cuts for wealthy individuals and corporations, and undoing many other practices that allow corporations to avoid taxes, are probably necessary foundations for other efforts to increase occupational, educational, and income equality.

Various measures to encourage unionization could also contribute to reducing income inequality. Workers in unionized jobs consistently earn more and have better benefits than workers in nonunionized jobs. Better enforcement of laws protecting the right to organize and new laws that put restraints on employers' use of consultants brought in to prevent unionization could have a long-term effect in raising wages.

Income security is achieved through measures that guarantee that income at an adequate level for basic provisioning does not stop when employment stops. Income security can be increased by strengthening some already existing programs. Unemployment insurance, workers' compensation, disability insurance including Supplementary Security Income (SSI) for the disabled and low-income elderly, sick pay, retirement benefits of various kinds, and welfare payments all provide income security. I have discussed these as the social safety net. Except for Social Security, all of these programs have limited coverage, and coverage, eligibility criteria, and levels and length of payment have eroded. Restoring unemployment insurance to its previous levels, for example, would increase income security and decrease poverty. The outcome of the battle over privatizing Social Security, which is going on as I am writing this, will have a decisive effect on income security in the future. But a major flaw in all these programs is that women, and some men, doing unpaid caring work do not have income security. Married women who are not in paid work have some derived Social Security coverage through their husbands' employment, but their unpaid, socially productive labor does not qualify them for any other benefits or protections. This is another way in which this work is devalued. This reveals another flaw: All these benefits, with the exception of SSI, are linked to paid work. Even Temporary Assistance for Needy Families, which replaced Aid to Families with Dependent Children, requires mothers, even of infants, to do paid work in order to be eligible. Most of the insurance-based schemes require continuous work over a considerable period of time to qualify for benefits. If, in a globalizing economy, increasing flexibility cannot guarantee continuous work, and if many jobs will not have wages high enough to provide a viable living, there is a problem with work-based income security supports (Standing 1999).

A universal basic income is a policy solution to the problem of income security that appears to be superior to other fragmented and inadequate safety net programs.[5] Such an income, in its purest form, would go to all adults, without eligibility requirements, over the entire lifetime. The amount of the guaranteed income would depend on the goals of the grant. If it were only a means to reduce poverty, the level of the income might be lower than if there were other goals. Both Guy Standing (1999) and Carole Pateman (2004) argue that the basic income should be a citizenship right, just as the right to vote is given by citizenship. Thus, the basic income would further democracy because "it would allow individuals more easily to refuse to enter or to leave relationships that violate individual self-government or that involve unsafe, unhealthy, or demeaning conditions" (Pateman 2004, 96). Individuals could more easily leave often undemocratic institutions such as marriage and the paid workplace. The basic income, then, would provide freedom not to work for money, allowing much more flexibility over the life course and more variation across the population in what people choose to do. Unpaid caring work might be one choice; community volunteer work, education, learning new skills, producing art, or simply loafing might be others. Many necessary activities are unpaid now, as Standing argues, and the opportunities for more people to engage in these could greatly enrich the society. Pateman argues strongly for a basic income as a step toward giving women equality as citizens by undoing some of the complex links between employment and marriage. Men's higher earning and women's obligations to do caring work perpetuate divisions of labor in caring and paid employment, still giving women weaker citizenship rights than men, not least in entitlement to such supports as Social Security. To achieve greater democracy, the basic income would have to be set at a level that provides "a modest but decent standard of life" (Pateman 2004, 92). A lower level would not support autonomy and choice.

A basic income could help to solve problems such as the deterioration of wages and increasing speed, intensity, and hours of work. Workers with this income security would be in a better position to demand changes in job conditions either directly or through refusing to take jobs that were clearly inferior. Both Standing and Pateman believe that most people would still choose to work. Some might choose to take part-time and/or low-wage jobs as a way to supplement the basic income. Many would choose to work full-time at demanding, high-income jobs, but their ability to influence the organization of work and work conditions might improve. Similarly, a basic income might encourage innovation and risk taking by providing a guarantee that failure would not lead to absolute poverty.

Many critics of a universal citizens' income have argued against it as too expensive, politically unfeasible, and as fatal to the work ethic, encouraging free-riding or taking without contributing. Many supporters answer that the funding of such a proposal is possible.[6] Politically, there are precedents in some European welfare state programs, such as universal, state-funded child allowances. To gather support and solve complicated questions about what other programs might be eliminated and possible funding sources, it would have to be introduced slowly. Political opposition would be vociferous in the United States and other countries in which neoliberal, free-market thinking dominates. There probably would be free-riders, but that is an endemic problem now. Wealthy people, who perhaps have never done any work, are free to ski in the Alps, relax on their yachts, and go to charity balls. They are free-riders. Pateman points to a more serious free-rider problem, the massive free-riding of husbands in the household. A basic income grant, particularly if the amount were not high enough to provide economic autonomy, could simply reinforce the traditional pattern in which the woman does the household work and the man earns the majority of the family income while he free-rides at home. Current ideas of reciprocity focus only on paid work as contributing to society. Pateman argues that discussions of reciprocity should also include the social contribution of family care work and volunteering in the community. A wide discussion of reciprocity and fair division of labor across the society, drawing on feminist analysis, could help to create a basic income program that does not reinforce the old gender division of unpaid labor. This may be a critical time at which to raise such issues in public debate, because the male breadwinner is in decline, the necessity and value of unpaid caring labor is more visible, and the difficulties of combining family and paid work are obvious to workers and employers alike.

In spite of many issues and problems, a basic income is a promising approach to income security that would guarantee an adequate level of provisioning even to those in the most insecure and lowest-wage jobs. It could further gender equality both at home and in the workplace, and it could provide the basis for increased democratic participation. In addition, as an unconditional right of citizenship, it would eliminate the surveillance and control inherent in most existing safety net programs.

Regulation of Markets and Labor Standards

Increasing insecurity, deterioration of job quality and stability, and increasing inequality in the United States are consequences of deregulation, privatization, and the development of global strategies of production by large corporations and the global capitalist class. These are global processes, and their consequences have been even more disastrous for large parts of the population of the developing world than in the wealthy countries such as the United States (Benería 2003). Measures to control and regulate corporations' global search for the lowest cost labor are essential if the other reforms discussed above are to be possible. Lourdes Benería (2003, 168) urges policy makers to "Take a global approach to the design of effective regulation of markets. In particular, work-related measures such as labor protection and labor standards will not be effective unless they are approached globally so as to avoid the current race to the bottom that results from countries competing through poor environmental and labor standards."

Representation or Voice

Democratic participation is necessary to achieve and maintain greater economic equality and security, to get recognition of the value of unpaid caring work, and to restructure work to accommodate the rest of life. Most work organizations are profoundly undemocratic. Standing (1999), as well as others, argues that the old forms of participation of workers in economic decision making, primarily through industrial and craft unions, are no longer adequate to express the interests of employees and citizens in globally organized, ever more "flexible" production. Moreover, unions, even where they are strong, have often subordinated the interests of white women and racial/ethnic minorities. Labor unions are still important, however, and feminists working in unions have made some progress in bringing women's issues to the forefront, as in the comparable worth efforts (Acker 1989a). Relatively new approaches to organizing are reaching low-paid service workers and retail employees in the United States. Older approaches to participation used in some European countries, such as participatory management in which workers hold a portion of seats on corporate boards, are still possible in some places. Still, new avenues to economic democracy and participation are essential. Some of these might be community based rather than company or workplace based. Some might be organized around particular issues, rather than around a wide range of issues. The living wage campaigns of the 1990s, essentially community campaigns to raise wages generally in a local area, is an example of a new form (Figart et al. 2002). Cross-national organizing to achieve "international agreements on core labor standards, social policies, and minimum wages" (Benería 2003, 130), as in the antisweatshop movement, is another example.

Political representation is essential to establish, maintain, or extend economic security and reduce inequality. All women as well as men of color need to have much better representation, as wealthy white men are now the primary political decision makers in the United States. Political representation at the federal level of middle- and working-class people is very weak, as corporate influence through large political donations and intensive lobbying dominate Washington politics. Numerous political reforms are needed. Reform of the campaign finance system might be a first step in reducing corporate influence and increasing the political representation of ordinary people, a goal that seems scarcely attainable at the beginning of the twenty-first century.

THE FUTURE OF CHANGE—THE END OF NONRESPONSIBILITY?

What are the possibilities of moving toward reforms that "place economic activity at the service of human or people-centered development . . . in which productivity and efficiency are achieved not for their own sake but as a way to increase collective wellbeing" (Benería 2003, 88)? Such a redefinition of the aims of production would require corporations to curb their nonresponsibility and drastically change their ways of functioning. And such basic changes could come only with national and global government interventions. Is this a totally utopian vision? Karl Polanyi's (1944) analysis has something to say about that. Polanyi argued that a "double movement," or two organizing principles, governed nineteenth- and early twentieth-century (U.S. and British) society. One principle was economic liberalism working to establish a self-regulating market; the other was the principle of social protection working to protect people, nature, and society from the destructive consequences of the free market. Polanyi observed that "the organization of capitalistic production itself had to be sheltered from the devastating effects of a self-regulating market" (132). Economic liberals had to call on the state to intervene to save freedom of trade from corporate actions that were destroying free trade through "trusts, cartels, and other forms of capitalistic combines" (148). Thus, the utopian vision was the idea of a self-regulating market: Only massive government interference could preserve the conditions of a "free market." He also noted that demands for social protections of other kinds could come from many sources in society, not only from organized labor or socialist groups. Similarities exist between the periods Polanyi analyzed and the last years of the twentieth century and the beginning of the twenty-first century.

The world, now largely capitalist, has been going through a period of free marketization, led by strong beliefs in neoliberal economics and involving the destruction in many countries of the old protections against the destructions of market society. Claims to nonresponsibility have been loud and persistent during this recent period of the triumph of neoliberalism and global capitalism, but they are beginning to be challenged in many different arenas. Now demands for new protections and new ways of organizing provisioning are arising from many sources—antiglobalization mobilizations such as that in Seattle, the World Social Forum and all its constituent groups, including feminist and environmentalist groups, the Zapatista movement, internationalist labor organizations and many others.[7] Feminist and women's organizing in many parts of the world (Bergeron 2001; Mohanty 2002; Gibson-Graham 2002) are particularly important. In addition, movements around specific issues, such as Justice for Janitors and the Living Wage movement in the United States, are also pushing for protections for working and middle class people. The goals of all these movements are diverse, and include protections for viable communities and ways of life that are threatened.

In the United States, some capitalist organizations are responding to the charges of nonresponsibility, as indicated by articles in the *Harvard Business Review* admitting that "a widespread expectation exists today that companies conduct themselves with at least a minimal degree of social responsibility" (Martin 2003, 102). The supporting legal foundations of the claims to nonresponsibility are not yet threatened. These foundations are in the existence of private corporations with the rights of individuals, free from effective public control, concentrating tremendous amounts of wealth and power, and able to "operate for the private good without a requirement that it consider the public good, including externalities such as pollution, congestion, waste of natural resources, and so on" (Perrow 2002, 36). And, I would add, including supporting, caring, and nurturing in the lives of ordinary people.

While the responses of corporations to charges that they are irresponsible may be primarily symbolic attempts to reduce public distrust, the responses show that demands for change are being heard. Sometimes extraordinarily vocal movements suddenly and unexpectedly escalate to levels that actually produce changes that make a difference. The civil rights movement and the women's movement are two twentieth-century examples in the United States. Global corporate capital seems to be in control at the moment, but changes toward radically restructuring gendered and racialized class practices, and reversing the race to the bottom in living and working conditions, could come as more and more people confront the realities that global market capitalism has brought affluence to perhaps the top 20 percent of the world's population, anxiety and insecurity to others who still are consuming and surviving, but deep poverty and desperation to the rest.

NOTES

1. Each one of these terms has generated a great deal of academic discussion. See Standing (1999) for some discussion within the policy proposal context.
2. This is the apparent assumption in the work of Jacobs and Gerson (2004) and many writing about the Scandinavian welfare states such as Leira (2002).
3. See Leira (2002) for a detailed description of various child care policies in Europe and Scandinavia.
4. The following discussion is based on Jacobs and Gerson (2004).
5. A basic income is an old idea that is again under discussion, with many contributors to the debate. Here I rely on the discussions by Guy Standing (1999, 337–70) and Carole Pateman (2004).
6. See Standing (1999) for a summary of many of the pro and con arguments. Pateman (2004) also discusses the ideas of supporters and opponents.
7. Peter Waterman (2004) gives a very interesting discussion of the relationship of the international labor movement to other movements in opposition to globalization.

References

Abramovitz, Mimi. 1996. *Regulating the Lives of Women (revised edition)*. Boston, Mass.: South End Press.

Acker, Joan. 2004. Gender, Capitalism and Globalization. *Critical Sociology* 30, no. 1: 17–42.

———. 2003. The Continuing Necessity of "Class" in Feminist Thinking. In Gudrun-Axeli Knapp and Angelika Wetterer, eds., *Achsen der Differenz. Gesellschaftstheorie und feministische Kritik II (Social Theory and Feminism)*. Münster: Westfälisches Dampfboot.

———. 2000. Revisiting Class: Thinking from Gender, Race and Organizations. *Social Politics*, Summer: 192–214.

———. 1999. Rewriting Class, Race, and Gender: Problems in Feminist Rethinking. In *Revisioning Gender*, ed. Judith Lorber, Beth Hess, and Myra Marx Ferree. Thousand Oaks, Calif.: Sage.

———. 1998. The Future of Gender and Organizations. *Gender, Work, and Organizations* 5, no. 4: 195–206.

———. 1994a. The Gender Regime of Swedish Banks. *Scandinavian Journal of Management* 10, no. 2: 117–30.

———. 1994b. Family, Gender, and Public Policy: The Swedish Case. In *The Family in Cross Cultural Perspective*, ed. Catherine Berheide and Esther Ling Chow. Albany: SUNY Press.

———. 1992a. The Future of Women's Work: Into the 21st Century. *Sociological Perspectives* 35, no. 1: 53–68.

———. 1992b. From Sex Roles to Gendered Institutions. *Contemporary Sociology* 21, no. 5: 565–69.

———. 1991. Thinking about Wages: The Gendered Wage Gap in Swedish Banks. *Gender & Society* 5:390–407.

———. 1990. Hierarchies, Jobs, Bodies: A Theory of Gendered Organizations. *Gender & Society* 4, no. 2 (June): 139–58.

———. 1989a. *Doing Comparable Worth: Gender, Class and Pay Equity*. Philadelphia: Temple University Press.

———. 1989b. The Problem With Patriarchy. *Sociology* 23, no. 2: 235–40.

———. 1988. Gender, Class, and the Relations of Distribution. *Signs* 13, no. 3: 473–97.

———. 1980. Women and Stratification: A Review of Recent Literature. *Contemporary Sociology* 9, no. 1 (January): 25–35.

———. 1978. Women and Class in Late Capitalism. Working paper, Center for the Sociological Study of Women, University of Oregon. Presented at a seminar on Women and Work, Inter-university Centre for Advanced Studies, Dubrovnik, Yugoslavia, April, 1979.

———. 1973. Women and Social Stratification: A Case of Intellectual Sexism. *American Journal of Sociology* 78: 936–45.

Acker, Joan, Kate Barry, and Johanna Esseveld. 1981. Feminism, Female Friends and the Reconstruction of Intimacy. In *The Interweave of Social Roles: Women and Men*, volume 2, ed. Helena Lopata. Greenwich, Conn.: J.A.I. Press.

Acker, Joan, and Sandra Morgen. 2001. Oregon Families Who Left Temporary Assistance to Needy Families (TANF) or Food Stamps: A Study of Economic and Family Well-Being from 1998 to 2000. Eugene, Ore.: Center for the Study of Women in Society, University of Oregon.

Acker, Joan, and Donald Van Houten. 1974. Differential Recruitment and Control: The Sex Structuring of Organizations. *Administrative Science Quarterly* 19 (June, 1974): 152–63.

Acta Sociologica 44, no. 3, 2001, and 45, no. 3, 2002.

Adkins, Lisa. 1995. *Gendered Work*. Buckingham: Open University Press.

Akst, Daniel. 2003. Look Underground, and Unemployment Is Low. *The New York Times*. September 7, Business: Your Money.

Alvesson, Mats. 1993. Gender Relations, Masculinities and Identity at Work: A Case Study of an Advertising Agency. Working paper, Department of Business Administration, University of Lund, Sweden.

Amott, Teresa, and Julie Matthaei. 1996. *Race, Gender, and Work: A Multi-cultural Economic History of Women in the United States*. Revised edition. Boston: South End Press.

Andersen, Margaret L., and Patricia Hill Collins. 2001. *Race, Class, and Gender*, Fourth edition. Belmont, Calif.: Wadsworth.

Anthias, Floya. 1998. Rethinking Social Divisions: Some Notes Towards a Theoretical Framework. *Sociological Review* 46, no. 3: 505–36.

Appelbaum, Eileen, Annette Bernhardt, and Richard J. Murnane, eds. 2003. *Low-Wage America: How Employers Are Reshaping Opportunity in the Workplace*. New York: Russell Sage Foundation.

Appelbaum, Eileen, and Peter Albin. 1990. Differential Characteristics of Employment Growth in Service Industries. In *Labor Market Adjustments to Structural Change and Technological Progress*, ed. Eileen Appelbaum and Ronald Schettkat, 36–53. New York: Praeger.

Appelbaum, Richard P., and Gary Gereffi. 1994. Power and Profits in the Apparel Commodity Chain. In *Global Production: The Apparel Industry in the Pacific Rim*, ed. Edna Bonacich, Lucie Cheng, Norma Chinchilla, Nora Hamilton, and Paul Ong. Philadelphia: Temple University Press.

Ashcraft, Karen Lee, and Dennis K. Mumby. 2004. *Reworking Gender: A Feminist Communicology of Organization*. Thousand Oaks, Calif.: Sage.

Axinn, June, and Herman Levin. 1992. *Social Welfare: A History of the American Response to Need*. New York: Longman.

Baca Zinn, Maxine, and Bonnie Thornton Dill. 1994. *Women of Color in U.S. Society*. Philadelphia: Temple University Press.

Badgett, M. V. Lee, and Jeannette Lim. 2001. Promoting Women's Economic Progress through Affirmative Action. In *Squaring Up: Policy Strategies to Raise Women's Incomes in the United States*, ed. Mary C. King, 179–99. Ann Arbor: University of Michigan Press.

Bailyn, Lotte. 2003. Academic Careers and Gender Equity: Lessons Learned from MIT. *Gender, Work and Organization* 10, no. 2: 137–53.

Bardhan, Ashok D., and Cynthia Kroll. 2003. *The New Wave of Outsourcing*. Berkeley, Calif.: Fisher Center for Real Estate and Urban Economics.

Barker, James R. 1993. Tightening the Iron Cage: Concertive Control in Self-Managing Teams. *Administrative Science Quarterly* 38: 408–37.

Baron, James N., and William T. Bielby. 1985. Organizational Barriers to Gender Equality. In *Gender and the Life Course I*, ed. Alice Rossi. Hawthorne, N.Y.: Aldine de Gruyter.

Baron, James N., Michael T. Hannan, Greta Hsu, and Ozgecan Kocak. 2002. Gender and the Organization-Building Process in Young High-Tech Firms. In *The New Economic Sociology: Developments in an Emerging Field*, ed. Mauro F.Guillén, Randall Collins, Paula England, and Marshall Meyer. New York: Russell Sage Foundation.

Barrett, Michèle. 1980. *Women's Oppression Today: Problems in Marxist Feminist Analysis*. London: Verso.

Barrett, Michèle, and Anne Phillips. 1992. *Destabilizing Theory*. Stanford, Calif.: Stanford University Press.

Bauman, Zygmund. 1998. *Globalization: The Human Consequences*. Cambridge: Polity.

Baumol, William J., Alan S. Blinder, and Edward N. Wolff. 2003. *Downsizing in America: Reality, Causes, and Consequences*. New York: Russell Sage Foundation.

Baxter, Janeen, and Mark Western, eds. 2001. *Reconfigurations of Class and Gender*. Stanford, Calif.: Stanford University Press.

Beck, Ulrich. 2000. *What Is Globalization?* Cambridge: Polity.

Beechey, Veronica. 1978. Women and Production: A Critical Analysis of Some Sociological Theories of Women's Work. In *Feminism and Materialism*, ed. Annette Kuhn and Ann Marie Wolpe. London: Routledge and Kegan Paul.

Bendix, Reinhard. 1962. *Max Weber: An Intellectual Portrait*. Garden City, N.Y.: Anchor Books, Doubleday.

Benería, Lourdes. 2003. *Gender, Development, and Globalization*. New York and London: Routledge.

———. 1999. Globalization, Gender and the Davos Man. *Feminist Economics* 5, no. 3: 61–83.

Benería, Lourdes, and Martha Roldán. 1987. *The Crossroads of Class & Gender: Industrial Homework, Subcontracting, and Household Dynamics in Mexico City*. Chicago: University of Chicago Press.

Benería, Lourdes, and Gita Sen. 1982. Class and Gender Inequalities and Women's Role in Economic Development—Theoretical and Practical Implications. *Feminist Studies* 8, no. 1: 157–76.

Benschop, Yvonne, and Hans Doorewaard. 1998. Six of One and Half a Dozen of the Other: The Gender Subtext of Taylorism and Team-Based Work. *Gender, Work and Organization* 5, no. 1: 5–18.

Benston, Margaret. 1969. The Political Economy of Women's Liberation. *Monthly Review* 21, no. 4: 13–27.

Bergeron, Suzanne. 2001. Political Economy Discourses of Globalization and Feminist Politics. *Signs* 26, no. 4: 983–1006.

Bergmann, Barbara R. 2003. The Economic Risks of Being a Housewife. In *Women and the Economy*, ed. Ellen Mutari and Deborah M. Figart. Armonk, N.Y.: M.E. Sharpe.

Berk, Sarah Fenstermaker. 1985. *The Gender Factory: The Apportionment of Work in American Households*. New York: Plenum Press.

Bernstein, Aaron. 2004. Shaking Up Trade Theory. *Business Week*, Dec. 6, Issue 3911, 116–20.

Bernstein, Jared and Jeff Chapman. 2003. Income Picture, September 26, 2003. Washington, D.C.: Economic Policy Institute. www.epinet.org.

Bernstein, Jared, Chauna Brocht, and Maggie Spade-Aguilar. 2000. *How Much is Enough? Basic Family Budgets for Working Families*. Washington, D.C.: Economic Policy Institute.

Besser, Mitch, and Ilya Ratner. 2004. Corporate H-1B Abuse. Oregon Association of Technology Professionals. www.ortech.org.

Bianco, Anthony, and Wendy Zellner. 2003. Is Wal-Mart Too Powerful? *Business Week*, Oct. 6: 100–110.

Bibby, Andrew. 2003. IT Outsourcing Goes Global: Job Exports Also Hit White-Collar Workers. *The Worlds of Work: The Magazine of the ILO*, no. 47: 13–15. Geneva: International Labor Office.

Bhavnani, Kum-Kum. 2001. *Feminism and "Race."* Oxford: Oxford University Press.

Blair-Loy, Mary. 2003. *Competing Devotions: Career and Family among Women Executives.* Cambridge, Mass.: Harvard University Press.

Blair-Loy, Mary, and Amy S. Wharton. 2004. Organizational Commitment and Constraints on Work-Family Policy Use: Corporate Flexibility Policies in a Global Firm. *Sociological Perspectives* 47, no. 3: 243–68.

Block, Fred. 1990. Political Choice and the Multiple "Logics" of Capital. In *Structures of Capital: The Social Organization of the Economy*, ed. Sharon Zukin and Paul DiMaggio. Cambridge: Cambridge University Press.

Bonacich, Edna, and Richard P. Appelbaum. 2000. *Behind the Label: Inequality in the Los Angeles Apparel Industry*. Berkeley: University of California Press.

Bookman, Ann, and Sandra Morgen, eds. 1988. *Women and the Politics of Empowerment*. Philadelphia: Temple University Press.

Boris, Eileen. 1999. When Work Is Slavery. In *Whose Welfare?*, ed. Gwendolyn Mink. Ithaca and London: Cornell University Press.

Bose, Christine. 1973. *Jobs and Gender: Sex and Occupational Prestige*. Baltimore: The Johns Hopkins University Center for Metropolitan Planning and Research.

Boserup, Ester. 1970. *Woman's Role in Economic Development*. London: George Allen and Unwin.

Bound, John, and Laura Dresser. 1999. Losing Ground: The Erosion of the Relative Earnings of African American Women during the 1980s. In *Latinas and African American Women at Work*, ed. Irene Browne. New York: Russell Sage Foundation.

Bourdieu, Pierre. 1987. What Makes a Social Class? On the Theoretical and Practical Existence of Groups. *Berkeley Journal of Sociology* 32: 1–18.

———. 1977. *Outline of a Theory of Practice*. Trans. Richard Nice. Cambridge: Cambridge University Press.

Boushey, Heather, and David Rosnick. 2003. *Jobs Held by Former Welfare Recipients Hit Hard by Economic Downturn*. Washington, D.C.: Center for Economic and Policy Research.

Bradley, Harriet. 1999. *Gender and Power in the Workplace*. New York: St. Martin's Press.

Braverman, Harry. 1974. *Labor and Monopoly Capital: The Degradation of Work in the Twentieth Century*. New York: Monthly Review Press.

Bremner, Robert H. 1956. *From the Depths: The Discovery of Poverty in the United States*. New York: New York University Press.

Brewer, Rose. 1993. Theorizing Race, Class and Gender: The New Scholarship of Black Feminist Intellectuals and Black Women's Liberation. In *Theorizing Black Feminisms: The Visionary Pragmatism of Black Women.* London: Routledge.

Brewer, Rose M., Cecilia A. Conrad, and Mary C. King, eds. 2002. *Feminist Economics: A Special Issue on Gender, Color, Caste, and Class* 8, no. 2.

Britten, Nicky, and Anthony Heath. 1983. Women, Men and Social Class. In *Gender, Class and Work*, ed. E. Garmarnikow et al. London: Heinemann.

Brodkin, Karen. 1998. Race, Class, and Gender: The Metaorganization of American Capitalism. *Transforming Anthropology* 7, no. 2: 46–57.

———. 1988. *Caring by the Hour: Women, Work, and Organizing at Duke Medical Center*. Urbana: University of Illinois Press.

Brown, Michael K., Martin Carnoy, Elliott Currie, Troy Duster, David B. Oppenheimer, Marjorie M. Shultz, and David Wellman. 2003. *White-Washing Race: The Myth of a Color-Blind Society*. Berkeley: University of California Press.

Browne, Irene, and Ivy Kennelly. 1999. Stereotypes and Realities: Images of Black Women in the Labor Market. In *Latinas and African American Women at Work*, ed. Irene Browne. New York: Russell Sage Foundation.

Budig, Michelle J., and Paula England. 2001. The Wage Penalty for Motherhood. *American Sociological Review* 66, no. 2: 204–25.

Burawoy, Michael. 1979. *Manufacturing Consent*. Chicago and London: University of Chicago Press.

———. 1985. *The Politics of Production*. London: Verso.

———. 2003. Revisits: An Outline of a Theory of Reflexive Ethnography. *American Sociological Review* 68, no. 5: 645–79.

Burawoy, Michael, and Katherine Verdery. 1999. *Uncertain Transition: Ethnographies of Change in the Post Socialist World*. Lanham, Md.: Rowman and Littlefield.

Burris, Beverly H. 1996. Technocracy, Patriarchy and Management. In *Men as Managers, Managers as Men*, ed. David L. Collinson and Jeff Hearn. London: Sage.

Butler, Judith. 1990. *Gender Trouble: Feminism and the Subversion of Identity*. New York: Routledge.

Callon, Michel, and Bruno Latour. 1981. Unscrewing the Big Leviathan: How Actors Macro-structure Reality and How Sociologists Help Them to Do So. In *Advances in Social Theory and Methodology*, ed. Karin Knorr-Cetina and Aaron V. Cicourel, 277–303. London: Routledge and Kegan Paul.

Catalyst. 2002. *Census of Women Corporate Officers and Top Earners*. www.catalyst women.org/knowledge.

Catanzarite, Lisa. 2003. Race-Gender Composition and Occupational Pay Degradation. *Social Problems* 50, no. 1:14–37.

Chapman, Jeff, and Jared Bernstein. 2003. *Falling Through the Safety Net: Low Income Single Mothers in the Jobless Recovery*. Washington, D.C. : Economic Policy Institute. Issue Brief 191. www.epinet.org/content.cfm/issuebriefs_ib191.

Charles, Maria, and David B. Grusky. 2004. *Occupational Ghettos: The Worldwide Segregation of Women and Men*. Stanford: Stanford University Press.

Christopher, Karen, Paula England, Timothy M. Smeeding, and Katherin Ross Phillips. 2002. The Gender Gap in Poverty in Modern Nations: Single Motherhood, the Market, and the State. *Sociological Perspectives* 45, no. 3: 219–42.

Cockburn, Cynthia. 1983. *Brothers* London: Pluto Press.

———. 1985. *Machinery of Dominance*. London: Pluto Press.

———. 1991. *In the Way of Women: Men's Resistance to Sex Equality in Organization*. Ithaca, N.Y.: ILR Press.

Cohen, Philip N., and Suzanne M. Bianchi. 1999. Marriage, Children, and Women's Employment: What Do We Know? *Monthly Labor Review* 122 no. 12: 22–31.

Cohn, Samuel. 1985. *The Process of Occupational Sex-Typing: The Femininization of Clerical Labor in Great Britain*. Philadelphia: Temple University Press.

Coll, Blanche D. 1969. *Perspectives in Public Welfare: A History*. Washington, D.C.: U.S. Department of Health, Education, and Welfare.

Collins, Patricia Hill. 1990. *Black Feminist Thought*. Boston: Unwin Hyman.

———. 1995. Comment on West and Fenstermaker. *Gender & Society* 9: 491–94.

———. 2000. *Black Feminist Thought*, second edition. New York and London: Routledge.

Collins, Sharon M. 1997. *Black Corporate Executives: The Making and Breaking of a Black Middle Class*. Philadelphia: Temple University Press.

Collinson, David L., and Jeff Hearn. 1996. Breaking the Silence: On Men, Masculinities and Managements. In *Men as Managers, Managers as Men*, ed. David L. Collinson and Jeff Hearns. London: Sage.

Combahee River Collective. 1983. A Black Feminist Statement. In *This Bridge Called My Back: Writings of Radical Women of Color*, ed. Gloria Anzaldúa and Cherrie Moraga. New York: Kitchen Table Press.

Conley, Frances K. 1998. *Walking Out on the Boys*. New York: Farrar, Straus, and Giroux.

Connell, R. W. 2000. *The Men and the Boys*. Berkeley: University of California Press.

———. 1995. *Masculinities*. Berkeley: University of California Press.

———. 1987. *Gender & Power*. Stanford, Calif.: Stanford University Press.

Cooper, Marianne. 2002. Being the "Go-To Guy": Fatherhood, Masculinity, and the Organization of Work in Silicon Valley. In *Families at Work: Expanding the Boundaries*, ed. Naomi Gerstel, Dan Clawson, and Robert Zussman. Nashville: Vanderbilt University Press.

Cornfield, Daniel B., Karen E. Campbell, and Holly J. McCammon. 2001. Working in Restructured Workplaces: An Introduction. In *Working in Restructured Workplaces*, ed. Daniel B. Cornfield, Karen E. Campbell, and Holly J. McCammon. Thousand Oaks, Calif.: Sage.

Crenshaw, Kimberlé Williams. 1995. Mapping the Margins: Intersectionality, Identity Politics, and Violence Against Women of Color. In *Critical Race Theory: The Key Writings that Formed the Movement*, ed. K. Crenshaw, N. Gotanda, G. Peller, and K. Thomas. New York: The New Press.

Crompton, Rosemary. 2000. The Gendered Restructuring of the Middle Classes: Employment and Caring. In *Renewing Class Analysis*, ed. Rosemary Crompton, Fiona Devine, Mike Savage and John Scott. Oxford: Blackwell.

———. 2001. The Gendered Restructuring of the Middle Classes. In *Reconfigurations of Class and Gender*, ed. Janeen Baxter and Mark Western. Stanford, Calif.: Stanford University Press.

———. 1998. *Class and Stratification*, second edition. Cambridge: Polity Press.

———. 1993. *Class and Stratification*. Cambridge: Polity Press.

Crompton, Rosemary, Fiona Devine, Mike Savage, and John Scott eds. 2000. *Renewing Class Analysis*. Oxford: Blackwell.

Crompton, Rosemary, and Michael Mann, eds. 1986. *Gender and Stratification*. Cambridge: Polity Press.

Crompton, Rosemary, and John Scott. 2000. Introduction: The State of Class Analysis. In *Renewing Class Analysis*, ed. Rosemary Crompton, Fiona Devine, Mike Savage, and John Scott. Oxford: Blackwell.

Czarniawska, Barbara, and Guya Sevón, eds. 1996. *Translating Organizational Change*. Berlin and New York: Walter de Gruyter.

Czarniawska-Joerges, Barbara. 1994. Editorial: Modern Organizations and Pandora's Box. *Scandinavian Journal of Management* 10, no. 2: 95–98.

Davies, Margery. 1982. *A Woman's Place Is at the Typewriter: Office Work and Office Workers, 1870–1930*. Philadelphia: Temple University Press.

Davis, Angela Y. 1981. *Women, Race & Class*. New York: Vintage Books.

Delphy, Christine. 1984. *Close to Home: A Materialist Analysis of Women's Oppression*. Amherst: University of Massachusetts Press.

DeNavas-Walt, Carmen, Bernadette D. Proctor, and Robert J. Mills. 2004. *Income, Poverty, and Health Insurance Coverage in the United States: 2003*. U.S. Census Bureau, Current Population Reports, P-60–226. Washington, D.C.: U.S. Government Printing Office.

Denison, Daniel R. 1997. Toward a Process-Based Theory of Organizational Design: Can Organizations Be Designed Around Value Chains and Networks? *Advances in Strategic Management* 14: 1–44.

Dill, Bonnie Thornton. 1979. The Dialectics of Black Womanhood. *Signs* 4, no. 3: 543–55.

———. 1988. Our Mother's Grief: Racial Ethnic Women and the Maintenance of Families, *Journal of Family History* 13: 415–31.

Dill, Bonnie Thornton, Maxine Baca Zinn, and Sandra Patton. 1999. Race, Family Values, and Welfare Reform. In *A New Introduction to Poverty: The Role of Race, Power, and Politics*, ed. Louis Kushick and James Jennings. New York: New York University Press.

Diprete, Thomas A. 1993. Industrial Restructuring and the Mobility Response of American Workers in the 1980s. *American Sociological Review* 58, no. 1: 74–96.

Drogin, Richard. 2003. *Statistical Analysis of Gender Patterns in Wal-Mart Workforce.* http://www.walmartclass.com/walmartclass94.pl?wsi=0&websys_screen=all_reports_view&websys_id=18.

Economic Policy Institute. 2004a. Economic Snapshots: High-paying Software Jobs Being Moved Abroad. March 24. www.epinet.org.

———. 2004b. Jobs Picture, November 5, 2004. www.epi.org.

———. 2004c. Offshoring. EPI Issue Guide. Washington, D.C.: Economic Policy Institute.

———. 2004d. Issue Guide. Unemployment Insurance. www.epi.org/content.cfm/issueguides_unemployment.

Edin, Kathryn. 2000. What Do Low-income Mothers Say about Marriage? *Social Problems* 47, no. 1: 112–33.

Edin, Kathryn, and Laura Lein. 1997. *Making Ends Meet.* New York: Russell Sage Foundation.

Edwards, Richard. 1979. *Contested Terrain: The Transformation of the Workplace in the Twentieth Century.* New York: Basic Books.

Eisenstein, Zillah. 1979. Developing a Theory of Capitalist Patriarchy and Socialist Feminism. In *Capitalist Patriarchy and the Case for Socialist Feminism,* ed. Zillah R. Eisenstein. New York and London: Monthly Review Press.

Elson, Diane 1994. Micro, Meso, Macro: Gender and Economic Analysis in the Context of Policy Reform. In *The Strategic Silence: Gender and Economic Policy,* ed. Isabella Bakker. London: Zed Books.

Ely, Robin J., and Debra E. Meyerson. 2000. Advancing Gender Equity in Organizations: The Challenge and Importance of Maintaining a Gender Narrative. *Organization* 7, no. 4: 589–608.

Enarson, Elaine. 1984. *Woods-Working Women: Sexual Integration in the U.S. Forest Service.* Tuscaloosa, Ala.: University of Alabama Press.

Engels, Frederick. 1972. *The Origin of the Family, Private Property and the State.* Edited, with an introduction by Eleanor Burke Leacock. New York: International Publishers.

England, Paula, Karen Christopher, and Lori L. Reid. 1999. Gender, Race, Ethnicity, and Wages. In *Latinas and African American Women at Work,* ed. Irene Browne. New York: Russell Sage Foundation.

Erikson, R., and J. H. Goldthorpe. 1988. Women at Class Crossroads: A Critical Note. *Sociology* 22: 545–53.

Esping-Andersen, Gøsta. 1993. *Changing Classes: Stratification and Mobility in Post-industrial Societies.* London: Sage.

———. 1990. *The Three Worlds of Welfare Capitalism.* Princeton: Princeton University Press.

Faux, Jeff. 2002. Global Economic Classes (Book Review). Economic Policy Institute, "Viewpoints." Washington, D.C.: Economic Policy Institute. www.epinet.org/webfeatures.html.

Featherstone, Liza. 2004. *Selling Women Short: The Landmark Battle for Workers' Rights at Wal-Mart.* New York: Basic Books.

Fenstermaker, Sarah, and Candace West, eds. 2002. *Doing Gender Doing Difference: Inequality, Power, and Institutional Change*. New York and London: Routledge.

Ferber, Marianne A., and Julie A. Nelson, eds. 1993. *Beyond Economic Man: Feminist Theory and Economics*. Chicago: University of Chicago Press.

Ferguson, Kathy E. 1984. *The Feminist Case Against Bureaucracy*. Philadelphia: Temple University Press.

———. 1994. On Bringing More Theory, More Voices and More Politics to the Study of Organization. *Organization* 1, no. 1: 81–100.

Ferguson, Sue. 1999. Building on the Strengths of the Socialist Feminist Tradition. *New Politics*, 7, 2 (new series), whole no. 26.

Ferree, Myra Marx, and Elaine J. Hall. 1996. Rethinking Stratification from a Feminist Perspective: Gender, Race, and Class in Mainstream Textbooks. *American Sociological Review* 61: 929–50.

———. 2000. Gender Stratification and Paradigm Change. *American Sociological Review* 65, no. 3: 475–81.

Ferree, Myra Marx, and Patricia Yancy Martin, eds. 1995. *Feminist Organizations*. Philadelphia: Temple University Press.

Figart, Deborah M., Ellen Mutari, and Marilyn Power. 2002. *Living Wages, Equal Wages*. London and New York: Routledge.

Fine, Michelle, and Lois Weis. 1998. *The Unknown City: The Lives of Poor and Working-Class Young Adults*. Boston: Beacon Press.

Folbre, Nancy. 1994. *Who Pays for the Kids? Gender and the Structures of Constraints*. London and New York: Routledge.

———. 2001. *The Invisible Heart*. New York: The New Press.

Folbre, Nancy, and Julie A. Nelson. 2003. For Love or Money—Or Both? In *Women and the Economy*, ed. Ellen Mutari and Deborah M. Figart. Armonk, N.Y.: M.E. Sharpe.

Foner, Philip S. 1947. *History of the Labor Movement in the United States*. New York: International Publishers.

Frankel, Linda. 1984. Southern Textile Women: Generations of Survival and Struggle. In *My Troubles Are Going to Have Trouble with Me*, ed. Karen Brodkin Sacks and Dorothy Remy. New Brunswick, N.J.: Rutgers University Press.

Frankenberg, Ruth. 1993. *White Women, Race Matters: The Social Construction of Whiteness*. Minneapolis: University of Minnesota Press.

Fraser, Nancy. 2003. Rethinking Recognition: Overcoming Displacement and Reification in Cultural Politics. In *Recognition Struggles and Social Movements*, ed. Barbara Hobson. Cambridge: Cambridge University Press.

———. 1998. Heterosexism, Misrecognition and Capitalism: A Response to Judith Butler. *New Left Review* 1, no. 228, March–April: 140–49.

———. 1997. *Justice Interruptus: Critical Reflections on the "Postsocialist" Condition*. New York and London: Routledge.

———. 1995. From Redistribution to Recognition? Dilemmas of Justice in a "Postsocialist" Age. *New Left Review* 212 (July/August): 68–93.

Freeman, Carla. Is Local: Global as Feminine: Masculine? Rethinking the Gender of Globalization. *Signs* 26, no. 4: 1007–38.

Freudenheim, Milt. 2003. Employees Pay 48% More for Company Health Plans. *The New York Times*, Business Section, September 10.

Friedan, Betty. 1963. *The Feminine Mystique*. New York: Dell Publishing Co.
Friedman, Milton. 1982. *Capitalism and Freedom*. Chicago: University of Chicago Press.
Galinsky, Ellen, and James T. Bond. 1998. *Business Work-Life Study*. New York: Families and Work Institute.
General Accounting Office. 2003. *Women's Earnings: Work Patterns Partially Explain Difference Between Men's and Women's Earnings*. Report to Congressional Requesters. Washington, D.C.: United States General Accounting Office. www.gao.gov/new.items.d0435.pdf.
Gardiner, Jean. 1975. Women's Domestic Labor. *New Left Review* 89: 47–58.
Garner, C. Alan. 2004. Offshoring in the Service Sector: Economic Impact and Policy Issues. *Economic Review (Federal Reserve Bank of Kansas City)*, 3rd quarter, 89, no. 3: 5–39.
Garten, Jeffrey. 2004. Offshoring: You Ain't Seen Nothing Yet. *Business Week*, June 21, issue 3888: 28.
Gersick, C. J. G., J. M. Bartunek, and J. E. Dutton. 2000. Learning From Academia: The Importance of Relationships in Professional Life. *Academy of Management Journal* 43: 1026–45.
Gerstel, Naomi, Dan Clawson, and Robert Zussman. 2002. *Families At Work: Expanding the Boundaries*. Nashville: Vanderbilt University Press.
Gibson-Graham, J. K. 1996. *The End of Capitalism (As We Knew It)*. Cambridge, Mass.: Blackwell.
———. 2002. Beyond Global vs. Local: Economic Politics Outside the Binary Frame. In *Geographies of Power: Placing Scale*, ed. A. Herod and M. Wrights. Oxford: Blackwell.
Giddens, Anthony. 1979. *Central Problems in Social Theory*. London: Macmillan.
———. 1973. *The Class Structure of the Advanced Societies*. New York: Harper & Row.
———. 1999. *Runaway World*. London: Profile Books
Gimenez, Martha E. 2001. Marxism, and Class, Gender, and Race: Rethinking the Trilogy. *Race, Gender & Class* 8, no. 2: 23–33.
Glass, Jennifer. 2004. Blessing or Curse? Work-Family Policies and Mother's Wage Growth Over Time. *Work and Occupations* 31, no. 3: 367–94.
Glazer, Nona Y. 1993. *Women's Paid and Unpaid Labor*. Philadelphia: Temple University Press.
Glenn, Evelyn Nakano. 1999. The Social Construction and Institutionalization of Gender and Race: An Integrative Framework. In *Revisioning Gender*, ed. J. Lorber, M. M. Feree, and B. Hess, 3–43. Thousand Oaks, Calif.: Sage.
———. 2002. *Unequal Freedom: How Race and Gender Shaped American Citizenship and Labor*. Cambridge: Harvard University Press.
Glucksmann, Miriam. 1990. *Women Assemble: Women Workers and the New Industries in Inter-war Britain*. London: Routledge.
———. 1995. Why "Work?" Gender and the "Total Social Organization of Labour." *Gender, Work and Organization* 2, no. 2: 63–75.
———. 2000. *Cottons and Casuals: The Gendered Organization of Labour in Time and Space*. Durham, UK: British Sociological Association, Sociology Press.

Goldin, Claudia. 1990. *Understanding the Gender Gap: An Economic History of American Women*. New York and Oxford: Oxford University Press.

Goldman, Abigail, and Nancy Cleeland. 2003. The Way of Wal-Mart: Sell More for Less . . . Even Less. *The Eugene Register Guard*, November 28: 1.

Goldman, Paul, and Donald R. Van Houten. 1980. Uncertainty, Conflict, and Labor Relations in the Modern Firm II. *Economic and Industrial Democracy* 1: 263–87.

Goldthorpe, John H. 1980. *Social Mobility and Class Structure in Modern Britain*. Oxford: Clarendon Press.

———. 1983. Women and Class Analysis: In Defense of the Conventional View. *Sociology* 17, no. 4.

———. 1984. Women and Class Analysis: A Reply to the Replies. *Sociology* 18, no. 4.

Goodman, Bill, and Reid Steadman. 2002. Services: Business Demand Rivals Consumer Demand in Driving Job Growth. *Monthly Labor Review*, April.

Goolsbee, Austan. 2003. The Unemployment Myth. *The New York Times*, November 30, Opinion.

Gordon, Linda. 1994. *Pitied But Not Entitled: Single Mothers and the History of Welfare 1890–1935*. New York: The Free Press.

Gottfried, Heidi. 1998. Beyond Patriarchy? Theorizing Gender and Class. *Sociology* 32, no. 3: 451–68.

———. 2003. Temp(t)ing Bodies: Shaping Gender at Work in Japan. *Sociology* 37, no. 2: 257–76.

Gottfried, Heidi, Stephen Rose, Heidi Hartmann, and David Fasenfest. 2004. Autonomy and Insecurity: The Status of Women Workers in the United States. Josei Roundou Kenkyu, *Bulletin of the Society for the Study of Working Women* 46: 17–39.

Gould, Elise. 2004. The Chronic Problem of Declining Health Coverage: Employer-Provided Health Insurance Falls for Third Consecutive Year. EPI Issue Brief #202. Washington, D.C.: Economic Policy Institute.

Gramsci, Antonio. 1971. *Selections from the Prison Notebooks*. Ed. and trans. Quintin Hoare and Geoffrey Nowell Smith. New York: International Publishers.

Greene, Anne-Marie, Peter Ackers, and John Black. 2002. Going Against the Historical Grain: Perspectives on Gendered Occupational Identity and Resistance to the Breakdown of Occupational Segregation in Two Manufacturing Firms. *Gender, Work and Organization* 9, no. 3: 266–85.

Grimshaw, Damian, Kevin G. Ward, Jill Rubery, Hu Beynon. 2001. Organisations and the Transformation of the Internal Labour Market. *Work, Employment and Society* 15, no. 1: 25–54.

Guillén, Mauro F., Randall Collins, Paula England, and Marshall Meyer. 2002. *The New Economic Sociology: Developments in an Emerging Field*. New York: Russell Sage Foundation.

Gustafsson, Bjorn, and Mats Johansson. 1999. In Search of Smoking Guns: What Makes Income Inequality Vary Over Time in Different Countries? *American Sociological Review* 64: 585–605.

Gutman, Herbert G. 1976. *Work, Culture Society in Industrializing America*. New York: Alfred A. Knopf.

Hacker, Andrew. 2003. *Two Nations: Black and White, Separate, Hostile, Unequal.* New York: Scribner.

Hall, John R., ed. 1997. *Reworking Class.* Ithaca and London: Cornell University Press.

Hammer, Michael, and James Champy. 1993. *Reengineering the Corporation: A Manifesto for Business Revolution.* London: Nicholas Brealey.

Handy, Charles. 2003. *What's a Business For? Harvard Business Review on Corporate Responsibility.* Boston: Harvard Business School Publishing Corporation.

Hansen, Karen V., and Ilene J. Philipson. 1990. *Women, Class, and the Feminist Imagination.* Philadelphia: Temple University Press.

Harding, Sandra. 1991. *Whose Science? Whose Knowledge? Thinking From Women's Lives.* Ithaca, N.Y.: Cornell University Press.

Hardt, Michael, and Antonio Negri. 2000. *Empire.* Cambridge, Mass.: Harvard University Press.

Hartmann, Heidi. 1976. Capitalism, Patriarchy, and Job Segregation by Sex. *Signs* 1, no. 3, part 2: 137–69.

Hartmann, Heidi, ed. 1981. *The Unhappy Marriage of Marxism and Feminism.* London: Pluto Press.

Hartmann, Heidi, and Roberta Spalter-Roth. 2003. *Survival at the Bottom: The Income Packages of Low-Income Families with Children.* Washington, D.C.: Institute for Women's Policy Research.

Hartsock, Nancy. 1983. *Money, Sex, and Power: Toward a Feminist Historical Materialism.* New York and London: Longman.

Hatcher, Caroline. 2003. Refashioning a Passionate Manager: Gender at Work. *Gender, Work, and Organizations* 10, no. 4: 391–412.

Hearn, Jeff. 1996. Is Masculinity Dead? A Critique of the Concept of Masculinity/Masculinities. In *Understanding Masculinities: Social Relations and Cultural Arenas,* ed. M. Mac an Ghaill. Buckingham: Oxford University Press.

———. 2004. From Hegemonic Masculinity to the Hegemony of Men. *Feminist Theory* 5, no. 1: 49–72.

Hearn, Jeff, and Wendy Parkin. 2001. *Gender, Sexuality and Violence in Organizations.* London: Sage.

Heath, Anthony, and Nicky Britten. 1984. Women's Jobs Do Make a Difference: A Reply to Goldthorpe. *Sociology* 18, no. 4: 475–90.

Heilbroner, Robert L., et al. 1972. *In the Name of Profit: Profiles in Corporate Irresponsibility.* Garden City, N.Y.: Doubleday.

Hennessy, Rosemary, and Chrys Ingraham, eds. 1997. *Materialist Feminism: A Reader in Class, Difference, and Women's Lives.* New York and London: Routledge.

Herbert, Bob. 2003. The White-Collar Blues. *The New York Times,* Op. Ed. page, December 29.

Higginbotham, Evelyn Brooks. 1992. African-American Women's History and the Metalanguage of Race. *Signs* 17, no. 2: 251–74.

Himmelstein, David U., Elizabeth Warren, Deborah Thorne, and Steffie Woolhandler. 2005. Market Watch: Illness and Injury as Contributors to Bankruptcy. *Health Affairs.* Feb. 2. www.healthaff.org.

Hochschild, Arlie Russell. 1997. *The Time Bind: When Work Becomes Home & Home Becomes Work.* New York: Metropolitan Books.

hooks, bell. 2000. *Where We Stand: Class Matters*. New York: Routledge.
———. 1984. *Feminist Theory: From Margin to Center*. Boston: South End Press.
———. 1981. *Ain't I a Woman: Black Women and Feminism*. Boston: South End Press.
Hossfeld, Karen J. 1994. Hiring Immigrant Women: Silicon Valley's "Simple Formula." In *Women of Color in U.S. Society*, ed. Maxine Baca Zinn and Bonnie Thornton Dill. Philadelphia: Temple University Press.
Howard, Christopher. 1999. *The Hidden Welfare State: Tax Expenditures and Social Policy in the United States*. Princeton: Princeton University Press.
Human Rights Watch. 2000. *Unfair Advantage: Worker's Freedom of Association in the U.S. Under International Human Rights Standards*. HRW Index # 2513. www.hrw.org/reports/2000/uslabor/.
———. 2005. *Blood, Sweat, and Fear: Workers' Rights in U.S. Meat and Poultry Plants*. HRW Index # 1–56432–330–7. www.hrw.org/reports/2005/usa0105.
Ingham, Geoffrey K. 2004. *The Nature of Money*. Cambridge: Polity.
Institute for Women's Policy Research. 2003. The Gender Wage Gap: Progress of the 1980s Fails to Carry Through. IWPR Publication #C353. Washington D.C.: IWPR.
———. 2004. Fact Sheet. Publication # C350 updated. Washington, D.C.: IWPR.
Jacobs, Jerry A., and Kathleen Gerson. 2004. *The Time Divide: Work, Family, and Gender Inequality*. Cambridge: Harvard University Press.
Jaggar, Alison. 1983. *Feminist Politics and Human Nature*. Totowa, N.J.: Littlefield Adams.
Janiewski, Dolores. 1985. *Sisterhood Denied: Race, Gender, and Class in a New South Community*. Philadelphia: Temple University Press.
———. 1996. Southern Honour, Southern Dishonour: Managerial Ideology and the Construction of Gender, Race, and Class Relations in Southern Industry. In *Feminism & History*, ed. Joan Wallach Scott. Oxford: Oxford University Press.
Jenkins, Rhys, Ruth Pearson, and Gill Seyfang. 2002. *Corporate Responsibility and Labour Rights: Codes of Conduct in the Global Economy*. London: Earthscan Publications.
Jennings, Ann L. 1993. Public or Private? Institutional Economics and Feminism. In *Beyond Economic Man: Feminist Theory and Economics*, ed. Marianne A. Ferber and Julie A. Nelson. Chicago: University of Chicago Press.
Johnston, David Cay. 2003. *Perfectly Legal: The Covert Campaign to Rig Our Tax System to Benefit the Super Rich—and Cheat Everyone Else*. New York: The Penguin Group (USA).
Joseph, Gloria. 1981. The Incompatible Ménage á Trois: Marxism, Feminism and Racism. In *Women and Revolution: The Unhappy Marriage of Marxism and Feminism*, ed. Lydia Sargent. Boston: South End Press.
Kalleberg, Arne, Barbara Reskin, and Ken Hudson. 2000. Bad Jobs in America: Standard and Nonstandard Employment Relations and Job Quality in the United States. *American Sociological Review* 65, no. 2: 256–78.
Kandiyoti, Deniz. 2002. *Agrarian Reform, Gender and Land Rights in Uzbekistan*. Geneva: United Nations Research Institute for Social Development.
Kanter, Rosabeth Moss. 1977. *Men and Women of the Corporation*. New York: Basic Books.

Kaplan, Temma. 2002. The Disappearing Fathers Under Global Capitalism. In *The Socialist Feminist Project*, ed. Nancy Holmstrom. New York: Monthly Review Press.

Keister, Lisa. 2000. *Wealth in America: Trends in Wealth Inequality*. Cambridge: Cambridge University Press.

Kelly, Erin, and Frank Dobbin. 1998. How Affirmative Action Became Diversity Management: Employer Response to Antidiscrimination Law, 1961 to 1996. *American Behavioral Scientist* 41 no. 7: 960–85.

Kelly, Joan. 1979. The Doubled Vision of Feminist Theory. *Feminist Studies* 5, no. 1: 216–27.

Kendall, Diana. 2002. *The Power of Good Deeds: Privileged Women and the Social Reproduction of the Upper Class*. Boston: Rowman and Littlefield.

Kessler-Harris, Alice. 1982. *Out to Work: A History of Wage-Earning Women in the United States*. New York: Oxford University Press.

———. 1990. *A Woman's Wage*. Lexington, Ky.: The University Press of Kentucky.

———. 1993. Treating the Male as "Other": Redefining the Parameters of Labor History. *Labor History* 34 (Spring/Summer): 190–204.

Kilbourne, Barbara, Paula England, and Kurt Beron. 1994. Effects of Individual, Occupational, and Industrial Characteristics on Earnings: Intersections of Race and Gender. *Social Forces* 72: 1149–76.

Kmec, Julie A. 2003. Minority Job Concentration and Wages. *Social Problems* 50, no. 1: 38–59.

Knights, David, and Darren McCabe. 1998. Dreams and Designs on Strategy: A Critical Analysis of TQN and Management Control. *Work, Employment and Society* 12, no. 3: 433–56.

Korpi, Walter, and Joakim Palme. 1998. The Paradox of Redistribution and Strategies of Equality: Welfare States, Institutions, Inequality, and Poverty in Western Countries. *American Sociological Review* 63, no. 5: 661–87.

Korvajärvi, Päivi. 2003. "Doing Gender"—Theoretical and Methodological Considerations. In *Where Have All the Structures Gone? Doing Gender in Organisations, Examples from Finland, Norway and Sweden*, ed. Ewa Gunnarsson, Susanne Andersson, Annika Vänje Rosell, Arja Lehto, and Minna Salminen-Karlsson. Stockholm: Center for Women's Studies, Stockholm University.

Krefting, Linda A. 2003. Intertwined Discourses of Merit and Gender: Evidence from Academic Employment in the USA. *Gender, Work & Organization* 10, no. 2: 260–78.

Kuhn, Annette. 1978. Structures of Patriarchy and Capital in the Family. In *Feminism and Materialism*, ed. Annette Kuhn and Ann Marie Wolpe. London: Routledge and Kegan Paul.

Kuhn, Thomas S. 1962. *The Structure of Scientific Revolutions*. Chicago: University of Chicago Press.

Kvande, Elin, and Bente Rasmussen. 1994. Men in Male-Dominated Organizations and Their Encounter with Women Intruders. *Scandinavian Journal of Management* 10, no. 2: 163–74.

Leidner, Robin. 1993. *Fast Food, Fast Talk: Service Work and the Routinization of Daily Life*. Berkeley: University of California Press.

Leira, Arnlaug. 1994. *Welfare States and Working Mothers: The Scandinavian Experience.* Cambridge: Cambridge University Press.

———. 2002. *Working Parents and the Welfare State: Family Change and Policy Reform in Scandinavia.* Cambridge: Cambridge University Press.

Leiulfsrud, H., and A. Woodward. 1987. Women at Class Crossroads: Repudiating Conventional Theories of Family Class. *Sociology* 21, no. 3: 393–412.

Lewis, Jane. 1992. Gender and the Development of Welfare Regimes. *Journal of European Social Policy* 3: 159–73.

———. 1997. Gender and Welfare Regimes: Further Thoughts. *Social Politics* 4, no. 2: 160–77.

———. 1985. The Debate on Sex and Class. *New Left Review*, no. 1/149: 108–20.

Lichtenstein, Nelson. 2004. Interview—What Are the Characteristics of the Wal-Mart Business Model? PBS, Frontline. www.pbs.org/wgbh/pages/frontline/shows/walmart/interviews/lichtenstein.html.

Logan, John. 2003. Consultants, Lawyers, and the "Union Free" Movement in the USA since the 1970's. *Industrial Relations Journal* 33, no. 3: 197–215.

Lovell, Vicky. 2004. *No Time to Be Sick: Why Everyone Suffers When Workers Don't Have Paid Sick Leave.* Washington, D.C.: Institute for Women's Policy Research.

Lown, Judy. 1983. Not So Much a Factory, More a Form of Patriarchy: Gender and Class during Industrialisation. In *Gender, Class and Work*, ed. Eva Gamarnikow, David H. J. Morgan, June Purvis, and Daphne E. Taylorson. London: Heinemann.

Lyter, Deanna M., Melissa Sills, Gi-Taik Oh, and Avis Jones-DeWeever. 2004. *The Children Left Behind: Deeper Poverty, Fewer Supports.* Washington, D.C.: Institute for Women's Policy Research.

Mackintosh, Maureen M. 1979. Domestic Labour and the Household. In *Fit Work for Women*, ed. Sandra Burman. New York: St. Martin's Press.

Marchand, Marianne H., and Anne Sisson Runyan. 2000. Introduction: Feminist Sightings of Global Restructuring: Conceptualizations and Reconceptualizations. In *Gender and Global Restructuring: Sightings, Sites and Resistances*, ed. Marianne H. Marchand and Anne Sisson Runyan. London and New York: Routledge.

Martin, Joanne, and Debra Meyerson. 1998. Women and Power: Conformity, Resistance, and Disorganized Coaction. In *Power and Influence in Organizations*, ed. R. Kramer and M. Neale, 311–48. Thousand Oaks, Calif.: Sage.

Martin, Patricia Yancey. 1996. Gendering and Evaluating Dynamics: Men, Masculinities, and Managements. In *Men as Managers, Managers as Men*, ed. David Collinson and Jeff Hearn. London: Sage.

———. 2003. "Said and Done" Versus "Saying and Doing": Gendering Practices, Practicing Gender at Work. *Gender & Society* 17, no. 3: 342–66.

Martin, Patricia Yancey, and David Collinson. 2002. "Over the Pond and Across the Water": Developing the Field of "Gendered Organizations." *Gender, Work & Organization* 9, no. 3: 244–65.

Martin, Roger L. 2003. The Virtue Matrix: Calculating the Return on Corporate Responsibility. *Harvard Business Review on Corporate Responsibility.* Boston: Harvard Business School Publishing Corporation.

Marx, Karl. 1906. *Capital: A Critique of Political Economy*. New York: The Modern Library.

Marx, Karl, and Frederick Engels. 1970. *The German Ideology*. Ed. C. J. Arthur. New York: International Publishers.

Mathieu, Nicole-Claude. 1976. Notes for a Sociological Definition of Sex Categories. *International Journal of Sociology* 5: 14–38.

Matloff, Norman. 2003. On the Need for Reform of the H1-B Non-Immigrant Work Visa in Computer-Related Occupations. *University of Michigan Journal of Law Reform* 36, no 4: 1–99.

Maume, David J. 1999. Glass Ceilings and Glass Elevators: Occupational Segregation and Race and Sex Differences in Managerial Promotions. *Work and Occupations* 26, no. 4: 483–509.

McCall, Leslie. 2001. *Complex Inequality: Gender, Class, and Race in the New Economy*. New York and London: Routledge.

McDonough, Roisin, and Rachel Harrison. 1978. Patriarchy and Relations of Production. In *Feminism and Materialism*, ed. Annette Kuhn and Ann Marie Wolpe. London: Routledge and Kegan Paul.

McDowell, Linda. 1997. A Tale of Two Cities? Embedded Organizations and Embodied Workers in the City of London. In *Geographies of Economies*, ed. Roger Lee and Jane Willis, 118–29. London: Arnold.

McIntyre, Robert S., and T. D. Coo Nguyen. 2004. *Corporate Income Taxes in the Bush Years*. A Joint Project of Citizens for Tax Justice and The Institute on Taxation and Economic Policy. www.ctj.org/corpfed04an.pdf.

Mead, Lawrence M. 1986. *Beyond Entitlement: The Social Obligations of Citizenship*. New York: Free Press.

———. 1992. *The New Politics of Poverty: The Nonworking Poor in America*. New York: Basic Books.

Mencher, Samuel. 1967. *Poor Law to Poverty Program*. Pittsburgh: University of Pittsburgh Press.

Metcalfe, Beverly, and Alison Linstead. 2003. Gendering Teamwork: Re-Writing the Feminine. *Gender, Work & Organization* 10, no. 1: 94–119.

Middleton, Chris. 1983. Patriarchal Exploitation and the Rise of English Capitalism. In *Gender, Class and Work*, ed. Eva Gamarnikow, David H. J. Morgan, June Purvis, and Daphne E. Taylorson. London: Heinemann.

Milton, David. 1982. *The Politics of U.S. Labor: From the Great Depression to the New Deal*. New York: Monthly Review Press.

Mink, Gwendolyn, ed. 1999. *Whose Welfare?* Ithaca and London: Cornell University Press.

Mishel, Lawrence, with Matthew Walters. 2003. How Unions Help All Workers. EPI Briefing Paper. Washington, D.C.: Economic Policy Institute.

Mishel, Lawrence, Jared Bernstein, and Heather Boushey. 2003. *The State of Working America 2002/2003*. Ithaca and London: Cornell University Press.

Mishel, Lawrence, Jared Bernstein, and Sylvia Allegretto. 2005. *The State of Working America 2004–2005*. Ithaca and London: Cornell University Press.

Mitchell, Juliet. 1971. *Woman's Estate*. New York: Pantheon Books.

Moen, Phyllis, ed. 2003. *It's About Time: Couples and Careers*. Ithaca and London: Cornell University Press.

Mohanty, Chandra Talpade. 1991. Cartographies of Struggle: Third World Women and the Politics of Feminism. In *Third World Women and the Politics of Feminism*, ed. Chandra Talpade Mohanty, Ann Russo, and Lourdes Torres. Bloomington and Indianapolis: Indiana University Press.

———. 2002. Women Workers and Capitalist Scripts: Ideologies of Domination, Common Interests, and the Politics of Solidarity. In *The Socialist Feminist Project*, ed. Nancy Holmstrom. New York: Monthly Review Press.

Moller, Stephanie, David Bradley, Evelyne Huber, François Nielsen, and John D. Stephens. 2003. Determinants of Relative Poverty in Advanced Capitalist Democracies. *American Sociological Review I* 68, no. 1: 22–51.

Molyneux, Maxine. 1979. Beyond the Domestic Labour Debate. *New Left Review* 116: 3–28.

Morgen, Sandra. 1988. "It's the Whole Power of the City Against Us!": The Development of Political Consciousness in a Women's Health Care Coalition. In *Women and the Politics of Empowerment*, ed. Ann Bookman and Sandra Morgen. Philadelphia: Temple University Press.

———. 1990. Conceptualizing and Changing Consciousness: Socialist-Feminist Perspectives. In *Women, Class, and the Feminist Imagination*, ed. Karen V. Hansen and Ilene J. Philipson. Philadelphia: Temple University Press.

———. 2002. *Into Our Own Hands: The Women's Health Movement in the United States, 1969–1990*. New Brunswick, N.J.: Rutgers University Press.

———. 2004. The Politics of Visibility and the U.S. Welfare State. Paper prepared for "The World Looks at Us: Rethinking the U.S. State" Conference, Harriman, N.Y., Oct. 8–10.

Morgen, Sandra, Kate Barry, and Joan Acker. 2003. Words and Deeds: Discourses of Welfare Reform. In *The Status of Women: Facing the Facts, Forging the Future*, 326–29. Washington, D.C.: Institute for Women's Policy Research.

Mutari, Ellen, and Deborah M. Figart. 2003. *Women and the Economy*. Armonk, N.Y.: M.E. Sharpe.

National Science Foundation. 2000. *Women, Minorities, and Persons with Disabilities in Science and Engineering: 2000*. Washington, D.C.: National Science Foundation.

———. 2004. *Women, Minorities, and Persons with Disabilities in Science and Engineering: 2004*. Washington, D.C.: National Science Foundation.

Nelson, Barbara. 1990. The Origins of the Two-Channel Welfare State: Workmen's Compensation and Mothers' Aid. In *Women, the State and Welfare*, ed. Linda Gordon. Madison: University of Wisconsin Press.

Nelson, Julie A. 2003. Separative and Soluble Firms: Androcentric Bias and Business Ethics. In *Feminist Economics Today: Beyond Economic Man*, ed. Marianne A. Ferber and Julie A. Nelson. Chicago: University of Chicago Press.

———. 1993. The Study of Choice or the Study of Provisioning? Gender and the Definition of Economics. In *Beyond Economic Man: Feminist Theory and Economics*, ed. Marianne A. Ferber and Julie A. Nelson. Chicago: University of Chicago Press.

Nelson, Robert L., and William P. Bridges. 1999. *Legalizing Gender Inequality: Courts, Markets, and Unequal Pay for Women in America*. Cambridge: Cambridge University Press.

Newsome, Kirsty. 2003. "The Women Can Be Moved to Fill in the Gaps": New Production Concepts, Gender and Suppliers. *Gender, Work & Organization* 10, no. 3: 320–41.

Northwest Policy Center. 2001. *Northwest Job Gap Study: Searching for Work that Pays.* Seattle: University of Washington, Evans School of Public Affairs. www.dept.washington.edu/npc/.

O'Brien, Mary. 1981. *The Politics of Reproduction.* Boston: Routledge and Kegan Paul.

O'Connor, Julia S., Ann Shola Orloff, and Sheila Shaver. 1999. *States, Markets, Families: Gender, Liberalism and Social Policy in Australia, Canada, Great Britain and the United States.* Cambridge: Cambridge University Press.

Ollilainen, Marjukka, and Joyce Rothschild. 2001. Can Self-Managing Teams Be Truly Cross-Functional?: Gender Barriers to a "New Division of Labor." *Research in the Sociology of Work,* volume 10. Greenwich, Conn.: JAI Press.

Omi, Michael, and Howard Winant. 1994. *Racial Formation in the United States.* New York: Routledge.

Orloff, Ann Shola. 1993. Gender and the Social Rights of Citizenship: State Policies and Gender Relations in Comparative Perspective. *American Sociological Review* 53, no. 3: 303–28.

Orrange, Robert M., Francille M. Firebaugh, and Ramona K. Z. Heck. 2003. Managing Households. In *It's About Time: Couples and Careers,* ed. Phyllis Moen. Ithaca and London: Cornell University Press.

Osterman, Paul, ed. 1996. *Broken Ladders: Managerial Careers in the New Economy.* New York: Oxford University Press.

Padavic, Irene, and Barbara Reskin. 2002. *Women and Men at Work,* second edition. Thousand Oaks, Calif.: Pine Forge Press.

Pahl, Jan M. 1999. *Invisible Money: Family Finances in the Electronic Economy.* Bristol, UK: Policy Press.

Pateman, Carole. 2004. Democratizing Citizenship: Some Advantages of a Basic Income. *Politics and Society* 32, no. 1: 89–105.

———. 1989. *The Disorder of Women: Democracy, Feminism and Political Theory.* Stanford, Calif.: Stanford University Press.

———. 1988. *The Sexual Contract.* Cambridge: Polity.

Pearce, Diana. 2004. The Statistical Measure of Poverty. In *Poverty in the U.S.: An Encyclopedia of History, Politics, and Policy,* ed. Gwendolyn Mink and Alice O'Connor. Santa Barbara, Calif.: ABC-CLIO.

———. 2003. Setting the Standard for American Working Families. Washington, D.C.: Wider Opportunities for Women.

———. 2001. The Self-Sufficiency Standard: A New Tool for Evaluating Anti-Poverty Policy. *Poverty and Race* 10, no. 2: 3–5, 7.

Perrow, Charles. 2002. *Organizing America.* Princeton and Oxford: Princeton University Press.

———. 1991. *Complex Organizations: A Critical Essay,* third edition. New York: Random House.

———. 1986. A Society of Organizations. *Theory and Society* 20: 725–62.

Perrucci, Robert, and Earl Wysong. 2003. *The New Class Society: Goodbye American Dream?* Lanham, Md.: Rowman and Littlefield.

Petchesky, Rosalind. 1979. Dissolving the Hyphen: A Report on Marxist-Feminist Groups 1–5. In *Capitalist Patriarchy and the Case for Socialist Feminism*, ed. Zillah R. Eisenstein. New York: Monthly Review Press.

Phillips, Anne. 1987. *Divided Loyalties: Dilemmas of Sex and Class*. London: Virago Press.

Phillips, Anne, and Barbara Taylor. 1980. Sex and Skill: Notes Toward a Feminist Economics. *Feminist Review* 6: 79–88.

Pierce, Jennifer L. 1995. *Gender Trials: Emotional Lives in Contemporary Law Firms*. Berkeley: University of California Press.

Piven, Frances Fox. 2002. Welfare Policy and American Politics. In *Work, Welfare and Politics: Confronting Poverty in the Wake of Welfare Reform*, ed. Frances Fox Piven, Joan Acker, Margaret Hallock, and Sandra Morgen. Eugene, Ore.: University of Oregon Press.

———. 1999. Welfare and Work. In *Whose Welfare?*, ed. Gwendolyn Mink. Ithaca and London: Cornell University Press.

Piven, Frances Fox, and Richard Cloward. 1993. *Regulating the Poor: The Functions of Public Welfare*. New York: Vintage Books.

Piven, Frances Fox, Joan Acker, Margaret Hallock, and Sandra Morgen, eds. 2002. *Work, Welfare and Politics: Confronting Poverty in the Wake of Welfare Reform*. Eugene, Ore.: University of Oregon Press.

Polanyi, Karl. 1944. *The Great Transformation*. Boston: Beacon Press.

Pollert, Anna. 1996. Gender and Class Revisited; The Poverty of "Patriarchy." *Sociology* 30: 639–59.

Porter, Michael E., and Mark R. Kramer. 2003. The Competitive Advantage of Corporate Philanthropy. *Harvard Business Review on Corporate Responsibility*. Boston: Harvard Business School Publishing Corporation.

Portes, Alejandro. 2000. The Resilient Importance of Class: A Nominalist Interpretation. *Political Power and Social Theory* 14: 249–84.

Portes, Alejandro, and Saskia Sassen. 1987. Making It Underground: Comparative Materials on the Informal Sector in Western Market Economies. *American Journal of Sociology* 93: 30–61.

Presser, Harriet B. 2003. *Working in a 24/7 Economy: Challenges for American Families*. New York: Russell Sage Foundation.

Quadagno, Jill. 1994. *The Color of Welfare: How Racism Undermined the War on Poverty*. New York: Oxford University Press.

Rasmussen, Bente. 2004. Between Endless Needs and Limited Resources: The Gendered Construction of a Greedy Organization. *Gender, Work & Organization* 11, no. 5: 505–25.

Reed, Rosslyn. 1996. Entrepreneurialism and Paternalism in Australian Management: A Gender Critique of the "Self-Made" Man. In *Men as Managers, Managers as Men*, ed. David L. Collinson and Jeff Hearn. London: Sage.

Reskin, Barbara F. 2002. Rethinking Employment Discrimination and Its Remedies. In *The New Economic Sociology: Developments in an Emerging Field*, ed. Mauro F. Guillén, Randall Collins, Paula England, and Marshall Meyer. New York: Russell Sage Foundation.

———. 2003. Including Mechanisms in Our Models of Ascriptive Inequality. *American Sociological Review* 68, no. 1: 1–21.

———. 2000. The Proximate Causes of Discrimination. *Contemporary Sociology* 29: 319–29.
———. 1998. *The Realities of Affirmative Action in Employment*. Washington, D.C.: American Sociological Association.
Reskin, Barbara F., Debra B. McBrier, and Julie A. Kmec. 1999. The Determinants and Consequences of Workplace Sex and Race Composition. *Annual Review of Sociology* vol. 25: 335–61.
Reskin, Barbara F., and Roos, Patricia A. 1990. *Job Queues, Gender Queues*. Philadelphia: Temple University Press.
Resnick, S., and R. Wolff. 1987. *Knowledge and Class: A Marxian Critique of Political Economy*. Chicago: University of Chicago Press.
Ridgeway, Cecilia. 1997. Interaction and the Conservation of Gender Inequality. *American Sociological Review* 62: 218–35.
Roach, Stephen S. 2003. The Productivitv Paradox. *The New York Times*, Opinion Page. November 30.
Roberts, Dorothy. 1999. Welfare's Ban on Poor Motherhood. In *Whose Welfare?*, ed. Gwendolyn Mink. Ithaca and London: Cornell University Press.
Romero, Mary. 1992. *Maid in the U.S.A.* New York: Routledge.
Rose, Sonja O. 1997. Class Formation and the Quintessential Worker. In *Reworking Class*, ed. John R. Hall. Ithaca and London: Cornell University Press.
Rose, Stephen J., and Heidi I. Hartmann. 2004. *Still a Man's Labor Market: The Long-Term Earnings Gap*. Washington, D.C.: Institute for Women's Policy Research.
Rosen, Ellen Israel. 2002. *Making Sweatshops: The Globalization of the U.S. Apparel Industry*. Berkeley: University of California Press.
Rosenfeld, Rachel. 2001. Employment Flexibility in the United States: Changing and Maintaining Gender, Class and Ethnic Work Relationships. In *Reconfigurations of Class and Gender*, ed. Janeen Baxter and Mark Western. Stanford, Calif.: Stanford University Press.
Rowbotham, Sheila. 1973. *Hidden from History*. London: Pluto Press.
Royster, Deirdre A. 2003. *Race and the Invisible Hand: How White Networks Exclude Black Men from Blue-Collar Jobs*. Berkeley: University of California Press.
Sacks, Karen Brodkin, and Dorothy Remy, eds. 1984. *My Troubles Are Going to Have Troubles With Me*. New Brunswick, N.J.: Rutgers University Press.
Sainsbury, Diane, ed. 1994. *Gendering Welfare States*. London: Sage.
Salzinger, Leslie. 2003. *Genders in Production: Making Workers in Mexico's Global Factories*. Berkeley: University of California Press.
Samuelson, Paul A. 2004. Where Ricardo and Mill Rebut and Comfirm Arguments of Mainstream Economists Supporting Globalization. *Journal of Economic Perspectives* 18, no. 3: 135–46.
San Francisco Chronicle. 2004. Business Section 1 and 12, March 7.
Sassen, Saskia. 2004. Immigration in a Global Era. *New Politics* 10, no. 4: 35–42.
———. 2002. Counter-geographies of Globalization: Feminization of Survival. In *Feminist Post-Development Thought*, ed. Kriemild Saunders. London: Zed Books.
Savage, Mike, and Anne Witz, eds. 1992. *Gender and Bureaucracy*. Oxford: Blackwell.
Scott, Ellen. 2000. Everyone Against Racism: Agency and the Production of Mean-

ing in the Anti-racism Practices of Two Feminist Organizations. *Theory and Society* 29, 6: 785–819.

Scott, Joan Wallach. 1988. *Gender and the Politics of History*. New York: Columbia University Press.

Seccombe, Wally. 1974. The Housewife and Her Labour Under Capitalism. *New Left Review* 83: 3–24.

Seidler, Victor J. 1989. *Rediscovering Masculinity: Reason, Language, and Sexuality*. London and New York: Routledge.

Sen, Amartya. 2002. How to Judge Globalism. *The American Prospect, Special Supplement: Globalism and the World's Poor* Winter: 2–6.

Sennett, Richard, and Jonathan Cobb. 1972. *Hidden Injuries of Class*. New York: Knopf.

Sheketoff, Charles. 2005. Beware the Snake Oil Salesman. *Center Points*, January. Salem, Ore.: Oregon Center for Public Policy. www.ocpp.org.

Shilling, A. Gary. 2003. Profits and Layoffs. *Forbes*. December 22, Vol. 172, no. 13: 224.

Siegel, Reva B. 1994. The Modernization of Marital Status Law: Adjudicating Wives' Rights to Earnings, 1860–1930. *Georgetown Law Journal* 82: 2127–2211.

Skeggs, Beverley. 1997. *Formations of Class and Gender*. London: Sage.

Skuratowicz, Eva, and Larry W. Hunter. 2004. Where Do Women's Jobs Come From? Job Resegregation in an American Bank. *Work and Occupations* 31, no. 1: 73–110.

Smith, Barbara Ellen. 1995. Crossing the Great Divides: Race, Class, and Gender in Southern Women's Organizing, 1979–1991. *Gender & Society* 9: 680–96.

Smith, Dorothy E. 1987. *The Everyday World as Problematic*. Boston: Northeastern University Press.

———. 1990. *The Conceptual Practices of Power*. Toronto: University of Toronto Press.

———. 1999. *Writing the Social: Critique, Theory, and Investigations*. Toronto: University of Toronto Press.

———. 1997. Comment on Hekman's "Truth and Method: Feminist Standpoint Theory Revisited." *Signs* 22, no. 2: 392–98.

Smith, Vicki. 1997. New Forms of Work Organization. *Annual Review of Sociology* 23: 315–39.

———. 2001a. Teamwork vs. Tempwork: Managers and the Dualisms of Workplace Restructuring. In *Working in Restructured Workplaces*, ed. Daniel B. Cornfield, Karen E. Campbell, and Holly J. McCammon. Thousand Oaks, Calif.: Sage.

———. 2001b. *Crossing the Great Divide: Worker Risk and Opportunity in the New Economy*. Ithaca and London: ILR Press, an imprint of Cornell University Press.

Spalter-Roth, Roberta, and Cynthia Deitch. 1999. "I Don't Feel Right-Sized; I Feel Out-of-Work Sized." *Work and Occupations* 26, no. 4: 446–82.

Spelman, Elizabeth V. 1989. *Inessential Woman: Problems of Exclusion in Feminist Thought*. Boston: Beacon Press.

Standing, Guy. 1989. Global Feminisation through Flexible Labour. *World Development* 17, No. 7: 1077–1095.

———. 1999. *Global Labour Flexibility*. New York: St. Martin's Press.

Stanworth, M. 1984. Women and Class Analysis: A Reply to John Goldthorpe. *Sociology* 18, no. 2: 159–69.

Stares, Paul B. 1996. *Global Habit: The Drug Problem in a Borderless World*. Washington, D.C.: Brookings Institution Press.

Steinberg, Ronnie J. 1992. Gendered Institutions: Cultural Lag and Gender Bias in the Hay System of Job Evaluation. *Work and Occupations* 19, no. 4: 387–432.

Taylor, Paul F. 1992. *Bloody Harlan: The United Mine Workers in Harlan County, Kentucky, 1931–1941*. Lanham, Md.: University Press of America.

Teichman, Judith A. 2001. *The Politics of Freeing Markets in Latin America: Chile, Argentina, and Mexico*. Chapel Hill: University of North Carolina Press.

Thomas, Dave A., and Robin J. Ely. 1996. Making Differences Matter: A New Paradigm for Managing Diversity. *Harvard Business Review*. September–October: 79–90.

Thompson, E. P. 1963. *The Making of the English Working Class*. New York: Vintage Books.

Thompson, Paul. 2003. Disconnected Capitalism: Or Why Employers Can't Keep Their Side of the Bargain. *Work, Employment & Society* 17, no. 2: 359–78.

Tilly, Charles. 1998. *Durable Inequality*. Berkeley and Los Angeles: University of California Press.

Tomaskovic-Devey, Donald. 1993. *Gender and Racial Inequality at Work*. Ithaca, N.Y.: ILR.

Uchitelle, Louis. 2003. A Missing Statistic: U.S. Jobs that Went Overseas. *The New York Times*. October 5. Business Section.

U.S. Census Bureau. 2003. *Statistical Abstract of the U.S.* Table No. 615. Employed Civilians by Occupation, Sex, Race, and Hispanic Origin, 1983 and 2002. www.census.gov/statab/www/.

———. 2004. Current Population Survey. Annual Social and Economic Supplement. www.census.gov/hhes/poverty/threshold/thresh03.html.

Uttal, Lynet, and Mary Tuominen. 1999. Tenuous Relationships: Exploitation, Emotion, and Racial Ethnic Significance in Paid Child Care Work. *Gender & Society* 13, no. 6: 758–80.

Vallas, Steven P. 2003. Why Teamwork Fails: Obstacles to Workplace Change in Four Manufacturing Plants. *American Sociological Review* 68, no. 2: 223–50.

Van Houten, Donald R., and Paul Goldman. 1977. Managerial Strategies and the Worker: a Marxist Analysis of Bureaucracy. *The Sociological Quarterly* 18: 108–25.

Wacjman, Judy. 1998. *Managing Like a Man*. Cambridge: Polity Press.

Walby, Sylvia. 1986. *Patriarchy at Work*. Minneapolis: University of Minnesota Press.

———. 1989. Theorising Patriarchy. *Sociology* 23, no. 2: 213–34.

———. 1990. *Theorizing Patriarchy*. Oxford: Blackwell.

Waldron, Tom, Brandon Roberts, and Andrew Reamer. 2004. Working Hard, Falling Short: America's Working Families and the Pursuit of Economic Security. Working Poor Families Project. www.aecf.org/publications/data/working_hard_new.pdf.

Wallerstein, Immanuel. 1974. *The Modern World System*. New York: Academic Press.

Waring, Marilyn. 1988. *If Women Counted: A New Feminist Economics*. San Francisco: Harper & Row.

Waterman, Peter. 2004. The International Labor Movement Between Geneva, Brussels, Seattle, Porto Alegre and Utopia. *New Politics* 10, no. 4: 53–72.

Weber, Lynn. 2001. *Understanding Race, Class, Gender, and Sexuality*. Boston: McGraw Hill.

———. 1995. Symposium on West and Fenstermaker's "Doing Difference." *Gender & Society* 9: 499–503.

Weber, Max. 1947. *The Theory of Social and Economic Organization*. New York: Oxford University Press.

West, Candace, and Sarah Fenstermaker. 1995a. Doing Difference. *Gender & Society* 9: 8–37.

———. 1995b. (Re)Doing Difference: A Reply. *Gender & Society* 9: 506–13.

Wharton, Amy S. 1994. Structure and Process: Theory and Research on Organizational Stratification. In *Current Perspectives in Social Theory, Supplement 1*, 119–48.

Williams, Colin C., and Jan Windebank. 2003. Reconceptualizing Women's Paid Informal Work: Some Lessons from Lower-Income Urban Neighborhoods. *Gender, Work & Organization* 10, no. 3: 281–300.

Williams, Eric. 1944. *Capitalism and Slavery*. Chapel Hill: University of North Carolina Press.

Williams, Fiona. 1995. Race/Ethnicity, Gender, and Class in Welfare States: A Framework for Comparative Analysis. *Social Politics* vol. 2, no. 2: 127–59.

Williams, Rhonda. 1997. Living at the Crossroads: Explorations in Race, Nationality, Sexuality and Gender. In *The House that Race Built: Black Americans, U.S. Terrain*, ed. Wahneema Lubiano. New York: Random House.

Willis, Paul. 1977. *Learning to Labor*. Farnborough, Eng.: Saxon House.

Winant, Howard. 1995. Symposium: On West and Fenstermaker's "Doing Difference." *Gender & Society* 9: 503–506.

Wright, Erik Olin. 1989. Women in the Class Structure. *Politics and Society* 17: 35–66.

———. 1997a. Rethinking, Once Again, the Concept of Class. In *Reworking Class*, ed. John R. Hall. Ithaca and London: Cornell University Press.

———. 1997b. *Class Counts: Comparative Studies in Class Analysis*. Cambridge: Cambridge University Press.

———. 2001a. Foundations of Class Analysis: A Marxist Perspective. In *Reconfigurations of Class and Gender*, ed. Janeen Baxter and Mark Western. Stanford, Calif.: Stanford University Press.

———. 2001b. A Conceptual Menu for Studying the Interconnections of Class and Gender. In *Reconfigurations of Class and Gender*, ed. Janeen Baxter and Mark Western. Stanford, Calif.: Stanford University Press.

Young, Iris. 1981. Beyond the Unhappy Marriage: A Critique of the Dual Systems Theory. In *The Unhappy Marriage of Marxism and Feminism*, ed. Heidi Hartmann et al. London: Pluto Press.

Young, Kate, Carol Wolkowitz, and Roslyn McCullagh. 1981. *Of Marriage and the Market: Women's Subordination Internationally and Its Lessons*. London: Routledge and Kegan Paul.

Zelizer, Viviana. 2002. Intimate Transactions. In *The New Economic Sociology: Developments in an Emerging Field*, ed. Mauro F. Guillén, Randall Collins, Paula England, and Marshall Meyer. New York: Russell Sage Foundation.

Index

About the Author

Joan Acker is a Professor Emeritus in the department of sociology at the University of Oregon. Her research and writing have focused on gender, class, and economic issues, including pay equity, gender wage differences, organizational processes and gender, and, most recently, welfare reform in the United States. She has had a number of visiting professorships, including a three-year stay as research professor at the Center for Working Life in Stockholm, Sweden. She was also a visiting Distinguished Professor at the Department of Sociology, Ontario Institute for Studies in Education, Toronto, Canada, a visiting professor at the University of Adelaide, Australia, and the Marie Jahoda International Guest Professor at Bochum University, Bochum, Germany. She has received the American Sociological Association Career of Distinguished Scholarship Award and the American Sociological Association Jessie Bernard Award for Feminist Scholarship.